WRITTEN CORRECTIVE FEEDBACK IN SECOND LANGUAGE ACQUISITION AND WRITING

> Thoughtful, well-researched, and well-reasoned, this book is a must-read for both researchers and practitioners in SLA and SLW.
> **Deborah Crusan**, *Wright State University*

What should language and writing teachers do about giving students written corrective feedback?

This book surveys theory, research, and practice on the important and sometimes controversial issue of written corrective feedback, also known as "error/grammar correction," and its impact on second language acquisition and second language writing development. Offering state-of-the-art treatment of a topic that is highly relevant to both researchers and practitioners, it critically analyzes and synthesizes several parallel and complementary strands of research—work on error/feedback (both oral and written) in SLA and studies of the impact of error correction in writing/composition courses—and addresses practical applications. Drawing from both second language acquisition and writing/composition literature, this volume is the first to intentionally connect these two separate but important lines of inquiry.

John Bitchener is Professor of Applied Linguistics at AUT University, Auckland, New Zealand.

Dana R. Ferris is Professor in the University Writing Program at the University of California, Davis.

WRITTEN CORRECTIVE FEEDBACK IN SECOND LANGUAGE ACQUISITION AND WRITING

John Bitchener and Dana R. Ferris

NEW YORK AND LONDON

First published 2012
by Routledge
711 Third Avenue, New York, NY 10017

Simultaneously published in the UK
by Routledge
2 Park Square, Milton Park, Abingdon, Oxon OX14 4RN

Routledge is an imprint of the Taylor & Francis Group, an informa business

© 2012 Taylor & Francis

The right of John Bitchener and Dana R. Ferris to be identified as authors
of this work has been asserted by them in accordance with sections
77 and 78 of the Copyright, Designs and Patents Act 1988.

All rights reserved. No part of this book may be reprinted or reproduced
or utilized in any form or by any electronic, mechanical, or other means,
now known or hereafter invented, including photocopying and recording,
or in any information storage or retrieval system, without permission in
writing from the publishers.

Trademark notice: Product or corporate names may be trademarks or
registered trademarks, and are used only for identification and explanation
without intent to infringe.

Library of Congress Cataloging in Publication Data
Bitchener, John.
  Written corrective feedback in second language acquisition and
  writing/John Bitchener and Dana Ferris.
  p. cm.
  Includes bibliographical references.
  1. English language—Study and teaching—Foreign speakers.
  2. English language—Rhetoric—Study and teaching. 3. Report
  writing—Study and teaching. 4. English language—Errors of usage.
  5. College prose—Evaluation. 6. Second language acquisition.
  I. Ferris, Dana. II. Title.
  PE1128.A2B4984 2011
  418.0071—dc22   2011013830

ISBN: 978–0–415–87243–0 (hbk)
ISBN: 978–0–415–87244–7 (pbk)
ISBN: 978–0–203–83240–0 (ebk)

Typeset in Bembo
by Florence Production Ltd, Stoodleigh, Devon

CONTENTS

Preface	viii
Acknowledgments	x

PART I
Theory and History of Error Treatment in SLA and Composition Studies   1

1   Perspectives on Error and Written Corrective Feedback
in SLA   3

Early Perspectives on Error and Written CF in SLA 4
Recent Perspectives on Error and Written CF in SLA 12
Perspectives of L2 Writing Theorists and Researchers on the
   Role of Written CF in SLA 20
Concluding Remarks 27

2   Perspectives on Error in Composition Studies: L1 and L2
Interactions and Influences   28

Historical Perspectives on Error in L1 Composition Research 28
Studies of Teacher Response to Error 35
The Influence of L1 Composition Studies on L2 Views of Error
   Treatment 40
Concluding Remarks 44
Notes 45

vi Contents

PART II
Analysis of Research on Written CF 47

3 Research on Written CF in Language Classes 49

Can Written CF Facilitate the Acquisition of L2 Forms and Structures? 50
Is Unfocused Written CF More Effective in Treating L2 Errors
than Focused Written CF? 53
Does Written CF Target Some Linguistic Error Domains/Categories
More Effectively than Others? 62
Are Some Types of Written CF More Effective in Treating L2 Errors
than Others? 64
Does the Educational and L2 Learning Background of Learners Determine
the Extent to which They Benefit from Written CF? 70
To What Extent Can the Proposals of Socio-cultural Theory Enhance
Our Understanding of Effective Written CF? 72
Concluding Remarks 73

4 Research on Written CF in Composition Studies 75

Approach and Analysis 76
General Studies of Teacher Response 77
Types of Errors Marked by Teachers 79
Effects of Written CF on Short-term Revision 82
Effects of Written CF on Long-term Improvement 87
Studies of Different Approaches to Written CF 90
Student Views of Written CF 92
Summary 95
Concluding Remarks 96
Appendix 4.1 97
Notes 98

5 Future Directions in SLA and Composition Research 99

Written CF in SLA Research 99
Summary 108
Written CF in Composition Research 108
Summary 119
Concluding Remarks 119
Notes 119

PART III
Practical Applications of Written CF Theory and Research 121

6 From Theory to Practice: Written CF for Language Learners 123

Purpose and Goals of Providing Written CF in a Language Learning
Program 124

Contents **vii**

The Timing and Frequency of Giving Learners Written CF 125
The Amount of Written CF to Provide 128
The Types of Linguistic Form and Structure to Focus On 130
Options in the Delivery of Written CF 131
The Providers of Written CF 134
How Written CF Can Be Supported with Other Approaches to Accuracy 135
How Learners Can Be Actively Involved in Accuracy-oriented Learning
  Outside the Classroom 137
Concluding Remarks 137

7 From Theory to Practice: Written CF for L2 Student Writers   138

Purpose and Goals of Written CF 139
Timing and Frequency of Written CF 141
Amount of Teacher-provided Written CF 144
Focus of Written CF 145
Form(s) of Written CF 147
Source(s) of Written CF 153
Support Beyond Written CF 159
Follow-up to Written CF 161
Summary 162
Concluding Remarks 162
Appendix 7.1 164
Appendix 7.2 168
Appendix 7.3 170
Notes 171

8 Preparing Teachers for Written CF in Language Learning and
   Composition Contexts   173

Preparing Language Teachers for Written CF 173
Preparing Composition Instructors for Written CF 183
Concluding Remarks 192
Appendix 8.1 193
Appendix 8.2 194
Appendix 8.3 194
Appendix 8.4 195
Notes 196

References   197
Index   213

PREFACE

This book surveys theory, research, and practice on the important and sometimes controversial practice of *written corrective feedback* (written CF), also known as "error/grammar correction," and its impact on second language acquisition (SLA) and second language (L2) writing development. Drawing from both second language acquisition (SLA) and writing/composition literature, it critically analyzes and synthesizes several parallel and complementary strands of research: work on error/feedback (both oral and written) in SLA and studies of the impact of error correction in writing/composition courses.

The volume begins with theory and history, surveying historical SLA views of "error" and what it means for short- and long-term acquisition as well as historical composition/writing views of the relative importance of error/language issues in overall writing development (Chapters 1–2). It then moves to a detailed analysis of the research that has been completed on oral corrective feedback, written corrective feedback following SLA research paradigms, and error correction work in L2 writing and composition studies (Chapters 3–4). This section concludes with discussion of a possible agenda for further research on this important topic (Chapter 5). The final section of the book focuses on pedagogical practice (Chapters 6–7). Based upon our understanding of the theory and current research findings, what should language and writing teachers do with regard to written CF? The book concludes with suggestions for teacher preparation for both language and writing instructors (Chapter 8). Each of the three major sections (theory, research, and practice) follows the same structure: a chapter looking at questions about written CF from the SLA perspective (Chapters 1, 3, 6) followed by one examining written CF through the lens of writing/composition concerns (Chapters 2, 4, 7). Chapters 5 and 8 are our synthesis chapters, where the two separate approaches to studies of written CF are brought together around the issues of a future research agenda and teacher preparation.

As Ferris (2010) wrote, "Although L2 writing and SLA researchers look at similar phenomena, often (but not always) in similar ways, it is important to understand that they do not necessarily ask the same questions" (p. 188). This is the first book to intentionally connect two separate but important lines of inquiry (SLA and L2 writing/composition studies) on the topic of corrective feedback. Though there have been volumes published on the topic in both arenas, no project to date has attempted to simultaneously analyze and synthesize both bodies of work. Ferris (2010) further noted:

> The two lines of research are not in competition; rather, they are complementary. There may be a methodological gap, but it is not a philosophical or theoretical chasm. L2 writing researchers and SLA researchers who investigate written CF—although they pose somewhat different questions—can and should learn from each other and build on one another's work.
>
> *(p. 192)*

The collaboration undertaken in this volume between an SLA researcher (Bitchener) and a writing researcher (Ferris) is thus our attempt to put the above philosophy into practice. Though we did author separate chapters (Bitchener wrote Chapters 1, 3, and 6; Ferris Chapters 2, 4, and 7), we read and commented extensively upon each other's work and co-authored Chapters 5 and 8.

In addition, this volume incorporates extensive recent research and reviews on written CF that have appeared in print since the publication of the abovementioned works, so it is an up-to-date and state-of-the-art treatment of a topic that is of importance and interest for both SLA researchers and writing researchers and practitioners. Finally, the sections on practice and future research should be of value to both instructors of L2 writers and to SLA/writing researchers. It should be a resource to researchers, to teacher educators, to classroom language and writing instructors, and to graduate students wanting to learn more about the topic of written CF and ways to study it. It could also be a useful addition to a reading list in courses on teaching composition, on second language teaching methods, on second language acquisition, on pedagogical grammar, or on the more specialized topic of response to student writing.

ACKNOWLEDGMENTS

John's Acknowledgments

I am indebted to a wide range of people who have played a role as co-researchers, co-writers, and reviewers of my research (presented at conferences and published in peer-reviewed journals). Without the input from my co-researcher (Ute Knoch) in many recent studies on the efficacy of written CF, the significance of this work may never have been realized. Equally, feedback from other colleagues interested in the potential of written CF for SLA, including Neomy Storch, has been influential in the shaping of my convictions about its role in the L2 teaching and learning process. Over the years, too, a range of anonymous reviewers of conference abstracts and journal articles have played an important role in sharpening my ideas. Without the generous support from my university (especially in the form of research and conference grants) to attend conferences where I received quality feedback, many of the projects and publications may not have seen the light of day. More than all of these people, I am greatly indebted to my co-author, Dana Ferris, who agreed to join me in the writing of this book and who has been my inspiration over a good number of years. As a colleague, she has challenged my thinking and, as a friend, she has introduced me to the pleasures of the Napa region. Finally, on a very personal level, I wish to thank my partner, Edwin Cheong, for keeping me "fed and watered" with many a culinary delight.

Dana's Acknowledgments

I am grateful to my faculty colleagues and graduate students at both my current (University of California, Davis) and former (California State University, Sacramento) institutions for their feedback and assistance as I have conducted primary research, designed classroom teaching and teacher preparation materials, and given workshops on the topic of written CF (or "the treatment of error") in L2 student writing. They have sharpened my thinking and given me a lot of great ideas. In particular, I would like to mention my faculty writing group at UC Davis, who gave me great feedback on Chapter 2: Professors Rebekka Andersen, Sarah Perrault, Chris Thaiss, and Carl Whithaus. I am also thankful for the insights provided by members of my two most recent research teams, all former or current graduate students: Jeffrey Brown, Daina Olseen Collins, Hsiang (Sean) Liu, Brigitte Rabie, Danielle Geist Schmidli, Manuel Senna, Aparna Sinha, and Maria Eugenia Arnaudo Stine. I am further grateful to the many other scholars—established and emerging—in the fields of SLA, L2 writing, and composition studies, whose work and conversation have inspired me. First on that list, of course, is my co-author, Professor John Bitchener, who not only has been a great collaborator but a fabulous host and guide to the beaches of Auckland and the sights of Wellington.

Finally, on a personal note, I'd like to thank my husband Randy and my daughter Melissa for their support during the months I worked on this book and Winnie the Pooch, who took me on walks when I needed a break.

Joint Acknowledgments

We are both extremely grateful for the support and guidance of our editor at Routledge, Naomi Silverman, and the entire editorial and production team. We are also appreciative of the anonymous reviews at earlier stages of the book's development; they were extremely thoughtful and useful to our composing and revision processes.

PART I

Theory and History of Error Treatment in SLA and Composition Studies

1

PERSPECTIVES ON ERROR AND WRITTEN CORRECTIVE FEEDBACK IN SLA

In this chapter, we survey a range of theoretical perspectives on the role and treatment of error in second language acquisition (SLA). In our preface, we explained that the focus of attention given to the role and treatment of error by theorists and educators in L2 composition studies and L2 language studies sometimes has differed and that the way in which this book is organized reflects these differences. Thus, in this opening chapter, we consider the role of error and written corrective feedback (CF) from an SLA language learning perspective. Chapter 2 then looks at the compositionist perspective on error and its treatment.

SLA theorists and researchers are interested in how individuals learn or acquire a second language. Consequently, they are interested in what can be done to help learners overcome the errors they make in the process of acquiring the target language. This raises the question about the extent to which errors should be seen in a negative or positive light. In other words, should errors be seen as linguistic acts that need to be prevented from occurring or as acts that should be viewed positively because of (1) the light they shed on a learner's current level of acquisition and (2) the role they can play in the development of the target language? In order to have an informed view on this issue, one needs to take into account the various theoretical positions that have been advocated in the literature. However, theoretical positions can only have validity if they are supported by research evidence. Therefore, this chapter will introduce the theoretical perspectives we consider to be most relevant to the role of error and written corrective feedback in the SLA process and conclude with an overview of some of the key research that has empirically investigated these perspectives and their associated pedagogical applications, leaving a more extensive and in-depth discussion of the individual studies to Chapter 3.

4 Theory and History of Error Treatment

Early Perspectives on Error and Written CF in SLA

Behaviorist Perspectives

During the 1950s and 1960s, errors were considered more negatively than they are today because they were seen to interfere with the learning process and so should be prevented from occurring. As Brooks (1960) put it, "error, like sin, is to be avoided and its influence overcome" (p. 58). Behaviorist accounts of language learning, prominent in these years, claimed that errors should not be tolerated because they can be habit-forming and that, if they are allowed to exist, will inevitably interfere with the learning of new target-like habits. It was believed that learning occurred when learners had the opportunity to practice making the correct response to the stimuli they received. If incorrect responses were made, corrective feedback was given. However, the focus of the behaviorist approach was more on error prevention than error treatment.

Not surprisingly, these beliefs led to a number of pedagogical initiatives. In order to help learners produce error-free statements, Brooks (1960) recommended that learners be given opportunities "to observe and practice the right model a sufficient number of times" and "to shorten the time lapse between the incorrect response and the presentation once more of the correct model" (p. 58). As teachers adopted the audiolingual approach to achieve these goals, they required their students to spend hours and hours memorizing dialogues, manipulating pattern drills, and studying a large number of grammatical generalizations. "Predictably," as Hendrickson (1978) explained, "most students who could not or did not make the effort to transfer audiolingual training to communicative use soon forgot the dialogue lines, the pattern drills, and the grammatical generalizations that they had studied or practiced in school" (p. 387). Somewhat surprisingly, though, many teachers never questioned the validity and feasibility of this mechanistic approach to error prevention.

Another approach that was recommended to help teachers treat learner errors was one involving Contrastive Analysis (CA). Believing it was interference from the learner's first language (L1) that was the primary source of errors, structural linguists spoke of the need to identify features of the L2 that differed from the L1 so that the negative transfer of the L1 could be prevented. CA involved describing comparable elements of both languages, identifying differences between the two, and predicting which errors learners would be likely to make. In doing this, it was believed that explanations would then be provided about why learners make errors and, therefore, about the role that teachers could play in their treatment. Although CA appeared to offer a positive way forward, it soon came under attack in the late 1960s and early 1970s as empirical evidence began to reveal its inability to predict the types of errors that were in fact being made by learners. A range of studies (Burt, 1975; Ervin-Tripp, 1970; Falk, 1968; George, 1972; Hendrickson, 1977; Hussein, 1971; Politzer & Ramirez, 1973; Richards,

1973a, 1973b; Selinker, 1969; Wilkins, 1968; Wolfe, 1967) revealed that, although interference from the learner's L1 is a major source of phonological errors, interference errors are only one of the many types of errors found in other areas of the learner's linguistic knowledge. Thus, the value of CA as the diagnostician and panacea of all ills was soon questioned.

At the same time, developments in the fields of linguistics (including L1 acquisition) and psychology began to attract the attention of theorists seeking alternative explanations about the source(s) of L2 learner error and how it should be treated. In the field of linguistics, structuralist accounts, describing the surface structure of a large corpus of language, were being replaced with a generative account, focusing on the rule-governed and creative nature of language. In the field of psychology, the prominent role of the environment in shaping children's language and behavior, advocated by Skinner (1957), was giving way to a more developmentalist view of learning, promoted by Piaget and colleagues (Piaget, 1970; Piaget & Inhelder, 1966). Each of these developments was reflected in Chomsky's (1959) beliefs about how children acquire their L1. He explained that children do not learn and produce a large set of sentences but create new sentences that have never been heard before, and that they do this because they internalize rules rather than strings of words. With regard to the complexity and abstractness of such rules, he explained that (1) children have an innate faculty that guides them in their learning of language; (2) they are programmed to discover the rules; and (3) they are guided in doing this by an innate knowledge of what the rules should look like. Underpinned by Chomsky's views, the L1 acquisition studies of the 1970s (e.g., Brown, 1973; Klima & Bellugi, 1966; Slobin, 1970) further revealed (1) that children go through stages; (2) that these stages are similar across children for a given language and across languages; (3) that child language is rule-governed and systematic; (4) that children are resistant to error correction; (5) that their processing capacity limits the number of rules they can apply at any one time; and (6) that they will revert to earlier hypotheses when two or more rules compete. These discoveries, together with the growing disillusionment with CA's ability to predict areas of difficulty, led to an interest in the language that is produced by L2 learners and, in particular, to an interest in the systematic investigation of second language learner errors, known as Error Analysis (EA).

The particular contribution of EA was its convincing discovery that the majority of L2 errors do not come from the learner's L1 or the L2 and that they must, therefore, be learner-internal. So, in order to understand them, error classifications were attempted by researchers and comparisons were made with errors that children were also making as they learned their L1. But, despite its practical focus, EA soon came under attack on theoretical grounds. On the one hand, it was being realized that the behaviorist belief of learning, as a response to external stimuli, was too limited in its focus and that it failed to account for what occurs in the learner's mind. On the other hand, it was argued that the dynamic and systematic nature of learner errors, revealed also in L1 acquisition

6 Theory and History of Error Treatment

studies, showed that learners actively construct their own rules about what is acceptable in the target language and that the language they produce develops over time. In 1972, Selinker coined the term "interlanguage" to describe this focus on the language produced by learners. It was characterized as a "system" in its own right, obeying its own rules, and as a "dynamic" system, evolving over time.

Early investigations into the nature of the learner's interlanguage were inspired by the L1 acquisition morpheme studies of Brown (1973) and de Villiers and de Villiers (1973). Examining the acquisition of fourteen grammatical morphemes in English, they found a consistent pattern in the order of emergence. This development then inspired SLA researchers to investigate the acquisition of the same morphemes by L2 learners. Dulay and Burt (1973) investigated the acquisition of eight of Brown's morphemes in Spanish-speaking children and Chinese-speaking children acquiring English as an L2 and found that children of different language backgrounds learning English in a variety of host country environments acquire grammatical morphemes in a similar order. Bailey, Madden, and Krashen (1974) also found that adult as well as child learners of English as an L2 develop accuracy in a number of grammatical morphemes in a set order, irrespective of the learning context. From this, they concluded that the existence of such an order indicated the operation of internal principles. Additional support for this observation came from studies reporting the systematic development of syntactic domains, including negative structures, interrogatives, and relative clauses.

In light of these findings, earlier theoretical perspectives about how an L2 is acquired and about the role of error in that process were rapidly being undermined. The role of error in the L2 learning process was, therefore, seen less in terms of a sinful act that must be prevented from occurring and more positively as an indicator of the mental processes that take place during the learning and acquisition of the target language. Before we discuss the role of error in second language development, it is important that we review the kind of research that was being undertaken in these early years on the role of written CF and the pedagogical advice that was being offered.

Early Written CF Research and Pedagogical Advice

Even from the early years of SLA research, studies of written CF had investigated pedagogically driven questions such as the reasons for correcting errors, which errors should be corrected and when, how they should be corrected, and who should do the correcting. Compared with the foci of more recent years, the early studies did not look at the more crucial underlying questions about whether or not, and the extent to which, written CF has the potential to help learners acquire the target language. Nevertheless, empirical questions were being asked about the treatment of written error even though, as Hendrickson (1978) wrote in his review essay, they were really "quite speculative and relatively scant" (p. 396). On the questions that this research did investigate, Burt (1975) reported that no current standards existed on whether, when, which, or how student errors should be corrected or who should correct them, and Robinson (1971) noted that there were few widely accepted linguistic criteria for grammatical and lexical correction in foreign language (FL) teaching. Although Hendrickson (1977) wrote of the immediate need for more research into these issues, he acknowledged that there was a body of literature that was beginning to think about the role of written CF in L2 learning and how it might be most effectively provided.

Should learner errors be corrected? The first question—should learner errors be corrected—was considered in a more limited way during these years than it has been more recently. In these early years, the focus was on reasons for correcting errors rather than on the more important question about whether it can be expected to "work" or play a role in the SLA process. According to Corder (1973), George (1972), and Kennedy (1973), correction was important because it was expected to help learners identify their own errors and discover the functions and limitations of the syntactical and lexical forms of the target language. In addition to these reasons, Cathcart and Olsen (1976) wrote of the importance of meeting learner expectations. They found, in their survey of college students' attitudes toward error correction, that they not only wanted to be corrected but that they wanted to be corrected more than teachers believed was necessary.

When should learner errors be corrected? Although the second question—when should learner errors be corrected—was largely under-researched, there was no shortage of opinion on the matter. As Hendrickson (1978) noted, there were at least 15 pieces of literature claiming that teachers had largely rejected the obsessive concern with error avoidance that characterized audiolingually orientated practice, and that there was a willingness to accept a wide range of errors and only correct those that they considered most problematic. But, because there was little empirical evidence on this issue during these years, Hendrickson (1978) called for more experimental research and suggested that, "it should focus on the cognitive effects of error correction based on different levels of language proficiency and relevant personality factors such as willingness to take risks" (p. 390).

Which learner errors should be corrected? The third question—which learner errors should be corrected—was considered more from a theoretical perspective than from an empirical perspective. Three broad categories of error were considered by teachers to be the most worthy of being corrected: those that impair communication significantly, those that have highly stigmatizing effects on the listener or reader, and those that occur frequently in learners' speech and writing. The few studies that investigated the question (Hendrickson, 1977; Olsson, 1972; Powell, 1973) found respectively that errors in French often resulted from reduction (especially in tense markers); that semantic errors in Swedish hindered communication more than syntactic ones; that global errors in intermediate

8 Theory and History of Error Treatment

English as a Second Language (ESL) learner writing resulted from inadequate lexical knowledge and misuse of prepositions and pronouns; and that most local errors resulted from misuse and omission of prepositions, lack of subject-verb agreement, and incorrect spelling and word choice. Although high-frequency errors were considered most in need of immediate error correction, the benefits of this approach were not tested empirically during these years.

How should learner errors be corrected? The fourth question—how should errors be corrected—received scarcely any empirical attention during these years despite the range of error correction methods being advocated. According to Hendrickson (1978), there was an urgent need for research into the value of using direct and indirect teacher correction, systematic methods of correction, the provision of selective feedback, the keeping of logs and charts, and the merits of focusing on individual student needs.

Who should correct learner errors? The fifth question—who should correct learner errors—was considered more from an intuitive perspective than from an empirical perspective. For instance, suggestions were made about the relative merits of teacher correction, peer correction, and self-correction but again, as Hendrickson (1978) pointed out, the relative effects of these approaches could only be "substantiated or refuted by conducting a series of carefully controlled experiments" (p. 396).

From this overview, it can be seen that pedagogical approaches to error correction in these early years were essentially based on intuition about what seemed to be effective practice. For each of the five questions referred to above, teachers had little empirical evidence on which to base their handling of learner errors but an exposure to plenty of theoretical and anecdotal views. This did not mean, however, that there was a reluctance by educators to publish pedagogical materials that were considered helpful for classroom teachers. For instance, three noteworthy publications, describing types and causes of learner error, appeared in the early 1970s, together with pedagogical suggestions on how they might be avoided and treated. George (1972) described three key causes of error (redundancy of the code, unsuitable presentation in class, and several types of interference) and explained how they could be treated in language classrooms. The second publication, *The Gooficon*, by Burt and Kiparsky (1972), was a collection of goofs and their explanations, designed to draw teachers' attentions to the systematic ways English can be used incorrectly and to ways in which error can be corrected. It also provided a taxonomy of error types (clausal, auxiliary, passive, temporal conjunctions, sentential components, and psychological predicates). Continuing the taxonomic approach of Burt and Kiparsky, Heaton and Turton's *Longman Dictionary of Common Errors* (1987) provided an alphabetically ordered list of 1,700 errors in English that are most frequently made by L2 learners, including those that the authors saw as characteristic of learners from specific L1 contexts (see Chapter 2 also). While each of these publications was considered helpful to teachers wanting direction and assistance in responding to learners' errors, they were justified on the belief that error was worth correcting and that written CF had a role to play in L2 acquisition. Little did early advocates of written CF realize that, at the beginning of the 1980s, there would be a swing in the opposite direction as Krashen and his advocates downplayed the role of error and its treatment in the SLA process. Krashen produced what has come to be regarded as the first comprehensive theory and model of SLA—the Monitor Model. It is to this landmark contribution that we now turn our attention.

The First General SLA Theory—Krashen's Monitor Model

Although Krashen's (1981, 1982, 1984, 1985) theoretical perspectives have received considerable criticism over the years, they have nevertheless been highly influential in shaping the direction of subsequent perspectives over the last three decades. Therefore, it is important that we consider this contribution in some detail before we look at more recent theoretical perspectives on how L2 acquisition can be explained and on the role of error and corrective feedback in the process.

Krashen's general theory comprised five basic hypotheses, each of which had implications for the way in which error was viewed and the extent to which it is worth treating. Although his arguments have been highly influential in shaping the direction of subsequent theoretical perspectives and their associated research agendas, none of his hypotheses has escaped a significant degree of criticism.

The Acquisition-learning Hypothesis. In this hypothesis, Krashen (1985) made a distinction between "acquisition" and "learning," claiming that they are two separate processes. He referred to "acquisition" as the "subconscious process identical in all important ways to the process children utilize in acquiring their first language" and to "learning" as the "conscious process that results in 'knowing about' language" (p. 1). He saw "acquisition" occurring as a result of learners interacting in natural, meaningful communication and "learning" occurring as a result of classroom instruction and activities in which the learner's attention is focused on form (i.e., what is considered accurate or target-like and what is erroneous and therefore not target-like). Krashen maintained that knowledge of the target language "acquired" and "learned" by these different routes cannot become integrated into a unified whole. In other words, he saw no role for CF in helping learners to develop their acquired knowledge (i.e., the type of knowledge that is used instinctively in online communication when there is little to no time available to reflect on one's learned knowledge). This means that he saw no value for acquisition in the learning that results from instruction and CF. Many, such as DeKeyser (2001, 2007) and McLaughlin (1978, 1980, 1987), disagreed with this position, claiming that there is an interface position—one in which "learned" knowledge can be converted into "acquired" knowledge. Nevertheless, the influence of Krashen's distinction has been pervasive in the theoretical perspectives advanced over the last 30 years and will be noted in later sections of this chapter.

10   Theory and History of Error Treatment

The Monitor Hypothesis. Given the specific ways in which Krashen saw acquisition and learning being used in target language production, it is not difficult to understand the claims of his second hypothesis—the monitor hypothesis. He believed that the only function learning has is one that enables a learner to monitor or edit what is produced by the acquired system. As McLaughlin (1987) explained it, "the monitor is thought to alter the output of the acquired system before or after the utterance is actually written or spoken, but the utterance is initiated entirely by the acquired system" (p. 24). This means, therefore, that the monitor will be able to operate when there is sufficient time (e.g., during written performance but not necessarily during oral performance), when a focus on accuracy is important to the learner, and when the learner has linguistic knowledge relevant to the form or structure in question. From both claims, it would seem that Krashen was not totally ruling out a role for error correction in the written context providing the target linguistic error category has been acquired. On the other hand, he did not see a role for error correction in either oral or written contexts if the linguistic form or structure is still being acquired. Despite any intuitive appeal this particular claim might have, it has, nevertheless, been criticized because attempts to test it empirically have failed. Another problem that critics have had with the monitor hypothesis is that it is impossible to tell when a learner is consciously applying a rule from the learned system and when the learner is applying, subconsciously, a rule from the acquired system.

The Natural Order Hypothesis. The third hypothesis stated that learners acquire the rules of language in a predictable order, with some coming early and others coming late. According to Krashen, the order does not appear to be determined solely by formal simplicity and the order is not dependent on the order in which rules are taught in language classes. Thus, he claimed that there is no value to be gained from classroom instruction and, therefore, error correction, if one's focus is on subconscious acquisition of the target language. This further implies that a focus on error and its treatment in the classroom is not going to aid the acquisition process so should be regarded as unnecessary. This position runs counter to those reviewed in the previous section of this chapter, which acknowledged the partial role, at least, of language transfer and of instructional attempts to treat error. It also fails to account for situations in which the learner is "ready" to acquire a new linguistic form or structure.

The Input Hypothesis. Arising from the natural order hypothesis is the Input Hypothesis. Here, Krashen (1985) claimed that L2 learners move along the developmental continuum by receiving comprehensible input. By this, he means input about the target language that is just a little beyond the learner's current level of syntactic complexity. He explained that, if a learner's current level is i, then comprehensible input for that learner will be $i + 1$, where 1 refers to the next stage in the developmental sequence. He claimed that, "if input is understood, and there is enough of it, the necessary grammar is automatically provided" (p. 2). Consequently, he went on to claim that, when learners are exposed to enough comprehensible input, there is no need for formal grammar instruction and thus, by implication, no need to focus a learner's attention on errors that have been made or to try to treat them in any way.

For Krashen, the Input Hypothesis was the central component of his overall theory. Clearly, however, the same value has not been attached to it by those advocating a role for conscious learning in the acquisition process. At least four criticisms of it have been made. First, its vagueness and imprecision with regard to how one might determine level i and level $i + 1$ have been highlighted. Second, the circular nature of the claims have been criticized. Krashen states, on the one hand, that "acquisition" takes place if a learner receives comprehensible input and, on the other hand, that comprehensible input is said to have been provided if "acquisition" takes place. Third, attention has been drawn to the impossibility of testing it without a clear definition of what constitutes comprehensible input and how it might relate to acquisition. Fourth, no consideration was given to the internal workings of the Language Acquisition Device (LAD) where Krashen claims that acquisition occurs. Each learner is believed to have a LAD that contains information about the possible form the grammar of any language can take.

The Affective Filter Hypothesis. Building on the Input Hypothesis, Krashen's next hypothesis states that the input a learner is exposed to must be "taken in" by the learner and, for this to occur, a learner's affective filter must sufficiently low. He claims that those whose attitudes are not optimal for second language acquisition will not only tend to seek less input, but they will also have a high or strong affective filter—even if they understand the message, the input will not reach that part of the brain responsible for language acquisition, or the LAD. He also refers to harmful effects that can arise from a high affective filter, including increased anxiety and low self-esteem. Although most would agree that affective variables play an important role in L2 acquisition, the hypothesis has been criticized on other grounds. Theoretically, it is faulty because self-conscious learners, who often suffer low self-esteem and who, therefore, have a high filter, are not necessarily poor language learners. Equally, confident learners who manifest outgoing attributes are not necessarily good language learners. Secondly, it has been criticized for its limited explanation about how the filter works.

Despite the criticisms that have been levelled against Krashen's claims, they have nevertheless been highly influential in pedagogy and, arguably, to a lesser extent, in a range of more recent theoretical and empirical developments. It is to these developments that we now turn our attention: (1) those that propose a more positive role than that advocated by Krashen for understanding the nature of learner error and how it might be used to facilitate SLA, and (2) those that, in essence, echo Krashen's beliefs.

12 Theory and History of Error Treatment

Recent Perspectives on Error and Written CF in SLA

Over the last 20 years, theoretical perspectives in second language learning/ acquisition, including the role of error and its treatment, have become more prominent. Continuing their interest in understanding how the learning/ acquisition process works and how the human brain processes and learns new information, theorists and researchers, working within various cognitive frameworks, have focused their attention on the learner as an essentially autonomous individual who, despite drawing upon input from his social environment, ultimately determines his own learning/acquisition path. Also interested in the cognitive processing of language input are socio-cognitive theorists and researchers who focus on the interacting roles of one's social environment and one's cognitive processes. Even more recently, socio-cultural theorists and researchers, following Vygotskyan beliefs and practices, have brought our attention to the socially mediated and socially constructed nature of learning. We will now examine what we consider to be the most influential of these perspectives in terms of their stated and implied inclusion of a role for CF in the SLA process.

Cognitive Perspective—Information Processing Models and Theories

Information processing models, developed by cognitive psychologists, have had a strong influence on two important L2 information processing models developed by McLaughlin (1987, 1990) and Anderson (1983, 1985). These models see SLA as a building up of knowledge systems that can eventually be called on automatically by learners.

McLaughlin's Model. Based on the view that complex behavior builds on simple processes, McLaughlin (1987) argues that it is appropriate to also view second language learning in this light because it involves the acquisition of a complex cognitive skill:

> To learn a second language is to learn a *skill*, because various aspects of the task must be practiced and integrated into fluent performance. This requires the automatization of component sub-skills. Learning is a *cognitive* process, because it is thought to involve internal representations that regulate and guide performance ... As performance improves, there is constant restructuring as learners simplify, unify, and gain increasing control over their internal representations. These two notions—automatization and restructuring—are central to cognitive theory.
>
> *(pp. 133–134, original emphases)*

This model accommodates the view that information may be processed in either a controlled or automatic manner and that learning involves a shift from controlled toward automatic processing. It explains that intentional learning, for example, by means of explicit instruction and corrective feedback, can play a significant role in the controlled phase and through "practice" or "repeated activation" over time become automatized.

The model shows how learners first resort to *controlled processing* in the L2—a process involving the temporary activation of a selection of information nodes in the memory, in a new configuration. Because this processing requires a lot of attentional control on the part of the learner, it is constrained by the limitations of the *short-term memory* (STM). But, through repeated activation, sequences first produced by controlled processing become *automatic*. Automatized sequences are then stored as units in the *long-term memory* (LTM) and so are made available very rapidly whenever the situation requires them, with minimal attentional control by the learner. As a result, automatic processes can work in parallel, activating clusters of complex cognitive skills simultaneously. Thus, *learning* is seen as the movement from controlled to automatic processing via practice. When this shift occurs, controlled processes are freed to deal with higher levels of processing (i.e., to the integration of more complex skill clusters), thus explaining the incremental nature of learning. McLaughlin is of the view that it is necessary for simple sub-skills and routines to become automatic before more complex ones can be considered. The ongoing movement from controlled to automatic processing results in a constant *restructuring* of the linguistic system of the L2 learner. However, as he also points out, restructuring can also destabilize some features of the interlanguage to the point where those that may have appeared to have been acquired later appear as errors.

It is not difficult to see a role for corrective feedback within the controlled processing component of this model. It accommodates the view that intentional learning, for example, by means of explicit instruction and CF, can play an important role in the controlled phase and ultimately lead to automatized processing. This view is corroborated by others who maintain that knowledge obtained as a result of controlled processing can be converted to automatized knowledge (referred to in our overview of the next model). As we can see, this model is quite different from Krashen's model where a role for CF was seen as non-facilitative of automatized processing, characteristic of a learner with "acquired" knowledge.

Anderson's Model. Anderson's ACT (Adaptive Control of Thought) model (1993) is similar to McLaughlin's model in that it centers on the belief that practice leads to automatization. As Anderson puts it, *declarative knowledge* (knowledge *that*) can become *procedural knowledge* (knowledge *how*). Declarative knowledge is the type of knowledge that Krashen refers to when he defines *learning* and the type of knowledge that he claims is not able to be *acquired* as automatized *procedural knowledge* and the type of knowledge that is processed during the controlled phase of McLaughlin's model. Although Anderson's model is a general model of skill acquisition, several SLA researchers (Johnson, 1996; O'Malley & Chamot, 1990; Schmidt, 1992; Towell & Hawkins, 1994) explain how it can be applied to aspects of L2 learning that require proceduralization and automatization. The following

14 Theory and History of Error Treatment

example from Mitchell and Myles (2004) explains how the model works in the language-learning context:

> If we take the example of the third person singular −*s* marker on present tense verbs in English, the classroom learner might initially know, in the sense that they have consciously learnt the rule, that *s*/*he* + verb requires the addition of an −*s* to the stem of the verb. However, the same learner might not necessarily be able to consistently produce the −*s* in a conversation in real time. This is because this particular learner has declarative knowledge of that rule, but it has not yet been proceduralized. After much practice, this knowledge will hopefully become fully proceduralized, and the third person −*s* will be supplied when the conversation requires it. This dichotomy between, on the one hand, knowing a rule, and on the other, being able to apply it when needed, is all to familiar to second language learners and teachers.
>
> *(p. 103)*

As we have already seen in our outline of Krashen's and McLaughlin's models, the more important (and controversial) issue is whether declarative knowledge can be converted into procedural knowledge in the L2 learning context. This has been keenly debated over the years because, if the former cannot be converted into the latter (the ultimate goal of SLA), the role of instruction and corrective feedback is brought into question. Anderson (1993) believes that it can be. He suggests that there are three stages in the process and illustrates these with reference to the third person singular −*s* example above:

1. The cognitive stage (a description of the procedure is learned—an −*s* must be added to the verb after a third person subject).
2. The associative stage (a method for performing the skill is worked out—how to add an −*s* when the context requires it).
3. The autonomous stage (the skill becomes more and more rapid and automatic—the learners adds an −*s* more and more automatically).

Other theorists and researchers (e.g., DeKeyser, 1997, 2001, 2007; Hulstijn, 1995; Schmidt, 1990, 1994, 1995; Schmidt & Frota, 1986; Swain, 1985; Swain & Lapkin, 1995) support the view that controlled activities, including instruction and corrective feedback, can facilitate the conversion of declarative knowledge into automatized procedural knowledge. DeKeyser's (1997) analysis, for example, revealed how explicit knowledge of L2 grammar rules can be gradually automatized through prolonged systematic practice but, as he mentions later (DeKeyser, 2003), "very little empirical evidence exists that systematically documents the change of L2 knowledge as a result of practice over a long period of time" (p. 328). That said, he nevertheless explains that "there is no evidence in the second language acquisition literature that explicit learning and practice cannot lead to automatized procedural knowledge, only a dearth of evidence that it can . . . (Relative) absence of evidence is not evidence of absence" (p. 328).

Cognitive Perspective—Pienemann's Model

The third information processing theorist we wish to refer to is Pienemann, whose processability and teachability theories address one of the potential constraints in the progress that learners can make as they move from the controlled processing of declarative knowledge to the automatized production of procedural knowledge. With regard to the role of written CF in this process, Pienemann, like McLaughlin and Anderson, is less explicit about the specific contribution of CF to the process than he is about the role of instruction. However, it is not difficult to make a connection to what he says about the learning and teaching of linguistic forms/structures and a role for CF within his processing claims and teaching possibilities. In his teachability hypothesis, Pienemann (1981, 1987, 1989, 1998) explained that grammar instruction can only be effective if it is provided when the learner is at a stage in his/her interlanguage that is close to the point when it could be acquired naturally. He adds that an L2 learner cannot progress if one stage is missing and that teaching can be constrained by the stage a learner is at.

Providing empirical validation of these claims, Johnston (1985) found no evidence to contradict Pienemann's stages when he investigated 12 grammatical rules and their predicted acquisition according to processability theory with a sample of adult Polish and Vietnamese immigrants in Australia. Similarly, Pienemann and Mackey (1993) found no evidence to contradict the theory when they tested it with 13 children who were learning English in an ESL context. It would seem, therefore, that a predictable order of acquisition does exist. Extrapolating this to a role for written CF, it would seem reasonable to conclude that written CF needs to be directed at grammatical features that learners are ready to acquire.

Reflecting on the contribution of these information processing perspectives, we can see that both McLaughlin's and Anderson's models explain that language learning and acquisition can occur, as the controlled processing of declarative knowledge is converted into automatized procedural knowledge as a result of practice. The controlled processing stage occurs as learners receive input (e.g., explicit instruction) and feedback (written CF) on their written output. However, as Pienemann explains, information processing is unlikely to occur if the targeted linguistic forms and structures lie outside a learner's stage of "readiness" or, as we will see later in our discussion of socio-cultural theory, outside his/her zone of proximal development.

Up to this point, our focus has been on cognitive, information processing perspectives and their focus on the learner primarily as an autonomous individual than as a social being, situated in a socially influential environment. From this

16 Theory and History of Error Treatment

point on, we explore other theoretical perspectives relevant to the role of error and its treatment in SLA, namely those that view language learning/acquisition in more social terms. First, we will consider those who see the social perspective interacting with the cognitive perspective—the interactionists.

Cognitive Perspective—the Interactionist Perspective

Interactionist perspectives on SLA have focused primarily on the role of oral interaction between learners and their interlocutors. Consequently, theorizing the role of interaction and testing its role in SLA have occurred more frequently in oral contexts than in written contexts. However, this does not mean that proposals and empirical findings arising from this context are irrelevant to the written context and the role of written CF in SLA. In completing our survey of this work, we will identify ways in which its significance for the written context has been noted and signal ways in which theoretical constructs and empirical findings might also be extrapolated to the written context.

Early interactionists identified negotiation of meaning between L2 learners and their interlocutors, as they interactionally modified their utterances to achieve mutual understanding when communication breakdowns occurred, as an important component of the learning/acquisition process. Long, in his 1996 Interaction Hypothesis, proposed that the use of conversational strategies such as repetitions, confirmation checks, comprehension checks, and clarification requests enable interlocutors to resolve communication difficulties, including those that may have arisen as a result of learner errors. As an extension of Krashen's Input Hypothesis (1985), Long argued that native speakers and L2 learners collaborate in such circumstances to ensure that the learner is receiving $i + 1$ rather than $i + 3$ or $i + 0$. He further argued that, if linguistic/conversational adjustments could be shown to promote comprehension of input and that this input was shown to promote acquisition, it could be concluded that linguistic/conversational adjustments promote acquisition. However, criticisms similar to those levelled against Krashen's original Input Hypothesis (its extreme generality and failure to specify the supposed psycholinguistic mechanisms by which comprehensible input might be analyzed and integrated into the learner's developing L2) were made of Long's Interaction Hypothesis. It was criticized for its focus on analyzing functional aspects of language rather than grammatical aspects and for the lack of empirical evidence about how interaction affects grammatical developments.

Long's reformulation of the Interaction Hypothesis (1996) placed a greater emphasis on linking features of input and the linguistic environment (i.e., the social dimension) with learner-internal factors (the cognitive dimension), explaining how these may facilitate subsequent language development:

> It is proposed that environmental contributions to acquisition are mediated by *selective attention* and the learner's developing L2 processing capacity, and

that these resources are brought together most usefully, although not exclusively, during negotiation of meaning. *Negative feedback* obtained during negotiation work or elsewhere may be facilitative of L2 development, at least for vocabulary, morphology and language-specific syntax, and essential for learning certain specifiable L1–L2 contrasts.

(p. 414, original emphases)

The case for including negative evidence (including CF) as well as positive evidence as input for language learning has been promoted by theorists because, even though those who explain that a constant diet of well-formed utterances provides the learner with evidence on structures that the target language does permit, input does not provide specific enough information on the limits to the system. Evidence that a role exists for negative evidence and CF in SLA has mainly arisen from classroom-based research, and it is this research base that we will document later in this chapter before we provide an introduction to written CF research.

The reformulated hypothesis also includes the beliefs that a learner's *processing capacity* and *degree of attention* to linguistic form may determine the extent to which L2 input becomes L2 intake (i.e., is incorporated into the learner's developing L2 system). Whereas Krashen stated that it was sufficient for a learner to pay attention to the meaning embedded in comprehensible input for acquisition to occur, interactionists such as Sharwood Smith (1981, 1993) and Schmidt (1990, 1994) explained that learners need to pay some attention to language form and structure if acquisition is to occur. Evidence of this need can be seen if we consider the French immersion programs in Canada, where it has been shown that, even though learners may develop fluency, functional abilities, and confidence in using the target language, they fail to achieve high levels of performance in some aspects of French grammar even after several years of full-day exposure to the target language (Harley & Swain, 1984). Consequently, interactionists explain the need to provide learners with negative evidence as well as positive evidence. The advent of focus on form (Long, 1991, 1996; Long & Robinson, 1998), which advocated spontaneous and brief attention to linguistic form in response to learners' problematic utterances within meaning-focused interaction, was one way in which this could be achieved.

In providing negative evidence and CF, Schmidt (1994) argued that it is important to distinguish between different types of attention: noticing, understanding, and awareness. *Noticing* refers to the process of bringing some stimulus into focal attention (i.e., registering its simple occurrence) while *understanding* and *awareness* refer to explicit knowledge (e.g., awareness of a rule). While he claimed that more noticing leads to more learning, he was less definite about the role of awareness. From empirical evidence, he noted that learners can make judgments about what is acceptable and unacceptable in target language data without necessarily being able to explain an underlying rule. However, he and others (e.g., Sharwood Smith, 1994) argued that *consciousness-raising* and *input enhancement*

18 Theory and History of Error Treatment

(through combinations of heightened saliency for target L2 items, meta-linguistic commentary, and negative feedback, including CF) may be important components of effective classroom learning for some forms and structures.

In summary, the interactionist perspective proposed a role for negative evidence (corrective feedback) in the SLA process. Insofar as its proposals were related to oral contexts, the literature has focused primarily on the role of oral CF in L2 development. We have seen that several mediating factors may impact upon the extent to which oral negative evidence can facilitate L2 development: the processing capacity of a learner; the degree of attention he/she gives to noticing, understanding, and awareness. This section has also referred to the roles that consciousness-raising and input enhancement (through a targeted or selective focus, the provision of meta-linguistic information, and corrective feedback) can play in facilitating the process. Although, as we have said, the focus of theorists and researchers has been on oral CF, it is not difficult to see where oral processes and conditions apply to written CF in L2 development. As we explain in Chapter 5, theorists and researchers interested in the potential of written CF for L2 development now need to more fully theorize and empirically test the commonalities between oral and written CF, and identify where any difference might lie. Piecemeal considerations have been offered in a few conference presentations, journal articles, theses, and dissertations, but published contributions of a comprehensive and systematic nature have yet to be offered.

Socio-cultural Perspective—a Different Interactionist Perspective

Socio-cultural theory of human mental processing, based on the work of Vygotsky (an early twentieth-century Russian psychologist), provides a very different perspective on the role of interaction in SLA. It assumes that all cognitive development, including language development, occurs as a result of social interactions between individuals, especially when learners have opportunities to collaborate and interact with speakers of the target language who are more knowledgeable than they are (e.g., teachers and more advanced learners). Lantolf and others (e.g., Lantolf & Thorne, 2007; Swain, Brooks, & Tocalli-Beller, 2002) suggested that L2 learners can achieve higher levels of linguistic knowledge when they receive appropriate scaffolding (i.e., the process of support that involves a shift from collaborative inter-mental activity to autonomous intra-mental activity). Thus, it is claimed that learners, with the assistance of *other regulation* (e.g., provided by teachers and more advanced learners) can eventually be *self-regulated* (i.e., able to use the L2 autonomously). In particular, it is believed to be most effective in the learner's *zone of proximal development (ZPD)* (i.e., the domain or skill where the learner is not yet capable of using the L2 autonomously as procedural knowledge but where, with the scaffolded assistance of the more proficient partner, level of performance can be raised). In this role, other regulators may draw upon strategies such as repetition, simplification, modelling, and corrective feedback (Lantolf & Thorne, 2007). Empirical evidence of L2 development in the zone of proximal development occurring during scaffolded teacher (expert)/student (novice) talk has been published by a number of researchers (e.g., Aljaafreh & Lantolf, 1994; Nassaji & Swain, 2000) in written contexts. A detailed discussion of the empirical studies will be given in Chapter 3.

Activity theory. Another component of socio-cultural theory that has relevance to both oral and written CF is *activity theory* (Lantolf & Appel, 1994; Leontiev, 1981). It sees all human actions, including mediated action, as configurations of both social and individual influences within a dynamic system—a system that must be investigated holistically rather than as discrete parts. This theory focuses on the individual goals that learners have when undertaking a particular task or problem. For example, when a teacher gives students a particular writing task, some learners may focus their attention on accuracy while others may focus on fluency. It may also be the case that the entry levels of knowledge and skill that individuals bring to the task vary and that these may also vary during the task itself. Although, as we will see in Chapter 3, the research base informing socio-cultural theory and activity theory is quite limited at this stage, its proposals are interesting and may well be helpful in advancing our understanding of why some learners benefit from written CF and others fail to do so.

Up to this point, we have focused our attention on some of the main theoretical explanations of how the L2 is acquired and have identified some of the ways in which theorists and researchers could more thoroughly and more systematically consider the role of written CF in existing and future frameworks. One of the reasons this has not happened so far is that attention has been given to theorizing primarily within oral contexts how and why SLA processes occur. This is understandable given that SLA is concerned with understanding how learners acquire and use automatized procedural knowledge in oral production. Online oral output is certainly a clear measure of a learner's SLA development, but it does not mean, however, that what occurs in the written context does not and cannot play a role in developing a learner's procedural knowledge. The questions are what role and to what extent written CF can play a role.

Another reason the role of the written context has tended to take a back seat in SLA theory construction is the relative absence of concern about this situation by writing theorists and researchers working within the SLA perspective. Researchers who have had an interest in written CF have tended to assume that there is a role for written CF in SLA and have, therefore, focused their attention on more pedagogically driven questions about how written CF might be most effectively provided. As we saw earlier in Hendrickson's review of questions that had been investigated prior to the early 1980s, attention had been given to questions about whether error should be corrected, when it should be corrected, which errors should be corrected, how errors should be corrected, and who should do the correction. While similar questions continue to be investigated, it was not until Truscott (1996) published his case against the practice of error correction in L2 writing that the attention of theorists, researchers, and teachers was jolted into an acknowledgement of the need to empirically test whether in fact it works. The debate that this call for abandonment has produced over the last 15 years has been highly influential in forcing theorists, researchers, and teachers to either accept Truscott's call or produce argument and evidence to refute it. It is to the specific theoretical claims made by Truscott and others that we now turn our attention.

Perspectives of L2 Writing Theorists and Researchers on the Role of Written CF in SLA

Considering the number of published theoretical perspectives on how the L2 is acquired since the first general theory was proposed by Krashen in the early 1980s, limited attention had been specifically given in the published literature to the role of written CF in the SLA process prior to Truscott's 1996 article in *Language Learning* in which he proposed that error correction be abandoned. His justification for this position was based on theoretical, empirical, and pedagogical arguments, many of which he continues to maintain (see Truscott, 1999, 2004, 2007, 2009) despite the range of counter-arguments and the growing empirical evidence that have been presented in journal articles and conference papers by other theorists, researchers, and teachers. In this section, we will discuss his theoretical arguments against the practice. In discussing his claims, we will be reflecting on the extent to which they support or run counter to the SLA theoretical perspectives reviewed above.

Truscott's first argument was that teachers, in providing their learners with error correction, did so in the belief that a simple transfer of information would enable their learners to correct their grammatical errors and hopefully not repeat them in future pieces of writing. He explained how a view such as this failed to acknowledge the complex learning processes underpinning the development of a learner's interlanguage: "The acquisition of a grammatical structure is a gradual process, not a sudden discovery as the intuitive view of correction would imply" (Truscott, 1996, p. 342). However, such a view seems to ignore a number of reasonable claims advanced by cognitive and socio-cultural theorists. It does not seem to take into account the possibility that some learners who are *ready*, in Pienemann's terms (see p. 15), Krashen's terms (see p. 10) and socio-cultural terms (the ZPD), to acquire the form or structure targeted with written CF may, over time, show that they are able to use the targeted linguistic form or structure with greater accuracy. This can occur regardless of whether or not teachers understand the processes underlying interlanguage development. It can occur irrespective of whether they understand, agree, or disagree with information processing and skill acquisition theories (wherein it is claimed that declarative knowledge, including that provided by written CF, can be automatized to the point where it becomes procedural knowledge and be applied accurately and consistently over time). The number of occasions in which written CF will be required may vary from learner to learner according to the linguistic domain of the error and to any number of individual difference variables (in both cognitive and socio-cultural activity theory terms). Some empirical studies within the cognitive psycholinguistic perspective (to be discussed in detail in Chapter 3) have found that a single provision of written CF is all that is necessary, even though it is also recognized that some learners may benefit from additional feedback.

Developing his case about the complex learning processes underpinning interlanguage development, Truscott argued that no single form of correction can be expected to help learners acquire knowledge of all linguistic forms and structures because the acquisition of syntax, morphology, and lexis require an understanding not only of form but also of meaning and use in relation to other words and other parts of the language system. He argued, for instance, that written CF cannot be expected to facilitate syntactic knowledge because the domain is not characterized by a collection of discreet items that can be learned one by one. Few would question such a position. But, even though teachers may sometimes fail to use appropriate and effective ways of responding to these different types of error, this is not a theoretical reason for suggesting that written CF cannot be expected to be effective when targeting different types of error. Research to date, as we will see in Chapter 3, has demonstrated that written CF can successfully treat some error categories. Interestingly, some of these studies have shown that accuracy improves irrespective of the type of written CF provided. It is important to realize that the absence of research and, therefore, evidence on the effect of written CF across different domains is not evidence of ineffectiveness. More research is required, and an outline of what might be included in such an agenda will be discussed in Chapter 5.

The second argument that Truscott presented against the practice concerns the feasibility of providing written CF at a time when the learner is "ready" to acquire a particular form or structure. Framed in this way, the argument could be seen more as a pedagogical reason than as a theoretical one. However, the focus of the case presented issues related to the readiness of the learner to benefit from a focus on linguistic forms and structures that may lie outside his/her ZPD (in terms of socio-cultural theory) or out of sequence with the natural order (in terms of Krashen's hypothesis three). Truscott focuses his attention here on the feasibility of providing learners with written CF at a time that coincides with their readiness, suggesting that the task is impossible. Teachers of language learners who are placed in classes according to their proficiency level usually have little difficulty identifying the most problematic and most recurring linguistic errors of their learners and identifying those that their learners are likely to be ready to respond to with written CF. Even less experienced teachers are able to consult commercially produced course books, designed for learners at various

22 Theory and History of Error Treatment

proficiency levels, where the linguistic forms and structures have been selected on the basis of their appropriateness for learning/acquisition at such levels.

Truscott continued his feasibility argument by suggesting that written CF is unlikely to be effective if it is provided on too comprehensive a range of error categories. This would seem to be a reasonable argument and one that would imply that a selective focus on error treatment is therefore the approach to take with L2 learners in language classes. As we have seen, the role of selective attention was also included in Long's revised Interaction Hypothesis. However, in the same section, Truscott also discounted a more selective approach, claiming that there is evidence to suggest its ineffectiveness. The evidence he cites is Hendrickson (1981). More recent evidence, to be discussed in Chapters 3 and 4, reveals that a selective approach in both oral and written corrective feedback is clearly effective.

The third argument that Truscott (1996) presented against the practice of written CF is that learning that results from the practice is likely to be only "pseudo-learning"—described as "a superficial and possibly transient form of knowledge" (p. 345). Truscott makes a valid point when he draws our attention to the fact that some learning may, in fact, be pseudo-learning if, over time, it fails to be acquired and therefore not used with consistent accuracy. He refers to a number of studies to make the point that "knowledge which students had apparently acquired actually disappeared in a matter of months, probably indicating that the teaching had produced nothing more than pseudo-learning" (p. 346). It is well understood that this can be the case but then to leap to the claim that, without any support, "there is no reason to believe that it (error correction) is producing anything other than pseudo-learning (if it has any effect at all)" (p. 346) is both amazing and illogical. Considering this argument, one is reminded, on the one hand, of the distinction between "learning" and "acquisition" presented by Krashen (1982). In suggesting that written CF is likely to result in little more than pseudo-learning, Truscott is implying that such learning will not be useful for acquisition. This would also mean that he discounts a role for written CF in information processing and skill acquisition theories. He concedes that written CF might be useful for editing even though he claims that editing "depends far more on intuitions or well-formedness, coming from the unconscious language system, than on meta-linguistic knowledge of points of grammar" (p. 347). He concludes his third argument against written CF by saying, "pseudo-learning, along with problems stemming from the existence of developmental sequences, provides good reason to doubt the value of grammar correction" (p. 349). While not totally debunking the practice, he acknowledges that "it is conceivable that the situation will eventually change as the result of future research, (but) we should not expect correction to be helpful, at least not as it is currently practiced" (p. 349).

As well as theorizing why error correction should not be provided in L2 writing classes, Truscott also claimed that there was empirical evidence of its ineffectiveness. However, as we will see in Chapter 3, the evidence he presented was extremely limited and the findings of the studies were conflicting.

Additionally, there were significant shortcomings with the design and analysis of the studies, meaning it is unwise to make definitive claims.

The third part of Truscott's case against the provision of error correction was pedagogically focused. On the one hand, he questioned the ability of some teachers to provide consistent and accurate error correction and the ability of some learners to understand what is meant by the feedback. On the other hand, he argued that providing learners with error correction could be counterproductive. For instance, he stated that teachers who provide error correction may cause learners to avoid using forms and structures they are unsure of and, therefore, discourage them from hypothesizing. He also argued, in the same way that Krashen (1984) did, that the time spent by teachers giving error correction and by learners responding to it takes their time and energy away from more important writing activities.

Not surprisingly, Truscott's call was responded to with equally strong counter-arguments. Ferris (1999) was the first to publish a rebuttal of his case, arguing that his conclusions were premature in light of the limited and conflicting evidence and that further research was required before a stand could be made one way or other. Her arguments were less theoretical than empirical and pedagogical, and will be discussed in Chapters 3 and 5, where our attention is given to these responses.

Over the last 15 years, Truscott has essentially maintained his stance against the practice, even though he has suggested that written CF may be effective in certain limited situations (Truscott, 1996, 1999, 2004, 2007, 2009; Truscott & Hsu, 2008).Whether or not he sees these minor and relatively "uninteresting" instances important enough to be considered evidence of the conversion of declarative knowledge to procedural knowledge is uncertain. For many SLA theorists and researchers, greater interest and importance is given to constructing a tenable theoretical platform for the practice and to investigating empirically the effectiveness of written CF in these terms as well as pedagogically (Bitchener & Knoch, 2010a, 2010b; Ferris, 2010; Hartshorn et al., 2010).

As we have already mentioned, theoretical perspectives underpinning written CF have been somewhat piecemeal. Nevertheless, some consideration has been given to questions concerning (1) whether or not written CF can be expected to be effective in helping L2 learners improve the accuracy of their writing over time and in facilitating the SLA process; (2) the circumstances/situations constraining levels of effectiveness; (3) pedagogical issues (e.g., type of feedback that is most effective, which errors should be corrected, when feedback should be provided, who should provide it, how it should be provided, who it should be given to, and so on); and (4) teacher and learner perspectives on the value of providing/receiving feedback. The first two of these questions have been of interest in more recent years, with the advent of SLA theories seeking to explain interlanguage processes and the role of error and corrective feedback in the various processes, whereas the third and fourth questions have been considered, to some extent at least (as we saw above), for more than 40 years.

24 Theory and History of Error Treatment

Before we turn our attention to an overview of the more recent research investigating theoretical issues (about the potential of written CF in the SLA process) and more pedagogically driven issues (about effective written CF practice), our next section will focus on an outline of some of the issues and findings in the oral CF literature. There are several reasons for doing this. On the one hand, oral CF research has received more attention, and for a longer period of time, than written CF research. In many respects, it is able to report more conclusive findings than is so far possible with written CF research. On the other hand, the design, execution, and analysis of oral CF research has been less flawed than the early written CF studies, and so researchers in the written CF context have been able to learn a lot from oral CF research about appropriate and effective design, execution, and analysis. Our focus will be on traversing the territory only; Chapter 3 will provide a detailed account of the individual studies.

Studies of Oral CF

Not surprisingly, a considerable body of oral CF research has focused on assessing the effectiveness for SLA. Although Krashen (1985) and Truscott (1999) doubted its value for L2 acquisition, a growing number of studies, including several meta-analyses (Li, 2010; Mackey & Goo, 2007; Russell & Spada, 2006) have reported positive findings for the practice. Equally positive findings have been reported for different types of feedback, including mixed types of feedback on various incidentally targeted linguistic items (Loewen, 2005), mixed types of feedback on specific linguistic items (Adams, 2007), and specific types of feedback (e.g., recasts) on specific linguistic structures (Révész & Han, 2006; Sachs & Suh, 2007; Trofimiovitch, Ammar, & Gatbonton, 2007). Other studies have compared different types of feedback together with a control group and, while finding feedback to be effective, discovered no difference in effect for feedback type (Ammar & Spada, 2006; Loewen & Nabei, 2007; McDonough, 2007). Several studies have found meta-linguistic feedback to have a significantly larger effect than other types of feedback like recasts (Dabaghi & Basturkmen, 2009; Ellis, Loewen, & Erlam, 2006; Sheen, 2007). Three studies (Ammar, 2008; Havranek, 2002; Yang & Lyster, 2010) have found prompts to be more effective than direct correction and recasts.

A smaller set of studies has investigated the mediating effect of other variables on the extent to which feedback is effective. Some studies (Ammar & Spada, 2006; Mackey & Philp, 1998; Trofimiovich et al., 2007) have found that higher-proficiency learners benefit more from oral CF than lower-proficiency learners. Sheen (2007) found that language analytic ability correlated with accuracy scores for learners who received meta-linguistic feedback but not for those who received recasts. Sheen (2008) also found that feedback was generally more effective for learners with lower levels of anxiety. However, Loewen (in press) explained that, "while these studies of individual differences are insightful, they are not sufficient in number to permit the types of generalizations made possible by synthetic analysis." Other factors, noted by Loewen (in press) that may also have an influence on the effectiveness of oral CF include the extent to which it is noticed, the salience of the different types of feedback provided, the linguistic item being targeted, the readiness of the learner to uptake from the feedback, the timing of the feedback, the amount of feedback provided, contextual variables such as the learning goals of the environment, and interlocutor variables such as gender, L1 status, and age.

A more detailed consideration of the extent to which the findings of oral CF studies are similar and different, and explanations for such patterns, will be provided in Chapter 3 when they are presented alongside correspondingly similar studies of written CF. Also in Chapter 3, we will identify the design, execution, and analysis lessons that can be learned from effective oral CF studies.

Studies of Written CF

As the various theoretical perspectives on SLA emerged in the post-Krashen years, researchers began to focus their attention on investigating the models and claims that were being made about how learners acquired a second language. This meant that some of the pedagogical beliefs and assumptions that had been held in earlier years came under the empirical microscope. The practice of providing learners with written CF on the errors they were making in their writing was no longer assumed by some to necessarily be effective for L2 acquisition. We note, in passing, that several of these studies became the evidence upon which Truscott (1996) made his call for the abandonment of error correction in L2 writing classes, but the extent to which each of these can be given this status will be assessed in Chapter 3. Studies investigating the efficacy of written CF have tended to look at the issue from two different perspectives. Some have investigated the effectiveness of written CF in terms of its ability to help learners accurately revise drafts (these will be referred to in Chapter 2 and discussed in detail in Chapter 4). Most often, these studies focused on writing that was done by L2 writers in composition classes where the focus of attention is specifically on writing. By comparison, other studies investigating the efficacy of written CF examined it more in SLA terms and were interested to see how effective written CF could be when learners wrote new texts. In language learning classrooms, attention is not only given to writing but also to the development of reading, speaking, and listening skills. It is believed that all four skill areas have a role to play in L2 development. Our focus in this overview, and again in Chapter 3, is on the empirical evidence that has been obtained about the potential of written CF to contribute to SLA.

The early studies cited by Truscott in 1996 (Kepner, 1991; Semke, 1984; Sheppard, 1992) were not only limited in number but also limited in terms of

26 Theory and History of Error Treatment

the robustness of their design and the consistency of their findings (Bitchener, 2008; Ferris, 2004; Guénette, 2007). In more recent years, a number of studies (Bitchener, 2008; Bitchener & Knoch, 2008, 2009a, 2009b, 2010a, 2010b; Chandler, 2003; Ellis, Sheen, Murakami, & Takashima, 2008; Sheen, 2007, 2010; Sheen, Wright, & Moldowa, 2009) conducted in language learning classrooms have sought to address the shortcomings of this earlier work, including most crucially the need for a control group that enables a comparison to be made between learners who receive written CF and those who do not. The findings of these studies reveal a more consistent level of evidence in support of the potential for written CF to contribute to the SLA process. While the findings of this research show that learners are able to retain levels of accuracy over time, the data has, to date, only investigated the effectiveness of the practice in a few linguistic domains (e.g., the use of the English article system, past tense, and prepositions).

Other studies in language learning classrooms have also investigated whether or not one type of feedback is any more effective than another type and whether some linguistic error categories are more responsive to written CF. Studies that have tested the relative effectiveness of direct and indirect types of feedback (Chandler, 2003; Frantzen, 1995; Lalande, 1982; Robb, Ross, & Shortreed, 1986) have not been able to produce consistent findings. Other studies have compared the effectiveness of different types of feedback within these two categories. For example, Bitchener (2008), Bitchener and Knoch (2008, 2009a, 2009b, 2010a, 2010b), Bitchener, Young, and Cameron (2005), and Sheen (2007) found that direct feedback with meta-linguistic explanation tends to have a more consistently positive effect than other types of direct feedback.

Studies of the effect of written CF on written complexity have, to date, yielded conflicting findings. Whereas Sheppard (1992) found a negative effect for written CF on structural complexity, Robb et al. (1986) found a significant positive effect for indirect CF on one of their complexity measures. On the other hand, Chandler (2003) concluded that written CF did not affect the complexity of L2 learner writing. Most recently, van Beuningen, de Jong, and Kuiken (2012) reported that written CF did not lead to simplified writing in either of their post tests.

From this cursory overview of key oral and written CF research, it can be seen that the same types of questions have been to the forefront of empirical investigation. The principal focus when considering the contribution of oral and written CF to L2 acquisition must certainly be the extent to which they play a role in the SLA process. Although, in both contexts, the research findings have yet to produce more definitive answers, there is growing evidence of a role even if the precise nature of the role has yet to be realized. Bitchener and Knoch (2010a), investigating ESL learners over 10 months, and van Beuningen et al. (2012), investigating multi-lingual Dutch learners over time, illustrate the type of evidence now emerging—evidence that attests to the level of retention that is possible when written CF is judiciously provided (e.g., when it takes into account the constraints referred to earlier in this chapter, such as cognitive load, selective attention, learner readiness, and so on). While the relative contribution of different types of written CF and other variables are less clear, the work being done in these areas is significant (as we will see in Chapter 3). Apart from a few studies, referred to earlier, within the socio-cultural perspective, most of the empirical testing of theoretical and pedagogical perspectives has been carried out within a cognitive and socio-cognitive perspective. The extent to which this approach can provide the field with all the answers it wants will be discussed in Chapter 5.

Concluding Remarks

This chapter has provided an essentially theoretical and historical overview of what we consider to be the main perspectives on error and written CF in SLA. We began with an account of the early behaviorist approaches, pointing out where they made a contribution to our understanding of the role of error in SLA and where they were unable to satisfactorily explain why learners continued to make errors in their use of the target language despite various types of intervention, including written CF. Then, when Krashen appeared in the early 1980s with his Monitor Model hypotheses about the conditions and processes he saw as crucial to SLA, it was as though the rug was being pulled out from under the feet of those who believed that progress was being made in understanding the role of error and its treatment. Believing in the sufficiency of comprehensible input for L2 development, Krashen saw little to no role for a focus on error and its treatment in this process. Following this first general SLA theory, a wide range of additional perspectives—from cognitive and socio-cognitive to those of a more socio-cultural nature—have been advanced. Each has made either a direct or indirect contribution to our understanding of the potential of written as well as oral CF in the SLA process. Empirical investigations into the efficacy of the theories and models presented in this chapter have been growing over recent years and are beginning to quell some of the early controversies about the efficacy of corrective feedback, both oral and written, for L2 learning/acquisition. The role of written CF in L2 development is an exciting and dynamic area of investigation, and, as such, is likely to continue engaging the energy and insights of established and emerging scholars.

2

PERSPECTIVES ON ERROR IN COMPOSITION STUDIES

L1 and L2 Interactions and Influences

Early histories of the theory and practice of L2 writing (e.g., Johns, 1990; Silva, 1990) have focused on how L1 composition research has influenced the practice of teaching L2 writers. It is easy to quickly conclude that the relationship between L1 and L2 composition is chronological and unidirectional: L1 composition came first, with L2 writing studies trailing a decade or so behind. However, recent examinations of the history of L2 writing in general (e.g., Ferris & Hedgcock, 2005; Matsuda, 2003a, 2003b) and of the specific issue of error in L1 composition (Santa, 2006) have painted a more complex picture of the interrelationships between L1 and L2 writing and between applied linguistics and composition. Interestingly, though, with regard to the particular question of error and the practical issue of written corrective feedback, we find a surprising trend: while L1 and L2 composition studies of error and error feedback have diverged widely in recent years as to *theory* about error and corrective feedback in student writing, actual classroom *practice* in L1 and L2 composition is more similar than one might predict.

This chapter traces the separate yet intertwined histories of L1 and L2 writing studies in views on error and corrective feedback, concluding with a description of the current status quo in theory and practice. We will argue that, contrary to what might be assumed, the field of L2 writing actually—at least at this point in time—has a more consistent and coherent theory/practice connection in the treatment of error in student writing than does L1/mainstream composition studies.

Historical Perspectives on Error in L1 Composition Research[1]

> After decades of scholarship and instructional advocacy in composition, many writing teachers feel as unsettled as ever about the role of error in response and evaluation.
>
> *(Anson, 2000, p. 5)*

As the above quotation suggests, there remains conflict and confusion among L1 writing scholars, and especially composition instructors, about the role and treatment of error in student writing. However, according to Connors (2003) and Santa (2006), for the first century of college-level composition, there was relatively little controversy around this question. On the contrary, it was assumed not only that writing teachers would diligently and assiduously correct their students' papers (or *themes*, as they were first known), but that such correction, in fact, was perhaps the primary job of the writing instructor.

Error as Character Flaw

The development of the undergraduate course requirement later known as "freshman composition" and currently "first-year composition" (FYC) is widely attributed to Harvard University (US) in the 1870s. The need for such a course arose because, after the American Civil War, a more diverse group of students began attending college, and "a perception that candidates . . . failed to meet acceptable standards of correctness in written English precipitated a transformation in admission policy" (Santa, 2006, p. 8). Historical documents from the late nineteenth century include scathing indictments of college student writing: "So ill-written, incorrectly spelled, ungrammatically expressed, and generally unworkmanlike—that it clearly shows the writer out of place in college" (Adams, Godkin, & Nutter, 1897, quoted in Brereton, 1995, p. 111). According to Harvard professor Adams Sherman Hill, good writing is characterized by "grammatical purity," which can be defined as the absence of "blunders which would disgrace a boy twelve years old" (Hill, 1879, quoted in Brereton, 1995, p. 46). In these early decades of college composition, there apparently was no concern over excessive attention to error at the expense of broader rhetorical issues, nor about the changing nature of language or subjective definitions of what constituted an "error." Rather, attention focused on the appalling lapses of student writers and the urgent but regrettable need to teach "those so-called student writers their mother tongue" (Adams, Godkin, & Quincy, 1892, quoted in Brereton, 1995, p. 75).

Because good writing was, by these scholars' definition, blemish-free, and because many student writers of that era (as in our era) failed to meet that standard, instructors thus were expected to assume "the task of disciplining student writers" (Santa, 2006, p. 19) by providing extensive, comprehensive correction of student themes on an almost daily basis. Santa (2006) described this as "clearly . . . an attempt . . . to mend the 'slovenly' English (and by inference—character) of college writers" (p. 20). This task was especially formidable because classes could include several hundred students, writing short, daily themes; by one estimate, a leading Harvard professor of that era read nearly 20,000 themes[2] in an academic year (Connors, 1997; Santa, 2006). Not surprisingly, nineteenth-century researchers reported that retention of English composition instructors was a problem (Connors, 1997).

30 Theory and History of Error Treatment

In their respective histories, Connors (1997) and Santa (2006) discussed the growing awareness in the first half of the twentieth century among composition theorists that perhaps such a single-minded fixation on error was not only unhealthy for all concerned but unrealistic, given shifting standards of correctness over time and in different regions. This awareness was facilitated by the work of linguists drawing distinctions between descriptive linguistics and prescriptive grammar (e.g., Bloomfield, 1933; Fries, 1940; Sapir, 1921) and articulated at various points by composition scholars such as Dykema (1940); Gilbert (1922), Leonard and Moffett (1927), McCrimmon (1939), and Wykoff (1939). A review of the early volumes of the journal *College Composition and Communication* (*CCC*, which began publishing in 1950) suggests ongoing controversy between more liberal views about the purpose of composition and the role or nature of error and conservative, back-to-basics adherence to time-tested (if not time-honored) prescriptions of correctness. As late as 1960, a representative of the latter contingent described a "typical" freshman writer thus:

> Technically he is slovenly and careless. More than three spelling errors to the standard page will occur; he may have more than five major errors in grammar in a six-hundred-word essay; he omits apostrophes, ignores the imp-personal pronoun, and uses contractions and colloquialisms. The form of his essay will often stop just short of being insulting.
>
> *(Baldwin, 1960, p. 111)*

Today's college writing instructors would no doubt recognize Baldwin's description of a freshman student writing as being accurate, even if they did not agree completely with his characterization of student writers as "slovenly and careless." The point here is that, as late as 1960, "error as character flaw" was a powerful paradigm that influenced teachers' attitudes, their instruction, and their response practices.

Error as Developmental Stage

Although, as noted above, composition scholars (often influenced by linguists) had for some decades taken issue with a rigid, prescriptivist approach to error in student writing, there was no major shift in attitude or practice until the landmark study by Mina Shaughnessy, *Errors and Expectations*, published in 1977. This second major era in the study of composition and error was ushered in, much as the first one was, by a major demographic change. Beginning in the 1960s, colleges began adopting "open admissions" policies that made college more accessible to a broader range of students; this change, together with the sheer numbers represented by the baby boomer generation, meant not only that more adults than ever before were attempting college but that these students had much more diverse cultural, socio-economic, and racial backgrounds than colleges and universities had seen previously. In her introduction, Shaughnessy described three groups of students that attended City University of New York (CUNY), a pioneer in the open admissions movement. The first two were traditional students, with the second group comprised of "academic stragglers," who perhaps were not mature enough to attempt college and who took remedial courses often referred to as "bonehead English" (Shaughnessy, 1977, p. 2). The newly welcomed third group, however, was unlike anything the college had previously experienced:

> they were . . . strangers in academia, unacquainted with the rules and rituals of college life, unprepared for the sorts of tasks their teachers were about to assign them. Most of them had grown up in one of New York's ethnic or racial enclaves. Many had spoken other languages or dialects at home . . .
>
> *(p. 3)*

When this third group of students began college, took placement examinations, and enrolled in their basic writing courses (the term used by Shaughnessy as preferred to "remedial" or even "bonehead" English classes), their teachers were overwhelmed by problems in the students' writing, which appeared to be "irremediable" and "illiterate" and the students themselves, sometimes described as "handicapped" or "disadvantaged" (Shaughnessy, 1977, pp. 3–4). Shaughnessy, an administrator in the CUNY basic writing program, undertook her book-length work to guide basic writing teachers by providing a precise description of students' written errors and materials that could help instructors to diagnose and remediate them. Her analysis, examples, and teaching materials were developed from a corpus of 4,000 freshman placement essays written at CUNY between 1970–74.

Analyzing student writing to identify, classify, and count student errors was not an endeavor that originated with Shaughnessy. Indeed, as noted by Connors and Lunsford (1988), between 1915–35, many such studies had been completed and published; in fact, Harap's (1930) review examines some 33 of these. However, what was unique about Shaughnessy's work was her analysis not only of the *types and frequencies* of student errors but of their possible *sources*. Santa (2006) noted that, "Prior to the 1960s, error was an aberration, an embarrassment, a sign of illiteracy, sloth, disrespect, a signal of membership in the underclass" (p. 60). In contrast, drawing on the work of socio-linguists (e.g., Cazden, John, & Hymes, 1972; Davis, 1972; Labov, 1972; Williams, 1970; Wolfram & Fasold, 1974), as well as psycholinguistic studies of first and second language acquisition and literacy development (e.g., George, 1972; Ginsburg & Opper, 1969), Shaughnessy argued that written errors made by basic writers were not, in fact, signs of carelessness, incompetence, or intellectual defectiveness, but rather rule-governed dialect variations[3] and/or signposts of developmental stages that inexperienced writers and language learners experienced as they acquired language

32 Theory and History of Error Treatment

and literacy in academic English. At the same time, because errors distract readers (or "carry messages which writers can't afford to send," Shaughnessy, 1977, p. 12) and thus can stigmatize writers, teachers must thoughtfully address error and help under-prepared students to develop academic language and literacy skills. To address these practical realities, *Errors and Expectations* carefully defined and exemplified various types of writing errors, suggested possible explanations for them, and provided specific classroom approaches for teachers to build knowledge and skills in areas of student weakness.

Shaughnessy's work was revolutionary in composition studies because of her compassionate and practical approach to the persistent problem of error in student writing. Because she simultaneously called for a broader, more informed perspective on why students make errors and a more effective strategy for helping students develop their language and writing skills, Shaughnessy's study of basic writing inspired several different lines of research and scholarly inquiry in the decades that followed it. For instance, Bartholomae (1980), directly referencing Shaughnessy's arguments as well as recent work in applied linguistics, called for a systematic use of EA (see Chapter 1), not only for research purposes but for classroom interventions with basic writers, so that teachers could more accurately assess what students do and do not know about language, as well as distinguish between errors of competence and performance. Similarly, Kroll and Schafer (1978) drew on their work with ESL writers to argue for a broader application of EA techniques in composition studies. In addition, following Shaughnessy's view that error is potentially stigmatizing to writers who produce it, researchers took up the issue of "error gravity," a line of research in which real-world academic and professional audiences are asked about their reactions to various types of written errors (e.g., Beason, 2001; Hairston, 1981; Wall & Hull, 1989). In short, Shaughnessy's work helped composition scholars and teachers—especially those who focus their efforts on under-prepared, basic, or second language writers—look more deeply for explanations or sources of written error and use their enlightened knowledge to better prepare students for the expectations of a sometimes harsh audience outside of the English composition class.

Error as Social Construct

Though Shaughnessy's work was and still is extremely influential in both the research and practice of composition, it was not without controversy—not, as one might expect, because she was seen as "coddling" students or "excusing" student errors, but because she did not, according to some, go far enough in challenging the status quo as to definitions of "error" or understanding its relative importance. For instance, Rouse (1979) claimed that Shaughnessy's work is an "assertion of authority," demanding that "students show themselves willing to learn the rules . . ." (p. 7). Though Shaughnessy provided a more sensitive and nuanced view of the sources of student error, the focus of *Errors and Expectations*

Error in Composition Studies **33**

is on helping students to remediate it, not asking whether or not it is appropriate to train students to avoid breaking rules that may not themselves be consistent, or violating reader expectations that may not be fair.

As previously noted, as early as the 1920s, composition scholars were drawing on descriptive approaches to linguistics to argue that perhaps the field's obsession with eradicating error in student writing (and placing harsh judgments on students who produce it) was not only out of balance but unrealistic, given the propensity of language to change and standards of usage to vary across contexts and discourse communities and to evolve over time. However, it was not until Shaughnessy's work led to the widespread acceptance of the notion that student error did not, in fact, simply signify a character flaw, that composition scholars began to question the notion of "error" as an absolute.

Santa (2006) claimed that "error is a *constructed* artifact" that "does not exist outside of agreed conventions of language, subjective criteria that readers bring to a text" (p. 10, emphasis in original). In a landmark essay published in *CCC* only a few years after Shaughnessy's book, Williams (1981) made a compelling argument that the idea of "error" resided primarily in the reader's mind rather than in the writer's incompetence—that readers, in a sense, "create" error by expecting it and noticing it, especially in student writing where teachers feel responsible for finding and eradicating it. As a dramatic illustration of his thesis, at the conclusion of the essay, Williams disclosed that he had deliberately placed over 100 common errors of grammar and usage ("errors" according to a popular composition handbook of the day) in his scholarly article.[4] The point, of course, is that readers most likely did not notice many (or any) of the errors before their attention was called to them *because they would not expect to find such errors in an essay by an accomplished writer in a respected journal.*

Williams' conclusion, in turn, leads to two related questions: (1) Do we only notice errors in student writing because we are looking for them, not because they are truly distracting or interfere with meaning? (2) If the "same" errors can be completely overlooked in a different context, how important are they, anyway? Williams' arguments have subsequently been taken up, in different forms, by scholars such as Anson (2000), Hartwell (1985), Horner (1992, 1994), and Santa (2006). Reader-response and critical theorists have taken these insights a step further by arguing against the pedagogy of accommodation ascribed to Shaughnessy and in favor of a pedagogy of "resistance to dominant language practices" (Santa, 2006, p. 119). Tying the views of social constructionists and critical theorists together, if "error" is a figment of the teacher-reader's imagination (or a function of his/her expectations) rather than a real problem, should practitioners perpetuate the myth by emphasizing error in their classrooms and their feedback, or should they (and their students) ignore or resist these irrelevant and even oppressive concerns?

At the same time, the "error gravity" argument raised by Shaughnessy (and others before and after her) persists. Beason's well-constructed 2001 study of how

34 Theory and History of Error Treatment

business professionals perceive and analyze error demonstrated that errors "harm the *image* of the writer" (p. 48). This study and the earlier ones by Hairston (1981) and Wall and Hull (1989) provide evidence in support of Shaughnessy's approach that is to this day compelling to writing instructors, particularly those who teach basic or multilingual writers: "[Resistance pedagogies] . . . may make it seriously difficult for students to ascertain the conventions of academic discourse, *conventions about which they have a functional and democratic right to know*" (Gray-Rosendale, 1998, p. 62, emphasis added; see also Johns, 1995). Even Santa, whose 2006 history clearly conveys his sympathy toward the reader-response/critical pedagogy camp, admitted that "a purely 'pedagogical' response to error that seals student writing from the scrutiny this work is likely to receive in a broader social context does a disservice to student writers, our pedagogy, and its desired outcomes" (p. 127). In other words, scholars from many different camps have cautioned that ignoring the effects of error on real-world readers may be negligent and even harmful to student writers.

Current Views of Error in Composition Theory and Practice

In Santa's recent (2006) historical overview of error in composition, he noted repeatedly that there is a clear discrepancy between what many composition theorists think about error and ongoing classroom practice: "Error has largely evaded successful theorizing . . . our response to error frequently deviates from what our own best thoughts on the matter dictate in response" (p. 131). In a similar vein, Anson (2000) noted that "many teachers continue to feel torn between denying attention to error in their response because of its incompatibility with newer theoretical perspectives, and experiencing the unavoidable effects of error as they read their students' writing."(p. 6). In short, theorists have argued for decades that:

(a) "a stultifying error hunt" (Connors, 1985, p. 61) or obsessive attention to error in teacher response, is fruitless and counterproductive;
(b) "error" is a socially constructed notion, anyway: what is considered an "error" in composition handbooks or by composition teachers might be perfectly acceptable in other contexts (or not even noticed, as Williams, 1981 demonstrated); and
(c) training students to avoid error (as advocated by Shaughnessy, 1977) inappropriately maintains a questionable status quo that teachers and students should be challenging, not accommodating.

Nonetheless, teachers continue to pay a great deal of attention to error in their response to student writing and in their classroom instruction. This is a theory/practice divide that clearly baffles and frustrates composition scholars interested in error and larger questions of response. Santa (2006), for instance, ends his book with this dour pronouncement: "We write error as readers; error writes us as a particular type of reader, as clinicians and diagnosticians, as composition practitioners. *Thus we continue to read students—and ourselves—in error*" (p. 132, emphasis added).

There are several pieces of evidence to support the claim that real-world teachers continue to focus on student error in their classes despite theorists' disdain for the practice. First, various artifacts of composition instruction, including widely used websites or online writing labs (OWLs), published handbooks and rhetorics, and grading rubrics used for local and large-scale assessment (Broad, 2003), seem based on the assumption that attention to correctness in grammar and usage should be of at least some concern for student writers and their teachers. While teacher-training materials typically suggest that instructors give less priority to marking errors than to other types of response (e.g., Bean, 1996; Glenn & Goldthwaite, 2008; see also Haswell, 1983), we do not find recommendations that teachers ignore error altogether. Second, two recent studies of teacher practices in responding to student writing (Ferris, Liu, & Rabie, 2011; Lunsford & Lunsford, 2008) clearly demonstrate that teachers in the present era give substantial attention to error in their feedback to student writers.

In sum, in L1 composition circles, there are two conflicting truths in tension: (1) where "the identification, eradication, and study of error was once a prime concern in the teaching of composition," among *researchers* "it is largely an afterthought" (Santa, 2006, p. vii); but (2) there remains among *teachers* a "recalcitrant response to error in student writing" (Santa, 2006, p. 104). This "recalcitrance" on the part of teachers appears to stem not from the earlier view that student error signifies a character flaw but rather from the pragmatic awareness that the real world outside the composition classroom expects and demands well-edited writing. To put it another way, though scholars feel that teachers should have gotten past their concern for error in student writing decades ago, practicing teachers continue to respond to error in their feedback—and there is little evidence that these teachers, as Anson (2000) claimed, indeed even "feel torn" about whether or not they should do so.

Studies of Teacher Response to Error

This theory/practice divide is evident in reviewing L1 composition research on error in response to student writing. Following Shaughnessy's (1977) landmark book, there was a great deal of research activity in the 1980s surrounding the study of error, research that was "arguably central to the establishment of composition as a discipline" (Santa, 2006, p. 68). However, once critical theorists began questioning the notion of error and especially whether teachers should focus on it, research on error became almost nonexistent in L1 composition, with the notable exception of Lunsford and Lunsford's recent (2008) study. Though, as previously noted, there was substantial work done in the first half of the twentieth

36 Theory and History of Error Treatment

century that described, categorized, and quantified error in student writing, "The literature on *students' production of error* is not paralleled . . . by equally comprehensive research on *teacher response to error*." (Anson, 2000, p. 6, emphases added). In this section, we first turn to broad investigations of teacher response (including, but not limited to, error treatment) and then discuss several studies specifically focused on how teachers respond to student error. The purpose of the discussion in this section is primarily to provide a historical perspective on response to error in L1 composition. We will take up critical analyses of the design and findings of specific studies in Chapter 4 of this volume.

Research on Teacher Response to Student Writing

The first major set of research studies and reviews on response to student writing appeared during the 1980s. This body of work is important because it reflects, among other trends, the changing attitudes toward error in student writing outlined in the first section of this chapter. In a state-of-the-art article originally published in 1981 by Knoblauch and Brannon (2006b), the authors' assessment of the entire endeavor of teacher commentary, including marking of student errors, was quite negative: ". . . we have scarcely a shred of empirical evidence to show that students typically even comprehend our responses to their writing, let alone use them purposefully to modify their practice" (Knoblauch & Brannon, 2006a, p. 69). However, the relatively limited amount of empirical work on the topic of response to student writing to that point was demonstrated by Knoblauch and Brannon's reference list: of the 15 studies cited, all but two were unpublished, and most were doctoral dissertation studies. Despite these negative findings, Knoblauch and Brannon (2006a) suggested that "intervening in the composing process . . . can measurably improve student writing, provided that a teacher adequately supports revising efforts" (p. 72), and concluded with a series of principles of response for both research and instructional purposes (p. 75).

As to the specific issue of teacher response to student error, one of the two published studies cited by Knoblauch and Brannon, a 1980 article by Searle and Dillon published in *Research in the Teaching of English* (also reprinted in Straub's 2006 anthology), reported that 12 elementary school teachers (of grades 4–6) focused their comments on "form" in 69 percent of the cases. Searle and Dillon further noted that teachers responded to different types of errors in various ways; for instance, "mechanical" errors were directly corrected while "structural" errors were given indirect feedback (e.g., "Watch your tenses," Searle & Dillon, 2006, p. 64). Returning to Knoblauch and Brannon's (1981) review, it is also worth noting that the same authors wrote a preface to Straub's 2006 anthology, in which they stated "We find nothing . . . to alter the fundamental impressions we formed twenty-five years ago" (Knoblauch & Brannon, 2006a, p. 1). Though they conceded that response to student writing "has always been, and remains, a valuable instructional activity" (2006, p. 6)—if only because it demonstrates the teacher's engaged investment in individual students' writing—they questioned whether there is any compelling empirical evidence that teacher commentary actually results in student improvement. This is a question that, as we shall see throughout this book, endures as well in the second language literature on written corrective feedback.

Other studies of teacher commentary appeared in the 1980s, most notably a pair of articles published in *CCC* in 1982 by Sommers, and Brannon and Knoblauch. Both articles drew upon research in which 35 university writing instructors both submitted samples of their own commentary and gave feedback on a set of three student papers provided by the researchers. Sommers described the teacher commentary as "arbitrary and idiosyncratic" and "hostile and meanspirited . . ." (1982, p. 149). She criticized error feedback that was given too early in the writing process, which gave students contradictory messages, and which failed to prioritize revision and editing concerns. Sommers concluded that "the news from the classroom is not good . . . We read . . . expecting to find errors . . . We find what we look for; instead of reading and responding to the meaning of a text, we correct our students' writing" (1982, p. 154). In short, according to Sommers, one of the primary ways in which teachers "appropriate" student texts and presumably confuse and demoralize student writers is through disproportionate and premature attention to errors.

Drawing upon the same research findings, Brannon and Knoblauch challenged the notion of the "Ideal Text," arguing that teachers disempower and demotivate students by using their commentary to lead students into producing the type of text teachers want to see rather than the meaning that student writers intended to convey. Response to error, according to the authors, contributes to this wholesale highjacking of student intentions: "By focusing on error, the teacher is the authority, a judge of the writing" (Brannon & Knoblauch, 1982, p. 162). Nor, according to Brannon and Knoblauch, does simply requiring multiple drafts and allowing revision solve the potential problems raised by a teacher's attention to error:

> It would be easy to point out errors, just as on single-draft assignments, and to require copyediting on the next draft. But the concern is not merely to ask for editing in order to make discourse look superficially better; rather, it is to work with the writer in examining the effectiveness of some intended communication and to initiate improvement where possible.
>
> *(p. 162)*

In other words, whereas Sommers challenged the ways in which teachers respond to student errors (i.e., on early drafts and in counterproductive and confusing ways), Brannon and Knoblauch raised the question of whether it is the teacher's place to correct errors at all (or require students to edit errors), when so doing might usurp "students' rights to their own texts" (Brannon and Knoblauch, 1982, p. 157). This latter view reflects the growing belief in the field

38 Theory and History of Error Treatment

(fueled by Williams' 1981 article) that attention to student errors was not especially important or relevant (and could even be counterproductive) to the larger concern of promoting student ownership and engagement in their writing.

These three papers—Knoblauch and Brannon's 1981 research review and the two research-based papers by Sommers (1982) and Brannon and Knoblauch (1982)—have been enormously influential, multiply reprinted, and ubiquitously cited. Other studies on response to student writing in the rest of the 1980s and into the 1990s (see especially Anson's 1989 edited collection) continued in the same vein, assuming that error correction, if done at all, should comprise a small, end-stage minor part of teacher response efforts. For instance, in a 1995 study by Straub and Lunsford, published as a book called *Twelve Readers Reading*, 12 noted scholars were given a set of 15 student papers and asked to respond to at least 12. One of the key findings noted in a summary of this study (Lunsford & Straub, 2006), is that "these teachers do not give a great deal of attention to error" (p. 177). Nonetheless, it is important to observe that the practices of these enlightened, well read experts—all of whom had helped to shape the field of composition studies in substantial ways—do not necessarily mirror those of real-world composition instructors. We cannot assume that practicing writing instructors do not give "a great deal of attention to error" in their feedback to students. In fact, in a recent study of the response practices of college/university writing instructors (Ferris et al., 2011), of 129 instructors surveyed, all said that they give at least some attention to error in their own feedback, and in the written commentary of 23 focal participants, many of the teachers focused on grammar much more than any other concern. In short, though composition scholars have for several decades urged teachers to focus little (or at least less) of their attention on student error, recent studies (Ferris et al., 2011; Lunsford & Lunsford, 2008) suggest that many or most writing instructors still mark error regularly and extensively.

Studies of Teacher Response to Student Error

Due largely to the historical trends described in the first part of this chapter, empirical studies on the specific issue of how teachers respond to student error have been few and far between over the past several decades. Here, we highlight the three most major and influential research efforts to date; as we will see, only the first of three (Haswell, 1983) highlights the *effects* of written corrective feedback on student writers.

Minimal Marking. In a brief piece published in *College English*, Haswell (1983) described an error correction method he called "minimal marking" and reported some research he had completed with his own students on the effects of the method. The philosophical justification for the minimal marking method was taken from Knoblauch and Brannon's 1981 research review; Haswell claimed that his "minimal marking" method embodied their principles for enlightened feedback.

He examined the effects of his approach with several of his own freshman writing classes, finding that students were successful in both self-editing their work after receiving feedback and reducing their overall percentage of errors from the beginning to the end of the semester.[5] Because Haswell's approach was so sensible and his findings so impressive, his short (five-page) paper has been extensively cited and drawn upon in teacher preparation materials (e.g., Bean, 1996). If teachers *must* mark errors (and, as the previous section suggests, it seems that they must and do), Haswell's approach at least showed them how to mark in ways that might actually help students in the long term, and that keep error treatment in its proper place in the composition class.

The Top Twenty Studies. Whereas Haswell's paper and research focused on tracing the effects of a particular classroom approach to error correction, the work of Connors and Lunsford (1988) and a follow-up study by Lunsford and Lunsford (2008) took a broader view, examining the error feedback methods of thousands of college writing instructors across the US. In their introduction, Connors and Lunsford summarized the dilemma felt by many composition instructors, circa 1980s:

> Marking and judging formal and mechanical errors in student papers is one area in which composition studies seems to have a multiple-personality disorder. On the one hand, our mellow, student-centered, process-based selves tend to condemn marking formal errors at all. Doing it represents the Bad Old Days . . . our more traditional pedagogical selves feel a touch guilty when we ignore student error patterns altogether, even in the sacrosanct drafting stage of composing. *Not even the most liberal of process-oriented teachers completely ignores the problem of mechanical and formal errors* . . . The world judges a writer by her mastery of conventions, and we all know it. Students, parents, university colleagues, and administrators expect us to deal somehow with those unmet rhetorical expectations, and, *like it or not, pointing out errors seems to most of us part of what we do.*
>
> *(1988, pp. 395–396, emphases added)*

As composition historians, Connors and Lunsford were interested both in examining how (or if) student error patterns had changed over time and in looking at how teachers marked errors. In the original (1988) study and its replication (Lunsford & Lunsford, 2008), large corpora of student papers with written teacher feedback were collected from writing instructors around the US; a "Top Twenty" list of frequent errors was generated from examination of a sample of the papers;[6] and raters were trained to analyze the corpus for errors from the Top Twenty list. In both studies, the authors noted that their participating teachers marked some but not all of the possible errors in student papers and had different approaches for marking various types of errors. Both studies also demonstrated that ratios of student errors had not changed substantially

40 Theory and History of Error Treatment

over the past century; though the *types* of errors shifted, the overall *proportions* of error stayed constant.

Connors and Lunsford concluded their paper by saying that their endeavor "has raised more questions than it has answered" (1988, p. 407). Ironically, positioned historically at the end of the 1980s—the end of the era in which error issues were studied intensively—the follow-up questions they posed (or that arise from a careful reading of their study) were not explored by other researchers. However, the "Top Twenty" list that was developed as a research instrument for this study took on a life of its own, cited in other teacher preparation works (e.g., Bean, 1996; Weaver, 1996) and used as a basis for materials in student handbooks later authored by Andrea Lunsford.

Twenty years later, a replication study by Lunsford and Lunsford (2008) added further insights about the ways in which composition pedagogy had changed: student papers were longer, responded to more complex tasks (persuasive and research-based assignments rather than narratives), and in many cases reflected a multiple-draft process approach. Besides changes in how writing was taught, the authors noted that the rapid spread of technology may have impacted the types and quantities of errors they found (e.g., the reduction of spelling errors) in the replication study. Despite these easily observable changes, however, Lunsford and Lunsford also noted with some surprise that "we are struck by how little some things have changed in terms of teacher comments" (2008, p. 794). The patterns of teacher marks and the types of errors to which teachers attended were quite similar to what Connors and Lunsford (1988) had found 20 years earlier.

Lunsford and Lunsford concluded their discussion by reminding readers of Williams' (1981) essay, which argued that readers most notice errors when they are looking for them: "The rate of error in our study, then, should also be seen as rate of *attention* to error. When readers look for errors, they will find them" (Lunsford & Lunsford, 2008, pp. 800–801, original emphasis). They argued that "mistakes are a fact of life" (p. 801). In short, even the few L1 composition researchers who have examined written corrective feedback since the early 1980s expressed some ambivalence and concern about the practice.

The Influence of L1 Composition Studies on L2 Views of Error Treatment

As noted earlier in this chapter, the influence of applied linguistics on composition studies and the relationships between L1 and L2 composition have been substantial and complex. With regard to perspectives on the treatment of error in student writing, some composition scholars in the first half of the twentieth century used the work of descriptive linguists as support for arguments against prescriptive views of language and error (Connors, 1997; Santa, 2006). Shaughnessy's (1977) landmark work was clearly influenced by the work of socio-linguists on non-standard varieties of English (most particularly Labov's studies of the variety known over the decades as Black English, Black English Vernacular, African American Vernacular English, or Ebonics) and by research on first and second language and literacy development. Bartholomae's (1980) article on "The Study of Error" drew not only from second language scholars' research on EA and natural order(s) of acquisition (e.g., Bailey et al., 1974) but also on primary research conducted with ESL student writers (Cohen & Robbins, 1976; Kroll & Schafer, 1978). Most recently, as student audiences have increasingly become more culturally diverse and multilingual in many instructional contexts (see Ferris, 2009; Harklau, Losey, & Siegal, 1999; Roberge, Siegal, & Harklau, 2009), L1 composition scholars have begun to consult L2 writing specialists and their work more frequently about all aspects of writing instruction, including, and perhaps especially, their perspectives on the treatment of error.

All that said, it is also important to note that L1 composition theory has also influenced L2 writing studies and pedagogy in significant ways. Until the appearance of the first major collections on second language writing (Johnson & Roen, 1989; Kroll, 1990) and the start-up of the *Journal of Second Language Writing* (*JSLW*) in 1992, most of the citations in articles on L2 writing came from L1 composition.[7] Some of the earliest pieces of scholarship on L2 writing instruction (e.g., Raimes, 1985; Zamel, 1976, 1982, 1983) drew strongly upon the work of L1 writing process researchers and theorists, arguing that L2 writing instructors should similarly focus less on error hunts and the Ideal Text and more on encouraging enlightened writing processes (see also Krashen, 1984; Zamel, 1985). Because of this pioneering work by Krashen, Raimes, and Zamel, L2 writing instruction began shifting in the mid-1980s toward process approaches (multiple-drafting, peer and teacher feedback at intermediate stages, postponing editing until final drafts, and so forth) (Ferris & Hedgcock, 2005; Johns, 1990; Matsuda, 2003a; Silva, 1990). Later, the work of critical theorists in composition studies similarly began to impact published work on L2 writing pedagogy in journals such as the *TESOL Quarterly* and *JSLW* (e.g., Atkinson, 1999, 2003; Benesch, 1993, 1999; Kubota, 2001; Ramanathan & Atkinson, 1999).

Despite these undeniable and substantial influences of L1 research on L2 writing theory, there has been ongoing debate among L2 writing scholars as to whether the findings of L1 composition studies can be uncritically applied to L2 writing pedagogy. In particular, scholars argued about whether expressivist and non-interventionist varieties of the process approach were appropriate for ESL writers (e.g., Eskey, 1983; Horowitz, 1986; Johns, 1995; Reid, 1994), whether L2 writers were essentially the same as monolingual L1 writers (Leki, 1990a, 1990b; Silva, 1988, 1993, 1997; Zamel, 1987), and whether specific pedagogical approaches such as peer response and teacher-student writing conferences could be used effectively with L2 writers (Ferris, 2003; Jacobs, Curtis, Braine, & Huang, 1998; Patthey-Chavez & Ferris, 1997; Zhang, 1995, 1999). While most L2 scholars recognized the value of L1 composition insights, they also wondered whether the endeavor of writing in an L2 was so intrinsically distinct from that of writing

42 Theory and History of Error Treatment

in the L1 that L2 writing research and pedagogy needed to be characterized differently, if not entirely separately.

With regard to perspectives on error in particular, while applied linguists, particularly SLA researchers, would assent to the L1 theorists' view that many errors are not especially important in interfering with meaning and that what constitutes an error may sometimes be a matter of taste and/or prescriptivism, they would not agree that *all* errors in student writing are invented by the reader. Rather, linguists have a theoretically and empirically grounded view of error: "errors" in writing are lexical, morphological, or syntactic deviations from the intuitions of a literate adult native speaker of the language (in whatever variety of that language is under consideration). For example, while the placement of a hyphen or a comma may indeed be a matter of stylistic debate, few competent speakers of English would disagree that "*Yesterday I go to the park"* is incorrect. Further, while Shaughnessy (1977) and others in L1 composition have argued that errors in student writing may be explained by dialect/variety differences from standard English and/or developmental stages in the acquisition of the academic written register, SLA scholars would add that the task of the L2 writer may be further complicated by L1 interference as well as L2 acquisition stages (or interlanguage; see Chapter 1). Thus, because L2 theorists have a complex view of the nature of written error and its sources, they have grappled more frequently than have L1 composition scholars—especially in recent years—with research questions concerning error.

L1 and L2 Composition Intersections in Error Treatment

The emergence of L2 writing as a major scholarly and pedagogical concern coincided historically with a marked decrease of interest in error in both L1 composition (see earlier sections of this chapter) and in second language acquisition studies (in large part due to the influence of Krashen, 1982, 1984; see discussion in Chapter 1). As discussed by Ferris in the preface to her 2002 book, *Treatment of Error in Second Language Student Writing*, ESL writing teachers in the 1980s:

> had been trained to be "process-approach" writing teachers . . . with attention to language issues . . . being intentionally postponed to the very end of the composing process. What this often meant, in practice, was that grammar and editing issues were almost never addressed by teachers or their students in the ESL writing classroom.
>
> *(p. xi)*

To be fair, L2 writing scholars such as Raimes (1987), Taylor (1981), and Zamel (1982) argued for a more effective *balance* between composing skills and language skills in L2 writing classes, rather than the abandonment of language instruction:

It should not be concluded . . . that engaging students in the process of composing eliminates our obligation to upgrade their linguistic competencies. Raimes (1979) talks about the numerous language skills that ESL composition teachers need to attend to. But what needs to be emphasized is that this obligation should not form the basis of our writing instruction.

(Zamel, 1982, p. 207)

Nonetheless, teachers trained in Krashen's (1982) five hypotheses of second language acquisition (see Chapter 1) along with process approach pedagogy often would leave the "upgrading" of students' "linguistic competencies" for another day—which frequently never arrived. The benign neglect of error and linguistic accuracy in L2 writing raised alarms among scholars (e.g., Eskey, 1983; Horowitz, 1986) and quiet resistance among L2 writing instructors (see Ferris, 2002, pp. xi–xii).

The points of alarm and resistance were similar to those raised by some L1 composition scholars (e.g., Beason, 2001; Hairston, 1981; Shaughnessy, 1977), focusing primarily on real-world accuracy expectations of readers outside the ESL classroom (Janopolous, 1992; Santos, 1988; Vann, Lorenz, & Meyer, 1991; Vann, Meyer, & Lorenz, 1984), but they also went further in two distinct ways. First, a number of researchers have noted that L2 students expect and want feedback on their written errors and will be made frustrated and anxious by its absence (see Ferris, 2002, 2003; Ferris & Roberts, 2001; Leki, 1991; see also rebuttals to this point by Truscott, 1996, 1999). Second, scholars have studied ways in which L2 students' texts are observably different from those produced by L1 writers (Ferris, 1994; Hinkel, 2002; Hyland, 2002; Silva, 1993, 1997) and argued that L2 writers, being still in the process of second language acquisition, need more attention to their errors than do L1 writers producing texts in their native languages (Eskey, 1983; Leki, 1990a; Zamel, 1982). Because of these various points of resistance, by the early 1990s, several grammar and editing textbooks for ESL writers had appeared (Ascher, 1993; Fox, 1992; Lane & Lange, 1993; Raimes, 1992) as well as "how-to" books and papers on treating ESL writers' errors (Bates, Lane, & Lange, 1993; Ferris, 1995b; Frodesen, 1991). In the present day, the question for most teachers of L2 writers is not *if* they should treat student errors but rather *how best* to do so (Ferris, 2010; Hartshorn et al., 2010). The current dialogue around the issue of error is thus quite different in L2 writing than it is in L1 composition.

Research on Written Corrective Feedback in L2 Writing

Until the 1990s, nearly all research on error correction in L2 writing was focused not on composition or writing classrooms but on language instruction (in foreign language or ESL classes or English as a Foreign Language (EFL) settings in non-English-medium settings). The history of this research is outlined in Chapter 1,

44 Theory and History of Error Treatment

and the studies themselves reviewed in Chapter 3. Beginning in the 1990s, as ESL composition developed into a distinct field of inquiry and as error treatment in L2 writing classes emerged from the underground, researchers began to examine ways in which writing instructors responded to L2 students' errors and the effects of these interventions. These studies examined short- and longer-term effects of error correction on student accuracy (e.g., Chandler, 2003; Ferris, 1995a, 1997, 2006; Polio, Fleck, & Leder, 1998), the impact of different correction techniques on immediate student revision (Ashwell, 2000; Fathman & Whalley, 1990; Ferris & Roberts, 2001; Sheppard, 1992), descriptions and self-reports about how teachers respond to student error (Ferris, 2006; Ferris et al., 2011; Lee, 2008, 2009; Montgomery & Baker, 2007), and student views of teacher response, including error correction (Ferris & Roberts, 2001; Leki, 1991; Montgomery & Baker, 2007). This body of work is examined and analyzed in more detail in Chapter 4; here, we simply note that there has been substantially more research done on error feedback in L2 writing over the past 20 years than in L1 composition.

We would be remiss, however, in leaving this section without mentioning again the criticisms raised of "grammar correction" in L2 writing by Truscott (1996, 1999, 2004, 2007, 2009; Truscott & Hsu, 2008). Truscott's persistent critiques of the practice of error feedback and the research that argues in its favor are discussed at some length in Chapter 1 and revisited in the light of specific studies reviewed in Chapters 3–4. To the extent that Truscott argued that too much attention to error is harmful because it takes teachers' and students' attention from more important concerns (Truscott, 1996; see also Krashen, 1984), most if not all L2 writing scholars and practitioners would agree. Whether written corrective feedback is an effective tool *among others* to help student writers build greater awareness of problematic error patterns and skills to self-edit or avoid them is a question that could still benefit from further research, but again, most L2 experts would likely assent to this moderate position (see Ferris, 2010; Hartshorn et al., 2010).

Concluding Remarks

Because L1 composition and research has unquestionably been intertwined with the development of L2 writing pedagogy, research, and theory, we reviewed the history of the notion of error and the relatively sparse research on error treatment in L1 composition studies. As we have seen, L1 composition research has gone through several different eras in its view of student written error, and these paradigm shifts have, at key points, been influenced by the work of applied linguists. At this point in time, there is a clear discrepancy between what composition scholars *believe* about error and what composition instructors actually *do*. Though scholars are aware of this divergence, there is little evidence that their concerns about error have impacted teacher practice in any substantial way.

Error in Composition Studies **45**

In contrast, though L2 composition went through its own dormant period in the 1980s as to research on error in student writing, the past 20 years or so have seen a flurry of research activity on this topic.[8] As Ferris has noted elsewhere (2010), it is ironic indeed that Truscott's (1996) essay, which strongly argued for the abandonment of written CF in L2 writing, actually led to increased interest by researchers in the topic. The convergence of focus-on-form and oral corrective feedback research in SLA (discussed in Chapter 1) with increased attention to error treatment in second language writing (written CF research) has yielded a set of findings that can be further explored empirically but which are already proving useful in classroom settings (see Chapters 3–4 for detailed discussion of these findings; see Chapters 6–7 for practical applications of the research). Among SLA and L2 writing researchers and L2 writing practitioners, there is much less of a sense of disconnect between research findings and actual practice, and little of the anxiety found in the L1 literature over the "recalcitrance" of classroom teachers in continuing to address error in their feedback and instruction.

Thus, as we stated at the beginning of this chapter, theory and practice on the issue of error treatment are much more connected in L2 writing studies than they are in L1 composition. It will be interesting to observe in the coming years whether the growing interest in L2 issues within L1 composition leads to yet another era in the examination of error in composition studies. Just as FYC courses were developed in response to demographic shifts in colleges and universities in the post-Civil-War period, and just as Shaughnessy's (1977) work with basic writers followed the advent of open admissions policies in the 1960s, perhaps the rapid mainstreaming of multilingual writers into composition programs will result in a felt need or at least a willingness among L1 researchers to look more closely again at the issue of error in student writing, and especially at how practitioners address it in their writing classes.

Notes

1. We are indebted in this section of the chapter to the book-length historical overview on error recently published by Santa (2006), which, in turn, builds on the previous historical work produced by Brereton (1995), Connors (1997, 2003), and Hillocks (1986), among others. Readers interested in a more in-depth treatment of the history of L1 composition and its approach to error are urged to consult these excellent sources.
2. Student themes in the nineteenth century were typically only 50–100 words long, but 20,000 in one year is, nonetheless, a daunting figure!
3. For another statement on the issue of dialects and language varieties in student writing that is contemporary to Shaughnessy's work, see National Council of Teachers of English's (NCTE's) (1974) "Resolution on Students' Right to Their Own Language."
4. We recognize that disclosing this here is akin to describing the surprise ending to a suspense film such as *The Sixth Sense*, and we apologize for the "spoiler" to readers who have not previously experienced Williams' brilliant essay.
5. It is also worth noting that Haswell's findings were loosely reproduced in a controlled quasi-experimental study focused on L2 writers nearly 20 years later (Ferris & Roberts, 2001).

46 Theory and History of Error Treatment

6. There was some variation between the two (1988 and 2008) Top Twenty lists. The specifics of these studies are discussed in more detail in Chapter 4.
7. Other second language writing historians will note that, prior to 1990, there was a fair amount of L2 writing research published in the area of contrastive (now called intercultural) rhetoric (especially the 1987 collection published by Connor and Kaplan). However, this work is largely descriptive rather than pedagogical.
8. Both of the authors review extensively for a wide range of journals and can attest firsthand to the steady stream of research projects and review/argument essays on this topic that cross our desks/inboxes. In addition, articles on error correction are among the most downloaded and cited in the *JSLW* database.

PART II

Analysis of Research on Written CF

3

RESEARCH ON WRITTEN CF IN LANGUAGE CLASSES

In this chapter, we outline and evaluate research that has investigated the role of written CF in language learning classrooms, including Foreign Language Learning (FLL), EFL, and ESL contexts, where the focus is on testing the efficacy of written CF for L2 acquisition (learning and development). As we have seen in Chapters 1 and 2, the role of written CF, on a theoretical level, has been controversial (Ferris, 1999, 2010; Krashen, 1982, 1984, 2003; Truscott, 1996, 1999, 2004, 2007), so the only way an attempt can be made to resolve the various issues and claims is by means of empirical investigation. This does not mean, however, that the findings and suggested implications of such investigations will not also be controversial, as we will show in our discussion of the critiques that have been offered. Any empirical test must be designed and executed in a way that is appropriate to the questions being investigated. When this is not the case, as we will show with some of the earlier studies in particular, debate is likely to arise when interpretations of data and findings are offered. Most of the research has been situated within a cognitive framework, so this will be the main focus of the chapter. However, as we explained in Chapter 1, a socio-cultural perspective has also been considered in some of the more recent research, so this contribution will be outlined towards the end of the chapter.

With these thoughts in mind, we describe and evaluate the extent to which the available research has managed to address the key questions/issues/claims outlined at the end of Chapter 1. These questions include:

1. Can written CF facilitate the short-term and long-term acquisition of L2 forms and structures?
2. Is unfocused written CF more effective in treating L2 errors than focused written CF?

50 Analysis of Research on Written CF

3. Is written CF more effective in targeting some linguistic error domains and specific error categories than other types?
4. Are some types of written CF more effective in treating L2 errors than others?
5. Does the educational and L2 learning background of learners determine the extent to which they benefit from written CF?
6. To what extent can the proposals of socio-cultural theory enhance our understanding of the effectiveness of written CF?

In looking at these questions, our descriptive outlines of the studies will include a discussion of similarities and differences across the studies, critical responses to the studies, and an evaluation of what we can conclude about each question from the available evidence. Pedagogical applications from the studies and recommendations for further research will be discussed in Chapters 5 and 6. In our discussion of each question, we provide a chart summarizing the key aspects of the studies being discussed.

Can Written CF Facilitate the Acquisition of L2 Forms and Structures?

The question of whether written CF can play a role in the L2 acquisition process is the most important question to be answered. If the answer is negative, all other questions cease to have importance. Thus, it is somewhat surprising that so little consideration had been given to this question prior to Truscott's (1996) call for the abandonment of the practice. On the one hand, this benign neglect can perhaps be explained by the prominence given in SLA theorizing and research to the role of oral interaction, including oral CF. This is understandable given that a learner's online use of procedural knowledge is a clearer indication of whether linguistic forms and structures have been acquired than is his/her explicit, declarative knowledge. On the other hand, however, there was a tendency among teachers to continue giving written CF on a range of written errors when there was no certainty that written CF can facilitate the acquisition of L2 forms and structures. The assumption that written CF "works" was quite rightly challenged by Truscott (1996), even though the evidence he cited in support of his claims was equally in need of being challenged. The particular value of Truscott's 1996 essay was the strength of its claims and the attention it gave to the importance of investigating whether, in fact, written CF can play a role in the SLA process. As we have mentioned above, it is important that studies are designed appropriately so that the question can actually be answered. Unfortunately, this has not always been the case with some of the early (pre-Truscott, 1996) studies. Before looking at the available research on this key question, we outline some of the more critical design flaws and execution shortcomings in the early studies so that, in discussing the findings that have been reported, the extent to which they can be relied upon as acceptable evidence will be understood. Thus, our next section outlines the key design flaws of the early research.

Design and Execution Flaws

In order to test whether written CF can play a role in the SLA process, it is necessary to test the effectiveness of the practice over time. In other words, when measuring an increase in learning, it is necessary to first establish the current performance level of a learner. This is most often established by means of a pre-test piece of writing of a learner's current level of accuracy in using whatever linguistic form or structure is being investigated. Having established this, accuracy improvement, as a result of written CF, can be measured if another piece of writing (i.e., a new text) is completed immediately after the written CF has been given. In some studies, researchers include a revision stage in which learners are required to revise their pre-test piece of writing, using the feedback they have received on their text. In order to determine the long-term effectiveness of written CF, one or more delayed post-test pieces of writing are then required so that the accuracy levels can be observed and compared with those of the immediate post-test and the pre-test pieces of writing. Unfortunately, some of these key design components have not been included in some of the early studies (reviewed in the next section).

Another design flaw identified in the literature has been the absence of a control group in some studies (i.e., a group of learners who did not receive written CF). In order to know whether accuracy improvements are the result of written CF alone, a comparison must be made between the accuracy performance of learners who receive written CF and those who do not receive written CF. A number of empirical studies have investigated the efficacy of written CF using this research design but other studies, claiming to have investigated the effectiveness of written CF, have not included a control group. This means that their findings cannot be used to answer the question of effectiveness. At best, they can be evaluated in terms of the relative effectiveness of different types of written CF.

A third issue concerns the measurement of accuracy in new pieces of writing. If post-test pieces of writing are to be a valid measurement of improvement, comparable writing tasks need to be administered at each test stage. Avoiding the use of different genres (e.g., journal entries for one piece of writing and argumentative essays in another) within a single study would have enabled valid text comparisons to be made in some of the early research (Bitchener, 2008; Guénette, 2007).

Arguably, these are the most critical design issues for studies investigating the efficacy of written CF. A range of additional issues including execution and analytical shortcomings have been identified in the literature (Bitchener, 2008; Ferris, 2003; Guénette, 2007) but the extent to which they might compromise the reported findings of a particular study is an issue that can only be considered in relation to that study. Some of these issues include the need to ensure (1) that learners within a single study are of the same L2 proficiency level, (2) that they are exposed to the same or closely similar classroom activities, (3) that

52 Analysis of Research on Written CF

teachers/researchers are consistent in the feedback they provide and in how they provide it, and (4) that data elicitation procedures are consistent across groups of learners. Some of these issues will be seen to be more widespread than others in our discussion of the research below.

The Short-term Effectiveness of Written CF

Many of the early studies that investigated the effectiveness of written CF focused on providing L2 writers with feedback that would enable them to revise a piece of writing. Most often, these studies were conducted in composition or writing classes (reviewed in Chapter 4) so the focus was on helping these writers improve the accuracy of their drafts. If writers were able to improve the accuracy of their writing, as a result of the feedback they had been given, these improvements were regarded as evidence of learning, or of short-term learning at least. However, such improvements may not necessarily be the result of learning if the feedback was direct and explicit (i.e., if direct error correction or explicit indirect feedback like meta-linguistic codes had been given) or if the error identified by the feedback had been a mistake or an oversight by the writer. The only way to know whether accurate text revisions are the result of learning is to look for evidence of improved accuracy in the writing of new texts and to compare the texts of writers who received and did not receive written CF.

Two studies (Truscott & Hsu, 2008; van Beuningen et al., 2008, 2012) have investigated by means of post-test analysis (the writing of new texts) the potential of text revisions to predict learning. Although these studies (see Figure 3.1 below) found that learners whose errors were corrected made significantly fewer errors than learners in the control groups (who had not received written CF during revision), the results of the studies are conflicting with respect to the role of written CF for learning. On the one hand, van Beuningen et al. (2008, 2012) found that written CF not only led to improved accuracy in the text revision but that it also constituted a learning effect (revealed in the improved accuracy of the new text). On the other hand, Truscott and Hsu (2008) reported that the accuracy improvement of their experimental group during revision did not lead to improved accuracy in the writing of a new text and therefore concluded that "the successful error reduction during revision is not a predictor . . . of learning" (p. 299). Figure 3.1 summarizes the reported findings of the researchers with respect to the effectiveness of written CF for text revision and new text writing (learning).

Reflecting on why the learners in the study by Truscott and Hsu (2008) failed to improve the accuracy of their writing in the new text, Bruton (2009) questioned whether there was, in fact, much room for improvement given that the learners had made few errors in their first piece of writing. Although this could be a reason, it is interesting to note, on the other hand, that advanced learners in Bitchener and Knoch (2010b) with high levels of accuracy can sometimes continue to benefit from additional written CF and raise their mastery and control

Studies	Revision effectiveness	Learning effectiveness
Truscott and Hsu (2008)	Error reduction	No error reduction
van Beuningen et al. (2008)	Error reduction	Error reduction
van Beuningen et al. (2012)	Error reduction	Error reduction

FIGURE 3.1 Studies of written CF for effective text revision and new text writing

of recurrent errors. Another reason might be that the underlining of all errors failed to sufficiently focus learner "attention" and may not have provided sufficient information for "understanding" to have occurred. As Schmidt (1994) and others have suggested, "attention" and "understanding" are prerequisite conditions of learning. A limited level of motivation with EFL learners to use the feedback they were given might be a further reason for the absence of a positive effect (Ferris, 2003). Reasons aside, Truscott and Hsu (2008) argued that written CF is not useful as a teaching tool even if it has some limited value as an editing tool. But, because van Beuningen et al. (2008, 2012) found a learning effect in their larger studies, the possibility exists that text revisions, depending on the type of feedback provided, may be able to contribute to learning. Further research of this type is therefore needed to examine its full potential.

Is Unfocused Written CF More Effective in Treating L2 Errors than Focused Written CF?

Few would disagree that the long-term effectiveness of written CF is the most important question to be answered. After all, the central goal of any language class teacher is to facilitate the long-term retention/acquisition of what he/she teaches and provides feedback on. In discussing the research that looked at this question, we divide the studies into three groups: those in which unfocused, focused and unfocused compared with focused written CF was provided.

Studies of Unfocused Written CF

Four of the early studies (Kepner, 1991; Robb et al., 1986; Semke, 1984; Sheppard, 1992) that sought to investigate the learning potential of written CF provided learners with unfocused, comprehensive feedback on a wide range of error categories whereas more recent studies of longitudinal effectiveness, with the exception of a study by van Beuningen et al. (2012), have tested the effectiveness of providing focused written CF on one or a few linguistic error categories. We now discuss each of the four studies, pointing to (1) the design and methodology issues that need to be considered when assessing the extent to

54 Analysis of Research on Written CF

which the studies provide clear evidence for or against the effectiveness of written CF and (2) the extent to which the findings may have occurred as a result of the unfocused feedback rather than focused feedback. Figure 3.2 distinguishes the written CF groups with those that have been interpreted as control group equivalents and indicates whether or not the researchers reported any differences between the two groupings.

Kepner (1991) investigated the effectiveness of giving one group of intermediate Spanish FL learners direct error correction on their linguistic errors and another group content comments on their texts (interpreted as the control group that did not receive written CF). Although there was no significant difference in the number of errors between the two groups after a 12-week period, a difference of opinion has been given about the type of conclusion that can be drawn from the findings. Ferris (2003, 2004) suggested that there was at least weak evidence of a beneficial effect for written CF because the correction group made fewer errors. Truscott (2007), on the other hand, concluded that there was "little to no value for correction" (p. 259). He based his position on the small and "unimpressive" mean difference (6.56) between the groups (in light of the pooled standard deviation of 16.89) and on the effect size (0.388) that fell in the middle of the "small" range. Taking a strict statistical perspective on this difference, one should conclude that this study does not provide evidence in support of the efficacy of written CF. Then again, one needs to also consider the gravity of other design and methodological shortcomings. Ferris (2003), for example, points out that:

> Kepner analyzed the sixth set of journal entries (out of eight total) for comparison purposes, (and that) she did not look at the first set of journal entries to see where the students started out on this type of writing.
>
> *(p. 60)*

Studies	Treatment	Control	Effectiveness
Kepner (1991)	1. Direct error correction	Content comments	No difference
Semke (1984)	1. Direct error correction 2. Direct error correction and content comments 3. Indirect coded feedback	Content comments	No difference
Robb et al. (1986)	1. Direct error correction 2. Indirect coded feedback 3. Indirect highlighting	Marginal error totals?	No difference
Sheppard (1992)	1. Direct error correction and conferences	Content comments and conferences?	No difference

FIGURE 3.2 Early studies of effectiveness of written CF on new texts

Clearly, this is a serious design omission because there is no way of knowing whether, in fact, the two groups of learners had the same initial level of accuracy. Additionally, as Ferris (2003) noted, "there was no control for the length of the journal entries (which were written outside class), a variable that could affect both error and proposition counts" (p. 60). The results of the study need to be interpreted, then, with caution and not presented as clear evidence of the ineffectiveness of written CF.

Semke's (1984) 10-week study of the journal writing of 141 German FL students in a US university also investigated the longitudinal effectiveness of written CF. Her study included four groups who received either direct error correction, coded feedback with self-correction by the students, comments-on-content only, or a combination of direct error correction and comments-on-content. The inclusion of a comments-on-content group in the design of the study means that this study, depending on one's point of view, may or may not qualify as one with a control group comparing learners who did not receive written CF and those who did (the other three groups). Semke reported no significant differences in accuracy between the three written CF groups and the comments-on-content group and so concluded that written CF was no more beneficial to those who received it than those who did not. Cautioning us against accepting this finding as clear evidence, Guénette (2007) pointed to the possibility that the findings may have been affected by the presence of an incentive for some participants. She explained that those in this study were graded according to the number of words written (the "content" group) or on a ratio of mistakes to the number of written words (the "form" groups). Consequently, in seeking to explain "the verve of the 'content' group," Guénette (2007, p. 50) suggested that this group may have not been "worried about losing points, while the other three groups probably needed to write less for fear of making too many mistakes." Considering these two issues (a real control group and an incentive), we should be careful about placing too much authority on the claims made by Semke about the absence of an effect for written CF.

The extent to which the study by Robb et al. (1986) qualifies as an investigation into the effectiveness of written CF is also debatable. This study of 134 EFL learners in Japan included four different groups of learners who received either direct error correction, coded feedback, highlighted feedback, or marginal feedback in the form of the total number of errors per line. Using the strict criterion that any indication an error has occurred (including the number of errors that have been made in a line of text) constitutes written CF, it would have to be concluded that this study does not qualify as one that investigates the question of effectiveness. Truscott (1996), taking a somewhat more relaxed position with regard to the categorization of the fourth group, argued that the study "was equivalent to a controlled study because the information presented to group (d) was so limited that it could not have been helpful . . ." (Truscott, 2007, p. 261). Robb et al. (1986), the researchers themselves, report that, even though all groups improved, there was no difference between the groups. In other words, learners

56 Analysis of Research on Written CF

who received written CF did not outperform those who did not receive it. Truscott (2007), however, claimed that the results of the study reveal more than this. He argued that they show the ineffectiveness of written CF because group (d) made slightly larger gains than the other three groups. Depending on the position one takes regarding the classification of group (d) as a control group or not, a reasonable conclusion would seem to be that the study does not provide clear, unequivocal evidence for or against the effectiveness of written CF. Casting more doubt on the extent to which we can rely of the findings of the study, Guénette (2007) pointed out the importance of adequately controlling against the possible effects of the classroom focus on grammatical form and sentence structure. She suggested that "all groups were perhaps attentive to form whether or not they were receiving corrective feedback" (p. 49).

It is similarly debatable whether Sheppard's (1992) study of 26 upper-intermediate ESL learners can be said to have included a no-correction control group and therefore be considered as offering evidence for or against the effectiveness of written CF. His study compared one group that received written CF over a 10-week period and another group that received comments relating to content (e.g., requests for clarification when the writing was difficult to understand). Additionally, learners in both groups had one-on-one conferences with their teacher. Those in the written CF group talked about the errors that had been made and those in the content-focused group talked about the meaning of the content that had been presented. Sheppard reports that no advantage was gained in terms of improved accuracy by the written CF group. It is unclear whether the learners in both groups received incidental instruction on linguistic errors during the 10-week period and whether the conferences between the teacher and the content-focused group avoided any discussion of difficulties in understanding meaning that may have arisen from linguistic error. Thus, it is unclear whether in fact the content-focused group was strictly a control group. Pointing to further reasons for being cautious about how the findings of this study might be used to argue for or against the efficacy of written CF, Ferris (2003, 2004) pointed out that there was an absence of inter-rater reliability checks on the coding of the data.

Considering these four early studies on the long-term efficacy of written CF, no significant differences between the correction and no-correction groups were reported. However, there is debate about whether studies that include a "content comments" group as a control group rather than a "no-correction" group as a control group can be accepted as having a real control group. This is because there is no certainty that "content comments" did not refer to issues of linguistic error and accuracy. This is the key issue to be considered when deciding whether or not two of the studies (Kepner, 1991; Semke, 1984) be classified as those with a control group. While there might also be debate about the extent to which the studies by Robb et al. (1986) and Sheppard (1992) include a real control group, a clearer case will be made for disqualifying these studies as ones that provide evidence for or against the effectiveness of written CF. Although Truscott (1996) maintained that evidence against written CF from these studies is compelling, the findings from further research that manage to avoid the shortcomings noted above will have the final say.

There is another factor that may have informed the absence of a positive effect for written CF. In each of these studies, the feedback was "unfocused" (i.e., it was provided on a wide range of linguistic error categories). This, therefore, raises the question about whether it was reasonable to have expected written CF to be effective when such a heavy cognitive load was placed on relatively low proficiency learners. To some extent, the work of van Beuningen et al. (2008, 2012) addresses this question. Their studies investigated the effectiveness of providing multilingual secondary school students (approximately 80 percent being from a non-Dutch language background) in the Netherlands with unfocused or comprehensive written CF on errors made in the use of the Dutch. The learners were divided into two treatment groups (direct written CF and indirect written CF) and two control groups (writing practice and revision without written CF). The studies found that unfocused written CF can be effective in improving accuracy: both treatment groups outperformed the control groups on the immediate post-test (one week after receiving feedback) and the direct written CF group outperformed the other groups in the delayed post-test (four weeks after receiving feedback). The researchers report medium-effect sizes for the treatment groups over the "control" groups. In light of critiques of the earlier studies referred to above, this study may also be said to have certain shortcomings. Questions may be asked about whether the researchers controlled for additional linguistic input between giving feedback and the one-week delay in administering the immediate post-test, and whether the self-correction group was a real control group given that the learners' attention was focused on accuracy when doing the self-correction and given that this occurred before the immediate post-test, one week later. The extent to which other shortcomings, identified by the researchers, might have impacted upon the findings is a further unknown. Nevertheless, the availability now of conflicting results about the effectiveness of providing learners with unfocused written CF means that further research is required on the relative benefits of unfocused feedback.

Studies of Focused Written CF

A growing range of recent studies have investigated the effectiveness of focusing written CF on only one or a few targeted linguistic errors. Within this category, "highly focused" feedback provides written CF on one category of error only and "less focused CF" restricts feedback to a limited number of targeted types of error (Ellis et al., 2008, p. 356). From a theoretical perspective, Schmidt (1994) and Ellis (2005) have pointed to the importance of "attention" and "understanding" in their work on cognitive theories of SLA, so it would seem that, if intensive

58 Analysis of Research on Written CF

written CF is provided on only one or a few targeted linguistic error categories, learners would be more likely to "attend" to such feedback, "understand" the cause or nature of the error, and "understand" how to correct it.

The first set of studies (Bitchener, 2008; Bitchener & Knoch, 2008, 2009a, 2009b, 2010a, 2010b; Ellis et al., 2008; Sheen, 2007; Sheen et al., 2009) were focused on investigating the effectiveness of providing ESL learners with written CF on one linguistic error category (i.e., "focused" feedback): two functional uses of the English article system (the use of the indefinite article "a" for first mention and the use of the definite article "the" for anaphoric mentions). These studies are summarized in Figure 3.3 below.

The rationale for focusing a range of studies on the English article system will be explained below when we discuss the effectiveness of written CF for treating different linguistic error categories. The reason so many studies have provided written CF on the same linguistic error category is not difficult to explain. In order to test the theoretical claims made against written CF, it is important that the claims be examined when feedback is given on the same linguistic domain rather than on a range of linguistic domains that may introduce a variable effect. The possibility of a resulting variable effect will be seen below in our discussion of different linguistic error categories.

The first study in the set (Bitchener, 2008) investigated the effectiveness of providing 75 low intermediate ESL learners with focused written CF on the two functional uses of the English article system. The participants were divided into one control group (that did not receive written CF) and three treatment groups that received either direct error correction with written and oral meta-linguistic feedback, direct error correction with written meta-linguistic feedback, or direct error correction. The study found that the accuracy of those who received focused written CF in the immediate post-test outperformed those in the control group and that this level of accuracy improvement was retained two months later. The study (Bitchener & Knoch, 2008) was then extended to 144 learners in order to see whether there was a differential effect for providing focused written CF to migrant and international learners (an issue that will be discussed in a later section). The extended study included the same four groups and again found that the treatment groups outperformed the control group.

Keeping the proficiency level and the treatment groups constant, Bitchener and Knoch (2010a) investigated the extent to which immediate gains made in accuracy by 52 learners, as a result of focused written CF, could be retained over a more extensive period of time (10 months). The importance of understanding the longitudinal potential of written CF for L2 acquisition cannot be underestimated given the possibility that short-term gains (e.g., one or two months) may not be retained when learners give their attention to other linguistic error categories in subsequent months of learning. The study found that all treatment groups outperformed the control group in the immediate post-test and that they retained this level of performance across the 10-month period.

Studies	Sample	Proficiency	Treatments	Findings
Bitchener (2008)	75	Low intermediate	1. Direct focused correction, written and oral meta-linguistic input 2. Direct focused correction and written meta-linguistic input 3. Direct error correction 4. Control	All three focused written CF groups outperformed control group in immediate and two months delayed post-test
Bitchener and Knoch (2008)	144	Low intermediate	1. Direct focused correction, written and oral meta-linguistic input 2. Direct focused correction and written meta-linguistic input 3. Direct focused correction 4. Control	All three focused written CF groups outperformed control group in immediate and two months delayed post-test
Bitchener and Knoch (2010a)	52	Low intermediate	1. Direct focused correction, written and oral meta-linguistic input 2. Direct focused correction and written meta-linguistic input 3. Direct focused correction 4. Control	All three focused written CF groups outperformed control group in immediate and three delayed post-test over 10 months
Bitchener and Knoch (2010b)	63	Advanced	1. Written meta-linguistic input 2. Indirect focused circling 3. Written and oral meta-linguistic input 4. Control	All three treatment groups outperformed control group in immediate post-test; both direct focused treatment groups outperformed indirect and control groups in 10 week delayed post-test
Sheen (2007)	91	Intermediate	1. Direct focused correction 2. Direct focused correction and written meta-linguistic input 3. Control	Both treatment groups outperformed control group on immediate and delayed post-test
Sheen et al. (2009)	80	Intermediate	1. Direct focused correction 2. Unfocused correction 3. Writing practice 4. Control	Groups 1–3 outperformed control group in immediate and delayed tests; group 1 made greater gains than group 2
Ellis et al. (2008)	49	Intermediate	1. Direct focused correction 2. Direct unfocused feedback 3. Control	All three groups performed with greater accuracy in immediate post-test; focused and unfocused groups outperformed control group in 10 week delayed post-test

FIGURE 3.3 Studies of focused written CF

60 Analysis of Research on Written CF

Keeping the same targeted focus (the English article system) but extending the investigation to a group of higher proficiency learners, Bitchener and Knoch (2010b) investigated the effectiveness of providing 63 ESL learners in the US with written CF. In this study, there was a control group (who did not receive written CF) and three different treatment groups who received either written meta-linguistic explanation, indirect circling of errors, or written meta-linguistic explanation with oral form-focused instruction. Significant differences between the control group and the three treatment groups were found on the immediate post-test. On the delayed post-test, significant differences were found between the two direct treatment groups and the indirect and control group. The delayed post-test result will be discussed below in our section on the relative effectiveness of different types of written CF.

Further evidence in support of the effectiveness of focused feedback targeting the use of English articles with written CF can be found in studies by Sheen (2007), Sheen et al. (2009) and Ellis et al. (2008). In the first of these studies, Sheen (2007) divided her 91 intermediate ESL learners into a control group and two treatment groups that received either direct written CF or direct written CF with meta-linguistic explanation. The study found that both treatment groups outperformed the control group on both the immediate and delayed post-tests. Building on this study, Sheen et al. (2009) investigated the effectiveness of providing 80 intermediate ESL learners with direct written CF, indirect written CF, writing practice alone, or no written CF. Again, this study found that the two groups that received written CF outperformed the control group in the post-tests. The study by Ellis et al. (2008), conducted in an EFL context with 49 intermediate Japanese male learners, also investigated the effectiveness of targeting the same two functional uses of the English article system studied by Bitchener (2008), Bitchener and Knoch (2008, 2009a, 2009b, 2010a, 2010b), Sheen (2007), and Sheen et al. (2009). All three groups (direct written CF on articles only; direct written CF articles and other error categories; control group) performed with higher levels of accuracy in the immediate post-test but the two treatment groups outperformed the control group in the delayed post-test.

Responding to the claims made by Truscott (1996), these studies demonstrate without exception the effectiveness of providing language class learners of English (in both ESL and EFL contexts) with focused written CF within certain linguistic environments. They show that (1) focused written CF is effective in treating at least certain types of linguistic error, (2) a single treatment can have a longitudinal effect (up to 10 months), and (3) written CF is beneficial for low- and advanced-proficiency learners. The extent to which focused written CF (even a single treatment) has a longitudinal effect on improving accurate use of other linguistic error domains and categories is not yet known.

Crucially, these studies have taken note of earlier design problems and, while not always managing to avoid every design and methodological issue, have attempted to avoid those that have been identified in the literature as having the most compromising effect on the robustness of results (e.g., the absence of a control group, the failure to compare initial texts with new texts, the limited assessment of longitudinal effectiveness, and inconsistency in the selection of consistent instrumentation such as the type or genre of writing tasks). Nevertheless, a few critiques of this work have commented on methodological issues that might be seen by some to have influenced the studies' findings.

First, Truscott (2007) argued that the findings supporting the effectiveness of written CF are biased because learners who are corrected tend to shorten and simplify their writing so that they avoid making too many errors. He suggested that such avoidance causes their error scores to rise. However, this argument is not really valid because the accuracy rates reported in all of the studies were calculated as a percentage of actual usage. Moreover, the nature of the writing tasks predisposed the learners to make quite extensive use of the targeted uses of the article system. We agree that, on some occasions, learners could have used other linguistic constructions to avoid uses they were uncertain about, but this would not have been possible on the majority of occasions.

Second, Xu (2009), referring specifically to Bitchener (2009) and Ellis et al. (2008), claimed that these studies, and, by implication, others with the same characteristics, have over-generalized their findings. Unfortunately, this claim reveals a misreading of the articles. However, as Bitchener (2009) said in his response to Xu, all claims concerning his study were made only in relation to the targeted focus of the study (i.e., the two functional uses of the English article system), and mention was made of the need for further research to explore the extent to which more general claims can be made about the effectiveness of written CF for treating other linguistic domains. Xu also expressed her concern with the narrow focus on two functional uses of the English article system and with the inability of this focus to advance our knowledge more generally. The rationale for the specific theory-testing focus of these studies has been explained earlier in this book and in the articles themselves. Similarly, attention has been drawn in article conclusions to the need for ongoing research into the effectiveness of written CF on other linguistic error domains and categories. Other issues raised by Xu have been responded to by Bitchener (2009) but are not considered to have impacted on the findings and claims reported.

Studies of Focused and Unfocused Written CF

Having reported on the studies that investigated the effectiveness of providing learners with unfocused or focused written CF, we reconsider now two studies (Ellis et al., 2008; Sheen et al., 2009) that compared the relative effectiveness of unfocused and focused written CF within a single study design. Our summary of these studies was provided in Figure 3.3 above. Ellis et al. (2008) compared the effectiveness of providing 49 Japanese male intermediate EFL learners with focused or unfocused written CF on the same two functional uses of the English

62 Analysis of Research on Written CF

article system as the several "focused" studies referred to above. The focused group received correction on article errors only while the unfocused group received correction on the article errors as well as correction on other error categories. The study reported that both types of feedback were equally effective, but, in saying so, the researchers were quick to point out that the two types of feedback were not sufficiently distinguished from one another because article corrections were highly represented in both. Consequently, the findings need to be interpreted in this light. Other issues that may have had an impact on the findings of this study were identified by Xu (2009), but we do not consider these to have had the same level of effect.

Seeking to address the methodological shortcomings of the Ellis et al. (2008) study, Sheen et al. (2009) investigated the effects of focused and unfocused written CF on both a single grammatical target (the English article system) and on a broader range of grammatical structures (articles, copula "be," regular past tense, irregular past tense, and prepositions). The study found that focused written CF on the English article system alone was more effective than unfocused written CF. Unfortunately, as the authors explained, this study was also affected by a methodological flaw. The written CF received by the unfocused group was somewhat unsystematic with some of the errors being corrected while others were ignored (Sheen et al., 2009), and, as van Beuningen et al. (2008) pointed out, "students might have been confused noticing that some of their errors were disregarded" (p. 282). Again, the findings of this study need to be read with this in mind.

The question of whether focused or unfocused written CF is more effective in helping learners acquire L2 forms and structures cannot, at this stage, be fully answered. We have seen that the recent findings of van Beuningen et al. (2012) on the effectiveness of unfocused, comprehensive feedback cast some doubt on what earlier unfocused studies were reporting. While the studies investigating the effectiveness of focused feedback have consistently shown that it can play a role in targeting a limited range of error categories, it is yet unclear how extensive its effectiveness might be. Perhaps more importantly, the question of the relative effectiveness of the two approaches is the one that is more crucial and, therefore, in greater need of further investigation. Two partly flawed studies that have investigated this issue provide a limited indication of how the question might ultimately be answered. Additionally, it may well be that the question will only be answered if it is investigated alongside other questions (e.g., those focusing on the interaction of feedback type and linguistic error domains and categories).

Does Written CF Target Some Linguistic Error Domains/ Categories More Effectively than Others?

Although there is growing evidence of the relationship between written CF and accuracy improvement over time, the research base has so far been limited to testing its effectiveness with certain linguistic error domains and categories. Thus, the extent to which written CF is effective for different domains and categories of linguistic knowledge has yet to be more fully explored. Truscott (1996) argued that no single form of correction can be expected to help learners acquire knowledge of all linguistic forms and structures because the acquisition, for example, of syntax, morphology, and lexis require an understanding not only of form but also of meaning and use in relation to other words and other parts of the language system. In fact, by 2007, his argument went further, claiming that written CF was only ever likely to have a positive effect in helping learners revise their initial texts and in treating errors that "are relatively simple and can be treated as discrete items" (Truscott, 2007, p. 258) such as non-grammatical errors. Referring to syntactic knowledge, he argued that written CF cannot be expected to facilitate the acquisition of such knowledge because it comprises more than a collection of discrete items. Additionally, he speculated (Truscott, 2004, 2007) that syntactic accuracy is unlikely to be the focus of written CF because learners would be more likely to avoid using complex structures that they were not confident in using accurately. On a theoretical level, these may be reasonable claims. Skehan (1998), for example, referred to limited capacity models of attention and explained that there will likely be a trade-off between accuracy and complexity, while Skehan and Foster (2001) suggested that learners are likely to focus their efforts on achieving greater control over more stable (interlanguage) elements and avoid extending their L2 repertoire. However, even if learners do avoid using more complex structures, this practice does not mean that written CF is unable to treat complex structures. Evidence from oral CF research has shown, for instance, that some complex structures can be targeted effectively. Studies by Mackey and Oliver (2002), Mackey and Philp (1998), and Mackey, Philp, Egi, Fujii and Tatsumi (2002) on syntactic structures such as question forms, and one study by McDonough (2006) on the use of dative constructions, have revealed positive effects when oral CF is provided. If the hypothesized advantages of written CF over some forms of oral CF prove to be true (see Sheen, 2010 for a discussion of differences between the two modalities), it may be that written CF is able to target complex forms and structures (e.g., syntax), as well as, and maybe better than, oral CF.

Only a limited amount of research has focused on the role of written CF for helping learners acquire specific linguistic forms and structures. Those that have been published have tended to investigate the effectiveness of written CF for treating discrete, rule-based items. One study (Bitchener et al., 2005) investigated the effect of written CF on three linguistic error categories (use of the English article system, the past simple tense, and prepositions) over a 12-week period and found it to be effective for helping L2 writers improve their accuracy in the first two, rule-based, categories but not in the more idiosyncratic use of prepositions. However, that study did not examine which particular functional uses of the article system were most effectively targeted with the feedback. Given the range of functional uses of the article system in English, it is important to know whether

64 Analysis of Research on Written CF

written CF is more effective in targeting certain uses rather than all uses. In a series of more focused studies, Bitchener (2008), Bitchener and Knoch (2008, 2009a, 2009b, 2010a, 2010b), Ellis et al. (2008), Sheen (2007), and Sheen et al. (2009) investigated its effect on two particular functional uses of the English article system (the use of the indefinite article for first mention and of the definite article for subsequent or anaphoric mentions) and found that writers who received written CF outperformed those who did not receive written CF. Gains were evident in both the immediate and delayed post-tests, thereby demonstrating that written CF can have an immediate effect on the writing of a new text and that the level of improvement can be retained over time. In short, this research base, limited as it is in terms of its target forms/structures, demonstrates, nevertheless, that written CF is effective in helping L2 writers improve the accuracy with which they use these particular rule-based, discrete items. Most recently, Bitchener and Knoch (2010b) also found that written CF enabled advanced proficiency L2 writers in the US raise further their already high levels of accuracy in using these two functional uses of the article system.

To date, the literature has not reported the findings of studies that have investigated whether written CF might also be effective in targeting more complex structures (e.g., syntactic structures). This is an important question for understanding the full potential of written CF for L2 acquisition. Although, as we have mentioned above, oral CF has proved to be effective in facilitating the acquisition of certain complex structures, doubt about the potential of written CF to do so has been expressed by Truscott (1996, 1999, 2007). While there is a very limited research base on the extent to which written CF can play a role in the acquisition of different linguistic forms and structures, there is a far more extensive base on the relative effectiveness of different types of written CF.

Are Some Types of Written CF More Effective in Treating L2 Errors than Others?

Research on the relative effectiveness of providing learners with different types of written CF has tended to dominate the written CF literature over the last 30 years. Most of the early studies examined whether *direct* forms of feedback are more effective than *indirect* types, but recently the categorization of feedback types has been expanded to include a more fine-grained consideration of sub-categories along the direct-indirect spectrum. Before we survey what this research has reported, we will describe the various categorizations and reflect upon the theoretical arguments that have been advanced to support each approach.

Categorization Definitions

Until recently, most of the studies into the relative effectiveness of different types of written CF were focused on comparing direct or indirect types of feedback.

Written CF in Language Classes **65**

Direct written CF has typically been defined as that which provides some form of explicit correction of linguistic form or structure above or near the linguistic error and usually involves the crossing out of an unnecessary word/phrase/morpheme, the insertion of a missing word/phrase/morpheme, and/or the provision of the correct form or structure. More recently, direct CF has included written meta-linguistic explanation (the provision of grammar rules and examples of correct usage) and, sometimes, oral form-focused instruction (to further clarify the written meta-linguistic explanation). On the other hand, *indirect* written CF has been defined as that which indicates an error has been made but it does not provide a correction or explicit meta-linguistic information. Typically, it has been provided in one of two ways: (1) underlining or circling an error; (2) recording in the margin the number of errors in a given line. Rather than the teacher providing direct feedback, writers are left to resolve and correct the problem that is drawn to their attention. In earlier research on written CF in composition classrooms, the provision of a code to show the category of error also tended to be included within the indirect category.

Theoretical Arguments

Theoretically, arguments have been advanced for both the direct and indirect approaches. Those supporting *indirect* feedback suggest that this approach is most useful because it invites L2 writers to engage in guided learning and problem-solving (Lalande, 1982) and, as a result, promotes the type of reflection on existing knowledge or partially internalized knowledge that is more likely to foster long-term acquisition and written accuracy. Considering acquisition in terms of the internalization of new linguistic knowledge, it is clear that indirect written CF would not be able to play a role in this regard. Those more in favor of *direct* feedback suggest that it is more helpful to writers because it (1) reduces the type of confusion that they may experience if they fail to understand indirect forms of feedback or fail to remember the feedback they have been given (e.g., the meaning of error codes used by teachers); (2) provides them with information to help them resolve more complex errors (e.g., syntactic structure and idiomatic usage); (3) offers more explicit feedback on hypotheses that may have been tested; and (4) is more immediate. We would suggest that the validity of each of these positions may reside in (a) the contexts under consideration (e.g., language learning classes or composition classes where the goals and foci of instruction may differ), and (b) the proficiency level of the writers.

Studies Comparing Direct and Indirect Written CF

Studies that have investigated the relative merits of different types of feedback have tended to be grouped according to those that have compared (1) direct and indirect types of feedback and (2) different types of direct feedback. Considering

66 Analysis of Research on Written CF

those that have *compared direct and indirect types*, Lalande's (1982) study of 60 intermediate German FL learners reported an advantage for indirect feedback (coding) over direct error correction, but the observed between-group difference in accuracy improvement was not statistically significant. It has also been noted by van Beuningen et al. (2012) that "the two treatments differed in more respects than just the method of CF provision; the indirect group was engaged in more form-focused activities than the group receiving direct CF" (p. 7). Robb et al.'s (1986) study of 134 EFL learners in Japan reported no advantage for any of their four feedback types (direct error correction; coded feedback; highlighting; marginal error counts). Similarly, in Semke's (1984) study of 141 German FL learners, no difference between the two approaches (direct error correction; comments; direct error correction and comments; coded feedback) was discovered. But, as Guénette (2007) noted, the groups in Semke's study were treated differently and this is likely to have had an effect on her findings:

> In that study, two different types of feedback on form were compared: one group saw their errors directly corrected and another group was asked to self-correct (errors were coded) and submit a rewrite one week later. However, the groups were "treated" differently. Because the correction group was asked to rewrite their essay rather than write a new one, students in that group wrote only half as much new material as the other groups. It is therefore very difficult to see the effect of the two different types of feedback on form—direct versus indirect corrections—because of a confounding variable (quantity of writing) that obscures the issue. In addition, correcting students' errors and asking them to recopy their essay is quite different, cognitively, from only pointing out the errors and asking them to self-correct.
>
> *(p. 49)*

On the other hand, three recent studies by van Beuningen et al. (2008, 2012) and Bitchener and Knoch (2010b), with secondary school learners in Dutch multilingual classrooms and advanced ESL learners respectively, managed to avoid significant design and execution issues. These studies reported that, even though there were positive short-term effects for both direct and indirect feedback, direct error correction had a more significant long-term effect than indirect written CF. Thus, the same finding was evident in two different settings (the Netherlands and the US) and with two different age groups (secondary school learners of Dutch and university learners of ESL). Figure 3.4 below summarizes the conflicting findings of these studies. Although the design and methodological issues of the first three studies might lead one to conclude that the findings of the three most recent studies are more robust and compelling, we believe that further research is required to confirm this view.

Studies	Feedback types	Effectiveness
Lalande (1982)	1. Direct error correction 2. Indirect coding	Advantage reported for indirect coding but not statistically significant
Semke (1984)	1. Direct error correction 2. Content comments 3. Direct error correction and content comments 4. Indirect coding	No difference
Robb et al. (1986)	1. Direct error correction 2. Indirect coding 3. Indirect highlighting 4. Indirect marginal error totals	No difference
van Beuningen et al. (2008)	1. Direct error correction 2. Indirect feedback 3. Writing practice 4. Self-correction revision	Direct error correction more effective long-term; both direct and indirect feedback effective short-term
van Beuningen et al. (2012)	1. Direct error correction 2. Indirect feedback 3. Writing practice 4. Self-correction revision	Direct feedback more effective for grammar but indirect for non-grammar items
Bitchener and Knoch (2010b)	1. Direct meta-linguistic explanation 2. Indirect circling 3. Direct meta-linguistic explanation and oral explanation 4. Control	Direct error correction more effective long-term; all direct and indirect feedback options equally effective short-term

FIGURE 3.4 Studies comparing direct and indirect written CF

Additional support for the effectiveness of providing direct written CF in language learning classrooms for long-term acquisition can be seen in the following section reporting on studies that tested the relative effectiveness of different types of *direct* written CF.

Studies of Direct Written CF

Several recent studies have examined the relative effectiveness of *different types of direct CF* on improved accuracy. Key features of these studies are summarized in Figure 3.5 below.

Bitchener et al. (2005), summarized in Figure 3.5, compared the effect of different direct feedback combinations typically practiced in advanced-proficiency

68 Analysis of Research on Written CF

Studies	Types of direct written CF	Effectiveness
Bitchener et al. (2005)	1. Direct error correction 2. Direct error correction and oral meta-linguistic explanation 3. Control	Group 2 more effective
Bitchener (2008)	1. Direct error correction, written and oral meta-linguistic explanation 2. Direct error correction and written meta-linguistic explanation 3. Direct error correction 4. Control	Groups 1 and 3 more effective than group 2 (only just) and group 4
Bitchener and Knoch (2008)	1. Direct error correction, written and oral meta-linguistic explanation 2. Direct error correction and written meta-linguistic explanation 3. Direct error correction 4. Control	No difference in types of written CF
Bitchener and Knoch (2010a)	1. Direct error correction, written and oral meta-linguistic explanation 2. Direct error correction and written meta-linguistic explanation 3. Direct error correction 4. Control	No difference in types of written CF
Sheen (2007)	1. Direct error correction 2. Direct error correction with meta-linguistic explanation 3. Control	Group 2 more effective

FIGURE 3.5 Studies comparing different types of direct written CF

classroom settings. They found that those in group one who received direct error correction and oral meta-linguistic explanation outperformed both groups two and three for the past simple tense and the definite article but found no such effect for prepositions. They suggested that the addition of oral meta-linguistic explanation may have been the crucial factor in facilitating increased accuracy. Limiting the investigation on the English article system to two functional uses (the indefinite article "a" for first mention and the definite article "the" for subsequent or anaphoric mentions), Bitchener (2008) investigated the effectiveness of other direct feedback combinations: (1) direct error correction with written meta-linguistic explanation (of the rule and an example of its use) and oral meta-linguistic explanation (in which discussion and clarification occurred); (2) direct error correction with written meta-linguistic explanation (of the rule and an example of its use); (3) direct error correction; and (4) no corrective feedback. Groups one and three outperformed the control group while group two only just failed to do so. When the study was extended (Bitchener & Knoch, 2008) to include an additional 69 learners, no difference was observed between the same three treatment combinations. Thus, it is possible that the larger sample size eliminated the difference in effect between group two and the other two treatment groups in the first study (Bitchener, 2008).

Another more longitudinal study by Bitchener and Knoch (2010a), investigating over a 10-month period the relative effectiveness of the same four feedback approaches, found that each of the groups who received one of the treatment options outperformed the control group and that there was no difference in effectiveness between the three treatment groups, suggesting therefore that none of the written CF options was any more effective than another. This study corroborates the findings of Bitchener and Knoch (2008). The special significance of this finding was its investigation over a 10-month period and therefore its longitudinal measurement of the effectiveness of different types of CF on accuracy retention.

Sheen's (2007) study of the relative effectiveness of two types of direct feedback (direct error correction alone; direct error correction and written meta-linguistic explanation) also found no difference between the two feedback options in the immediate post-test but, in the delayed post-test conducted two months later, found an advantage for written meta-linguistic explanation and direct error correction over direct error correction alone. Sheen suggested that the passage of time may have been the critical factor in facilitating this delayed effect for the inclusion of meta-linguistic explanation. These results corroborate those of Bitchener et al. (2005) in that there appears to be an advantage if meta-linguistic explanation accompanies direct error correction. However, in Bitchener and Knoch (2010a), the inclusion of written meta-linguistic explanation failed to provide learners with an advantage over those who only received direct error correction. Thus, a firm conclusion about the extent to which learners who receive written and/or oral meta-linguistic are able to increase their level of accuracy more than those who only receive direct error correction cannot be made at this stage. Further research into this issue is required. Investigations that separate the treatment variables within single study designs and examine their interaction with learners of different proficiency levels may produce more definitive results.

Looking at the studies of different types of feedback as a whole, we can see that there has been a growing interest in testing the relative effectiveness of delivering written CF in different ways but that firm conclusions are still somewhat elusive. Acknowledging that more studies need to examine the effectiveness of these different types, it is nevertheless tempting to suggest, on the basis of the

70 Analysis of Research on Written CF

more well-designed recent studies, that some form(s) of direct written CF may be more helpful for improving learner accuracy. Whether or not an advantage is to be gained if (1) meta-linguistic explanation is provided or (2) meta-linguistic explanation with direct error correction over direct error correction alone will not be known until further research is conducted.

Does the Educational and L2 Learning Background of Learners Determine the Extent to which They Benefit from Written CF?

Another variable in the written CF literature that has been identified but under-explored for the potential it might have in determining the effectiveness of written CF is subject/participant classification (Ferris, 2003, 2004). Hedgcock and Lefkowitz (1994) suggested that a distinction can be made between SL and FL writers because of differences in the purposes for which they are writing and in the pedagogical contexts in which they have acquired their first and second language literacy. They posit the view that FL writers may be less motivated than SL writers to attend to written CF because they are studying to meet a qualification requirement rather than studying to improve the accuracy and clarity of their English so that they can become fully active members of an English-speaking community. Additionally, they suggest that a third group— EFL students—who study English in non-English speaking countries may have varying degrees of motivation when it comes to the level of attention they give to written CF.

The educational background of learners has also been identified as a subject variable that might have an effect on the receptiveness of some students to written CF (Hedgcock & Lefkowitz, 1994). They suggest that, if students have received summative feedback (as a result of product-oriented instruction where feedback is provided in order to justify a grade rather than to help them revise their texts and focus on improving accuracy in new pieces of writing) as opposed to formative feedback (as a result of process-oriented instruction where feedback is provided with the opposite intention), they may not be highly motivated to attend to written CF.

A second background factor that has been identified for the potential it might have on a student's receptiveness to written CF is the level of exposure the student has had to formal and acquired knowledge of the target language (Ferris, 1999; Reid, 1998, 2005; Roberts, 1999). It has been suggested that international (visa) students, who are likely to have studied the target language in an EFL context, may have a strong explicit knowledge of terms and rules of English grammar but less of an acquired awareness of how to apply such knowledge to their own writing. On the other hand, it has been suggested that immigrant students (who, it is assumed, have not been exposed to formal instruction in the target language but who have picked up the language through participation in informal, conversational contexts) may rely on their acquired knowledge of the language to self-correct their writing, but have limited or perhaps no awareness of how to reference the formal system of grammar elicited by written CF.

One study (Bitchener & Knoch, 2008) attempted to investigate the extent to which these background factors might impact on a learner's response to written CF. Bitchener and Knoch (2008) divided their 144 participants into two groups: 75 international (visa) students and 69 migrant students. The international students, primarily East Asian students, were used to receiving written CF and focusing on accuracy in their L2 classrooms but the migrant students, a more heterogeneous group, were less accustomed to formal classroom learning and, therefore, potentially less attuned to focusing on written CF. Errors in the use of the same two functional uses of the English article system, targeted in other studies referred to above, received written CF. A control group did not receive written CF.

They found that the international students were no more able than the migrant students (and vice versa) to improve the accuracy of their writing as a result of receiving written CF. This is an interesting finding because earlier suggestions (Ferris, 1999; Hedgcock & Lefkowitz, 1994; Reid, 1998, 2005; Roberts, 1999) on the receptiveness of international visa students (essentially EFL students who are likely to have received most of their English instruction in a non-English speaking environment) to written CF have been that students from this background (one in which there would have been a high level of exposure to formal and acquired knowledge of the target language) might be more attuned to focusing on grammatical accuracy than migrant students. It is a popularly held view that migrant students may have a stronger desire to focus on general communicative competence so that they can become active members of their new English-speaking environment. Also, because many of them may have had less formal instruction in the target language, they may be less able to focus their attention on explicit grammatical knowledge than EFL students. However, as the results of this study reveal, this was not the case. One reason for this might be that neither of the two groups comprised students exclusively from one of these backgrounds. In other words, there may have been an overlap in the membership of the two groups. Migrant students may or may not have had formal instruction in the target language. International visa students may or may not have had opportunities to study the target language in an English-speaking environment (e.g., during term holidays). Future research may be able to categorize its subjects more strictly and determine whether those exclusively from one background are more able than those from another to improve upon the accuracy of their writing once they have received written CF. Even if a difference is found, the value of the finding might be questioned if typical classroom groupings contain students from a range of backgrounds. It may be that other individual, contextual, and language learning task-based factors play a significant role in the extent to which learners benefit from written CF. Although the findings of socio-cultural studies are so far limited in number, they nevertheless point to the effect that such factors

72 Analysis of Research on Written CF

can play as language learning occurs in the written context. It is to this empirical work that we now turn our attention.

To What Extent Can the Proposals of Socio-cultural Theory Enhance Our Understanding of Effective Written CF?

Empirical evidence of L2 development in the zone of proximal development (ZPD) occurring during scaffolded teacher (expert) student (novice) talk has been published by a number of researchers, and two of these studies (Aljaafreh & Lantolf, 1994; Nassaji & Swain, 2000) have been conducted in written contexts. In their longitudinal study of adult L2 learners receiving one-to-one written feedback from their language tutor (other regulator) on weekly writing assignments, Aljaafreh and Lantolf (1994) used a "regulatory scale" (scaffolding) to illustrate how the tutor's interventions could be ranged on a continuum from explicit to implicit corrective feedback. When the feedback needed by the individual students moved closer to the implicit end of the scale, they were considered to be moving toward more independent and self-regulated performance, and this was consequently taken as positive evidence of learning. The researchers argue that this reduced need for other-regulation constitutes evidence of language development within the learner's ZPD. Nassaji and Swain (2000), also using the regulatory scale to scaffold appropriately in their learners' ZPD, conducted a more formal testing of the claim that effective scaffolding is contingent on the state of the learner's ZPD. One Korean ESL learner was given randomly selected feedback and another was given negotiated ZPD-related feedback. The former was found to not be helpful in moving the learner toward self-regulation whereas the latter was. Further research employing this approach is needed to help us understand effective ways of providing ongoing written CF to learners who fail to benefit immediately from one-off feedback treatments. It is also likely to aid our understanding of why some learners benefit from written CF while others fail to, and of when direct and indirect forms of feedback might be most effective for individual learners.

Additional evidence of L2 development in ZPD interaction involving pair work and group work among pairs has been reviewed by Lantolf (2000) and Swain and Lapkin (2002). These studies focused on how learners support each other during oral L2 production, how they work together during "focus on form" activities and how they collaborate around L2 activities. Ohta (2000, 2001) provides some evidence of learners prompting and scaffolding others with language material that they are not yet capable of producing reliably by themselves during their own oral production. Donato (1994), investigating peer interaction during performance of classroom activities with a focus on form, and Swain and Lapkin (1998), investigating pairs of immersion learners doing a jigsaw task in L2 French, reported how learners work collaboratively to a point where there is a reduction in supportive scaffolding and transfer of L2 knowledge. Storch (2002), on the other hand, found that learners can also act competitively during pair work and that such modes of interaction may not be conducive to language learning. In two of their recent studies, Storch and Wigglesworth (2010a, 2010b) found that learners' uptake and retention of feedback may be mediated by their beliefs about language conventions (shaped by their learning experience), attitudes to the type of feedback provided, the activity of revising, and their goals.

Evaluating the contribution of socio-cultural theories to L2 development, it is important to note that the studies have been quite small, local, close-up short-term accounts of learner activity, and that they are generally qualitative and interpretative. To date, little attention has been given to causal explanations and the extent to which findings can be generalized. While Nassaji & Swain (2000) and Storch (2002) reported that learners who get timely and effective scaffolding or means of mediation are more likely to learn, the research has not addressed whether intervention in the ZPD simply scaffolds learners more rapidly along common routes of interlanguage development or whether it can bypass or alter the route by skilled co-construction, and thereby possibly challenge or, at least, suggest that Pienemann's teachabilty recommendations be modified. Socio-cultural research has yet to focus on learners from less advanced proficiency levels, the route of development, and the process of internalization. Nevertheless, the contribution of socio-cultural theorists and researchers is being realized. In terms of its specific contribution to explaining how written CF can play a role in SLA, the literature has already demonstrated why we need to take note of its proposals.

Concluding Remarks

In this chapter, we have considered the research that has attempted to answer the key questions arising from both the cognitive and socio-cultural perspectives on SLA. We have shown that recent studies have attempted to address the key design and methodological shortcomings of earlier research and that these studies are beginning to provide clearer answers to some of the questions. We have also identified where further research needs to be undertaken, but our discussion of these recommended directions will be discussed more fully in Chapter 5. We conclude this chapter with a summary of the key findings reported above.

- *The Short-term Effectiveness of Written CF*
  Accuracy in text revision may not necessarily be the result of learning from written CF and so may not necessarily be a predictor of long-term acquisition. To date, the findings are limited and conflicting.
- *The Long-term Effectiveness of Unfocused and Focused Written CF*
  The long-term effectiveness of providing a single treatment of unfocused written CF is uncertain, as the findings are conflicting, but the long-term effectiveness of providing a single treatment of focused written CF on

74 Analysis of Research on Written CF

discrete, rule-based linguistic categories of error is clear and compelling for the limited linguistic environments investigated so far. It is unclear whether focused or unfocused written CF is the more effective.

- *The Relationship Between Linguistic Error Domains/Categories and Written CF*
  Written CF appears to be effective in targeting discrete, rule-based linguistic categories such as English article and past tense use, but studies have yet to focus on more complex, idiosyncratic forms and structures.

- *The Relative Effectiveness of Direct and Indirect Types of Written CF*
  Early comparisons of the relative effectiveness of direct and indirect types of written CF reported no differences but recent studies report a clear advantage for direct forms of feedback. Studies of the relative effectiveness of different types of direct feedback are conflicting with some reporting an absence of effect and others suggesting an advantage for the provision of meta-linguistic feedback.

- *The Influence of Background Factors on Effective Written CF*
  The extent to which different background factors (e.g., educational and L2 learning backgrounds) impact upon the effectiveness of written CF have been under-researched. One study failed to find any differences in effect for written CF with migrant and international learners.

- *Socio-cultural Contributions to Understanding Effective Written CF*
  The few studies that have investigated the effectiveness of scaffolding learners with direct and indirect written CF (using a regulatory scale) and the impact of individual factors (such as personal goals, motives, beliefs, etc.) on tasks/ activities requiring a response to written CF have not reported any clear conclusions but have identified a range of areas and factors that further research should investigate to help us understand how and why learners benefit or fail to benefit from written CF.

While considerable progress has been made in finding answers to a range of key written CF questions, it is clear that some of these require further evidence and that others, not yet identified, will also need to be investigated. Our discussion in Chapter 5 will identify what we consider to be the important questions for further research.

4
RESEARCH ON WRITTEN CF IN COMPOSITION STUDIES

In this chapter, we look carefully at written CF research that has been conducted in composition/writing class settings. As previously noted (see Preface and Chapter 3), we have intentionally divided the discussion in this book between written CF delivered in language class settings that is primarily for the purposes of SLA and written CF delivered in writing/composition contexts for the purposes of long-term development in L2 writing.

We make this division to address concerns raised in previous research reviews on written CF about the indiscriminate mixing of studies conducted in widely different contexts. For instance, a good portion of the research done in the 1980s and 1990s on written CF took place in FL contexts, such as English-speaking students learning German or Spanish in US college courses (e.g., Kepner, 1991; Lalande, 1982; Semke, 1984), or in EFL contexts such as Japan (Robb et al., 1986). Hedgcock and Lefkowitz (1994, 1996) demonstrated that students in ESL/L2 and FL settings often have differing goals and motivations for writing in the L2, which may directly impact their willingness to attend to and learn from written CF provided by their teachers.

Besides the highly relevant issue of student goals and motivations (which are also reflected in course goals and instructional activities), another problematic issue for reviews on written CF is the way in which composition/writing is taught and feedback is delivered in these divergent contexts. For example, in Kepner's (1991) study, the student writing that was collected and received feedback consisted of journal entries that were not revised nor individually graded. It is, therefore, unlikely that the learners in Kepner's study were paying close attention to whatever feedback they received on their journal entries. It is problematic to use students' lack of attention to feedback on exploratory writing tasks as evidence that such feedback is ineffective for other types of writing assignments. For further

76 Analysis of Research on Written CF

discussion of problems raised by the mixing of studies from different contexts, see Ferris (2003, 2004).

We hope in this book to move beyond these methodological criticisms and to take a more finely tuned approach. Thus, all of the studies discussed in this chapter are concerned with error/written CF as it is implemented in composition/writing courses rather than in language courses. With this limitation placed on discussion, we minimize some of the issues just raised. Some of the studies discussed here focus on L1 contexts, others focus on L2 contexts, and many likely also include student populations with both L1 and L2 learners in the same courses. What they have in common is their focus on written CF for the sake of writing instruction and improvement rather than for general language acquisition (as discussed in Chapter 3).

While this division of labor between chapters sounds straightforward enough, for a few of the studies it was harder to tell which study belonged in which group or chapter. For example, several studies (e.g., Hartshorn et al., 2010; Montgomery & Baker, 2007) were conducted in writing courses housed in university intensive English programs (IEPs) in the US. The goals and audiences of such programs tend to be mixed and can vary not only from one institution to another but even from one class to another within the same program. For the most part, we resolved the uncertainties by assigning studies of written CF from EFL or IEP contexts to the language side of the divide (Chapter 3), but, because of these problems in definition, there will occasionally be passing references to several of them in this chapter as well.

Approach and Analysis

Our discussion of the written CF studies in composition is divided into several subsections. Each subtopic includes a chart summarizing the studies discussed in that section for easy reference, and each subsection ends with a brief analysis of what the group of studies discussed there suggests about written CF and possible limitations of or problems with the studies available at this point in time. We discuss implications of our reviews for future research and for instruction in some detail in later chapters.

Our review in this chapter on written CF in composition/writing contexts is structured around several questions about the written CF research base:

- How much teacher feedback on student writing is devoted to error (or written CF)?
- What types of student errors do writing teachers mark?
- What does the research show about the effects of written CF on short-term revision or editing skills of L2 student writers?
- What does the research show about the long-term effects of written CF on student writing development?

- What does research suggest about different specific approaches to written CF in writing course contexts?
- How do L2 writing students feel about written CF?

Where applicable, we also cite and discuss comments made by previous reviewers on some of these studies.

General Studies of Teacher Response

Studies of response or teacher feedback in writing courses go well beyond discussions of error correction or written CF, covering issues of how teachers respond to concerns about content or organization, whether they make marginal or terminal comments, whether they focus on praise or criticism, and so forth. In this section, we review studies that, while not exclusively focused on written CF, do touch specifically on issues of grammar or error, at least in passing. However, we do not include here sources that are secondary research reviews, advice for practitioners, or opinion pieces. We discuss only sources in which some empirical data were collected and discussed.

The Foci of Teacher Feedback in Writing Courses

A number of researchers have described the types of responses given by teachers to their student writers and categorized written commentary by the areas of concern teachers addressed. Figure 4.1 summarizes these studies; they are presented chronologically.

In most of the studies in this chart, the primary focus of teacher feedback was on global issues of content/ideas/organization rather than local issues of grammar, vocabulary, or mechanics.[1] This was true even in ESL contexts (Ferris, 1997; Ferris, Pezone, Tade, & Tinti, 1997; Hyland & Hyland, 2001), and the proportions of teacher-provided written CF were fairly similar across a range of pedagogical contexts and research designs. The main exceptions to the above generalization were the early study of elementary school teachers (Searle & Dillon, 1980) and the recent study of ESL writing teachers in an IEP in the US (Montgomery & Baker, 2007). The earliest study may reflect now out-of-date pedagogical practices (i.e., limited emphasis on process or revision). As to the later study, Montgomery and Baker noted that their teacher-participants were surprised by the heavy proportions of grammar commentary in their responses, which conflicted with their own self-reported beliefs and perceptions about how they responded to student writing, particularly on earlier drafts in a portfolio assessment context. The authors suggested that the teachers may have unconsciously reverted to responding behaviors that they believed would be most likely to facilitate student improvement (see Montgomery & Baker, 2007, p. 93).

78 Analysis of Research on Written CF

Study	Description	Findings relevant to written CF
Searle and Dillon (1980)	135 papers marked by nine teachers (US grades 4–6); 1,146 teacher responses (including checkmarks) categorized	At least 69 percent of the teacher responses focused on form
Connors and Lunsford (1993)	3,000 college student papers submitted by teachers around the US; "global" comments categorized as to purpose and focus	22 percent of the global comments focused exclusively on form (other types of error correction had been examined in an earlier study)
Straub and Lunsford (1995)	Twelve composition experts responded to a sample of 12 papers each; responses were categorized as to focus and mode	21 percent of the responses focused on "sentence structure, wording, and error"
Ferris et al. (1997); Ferris (1997)	1,526 comments by one teacher on 111 first drafts written by 47 university-level ESL students; categorized for purpose and form of comments	15 percent of all verbal comments (marginal and end notes) focused on grammar/mechanics (in-text corrections and symbols were not analyzed)
Straub (2000)	Analyzed comments made by six classroom teachers ("new compositionists") on their own students' papers; looked at focus and mode as in Straub and Lunsford (1995)	Newer teachers gave more comments on "local concerns" and more corrections than the experts in Straub's previous study, but the overall percentage of written CF was still low (around 25 percent)
Hyland and Hyland (2001)	Feedback given to six students by two teachers over a 15-week semester in an ESL program in New Zealand (17 texts; 500 feedback acts); categorized for focus and form	19 percent of the feedback points focused on form
Montgomery and Baker (2007)	13 teachers in US IEP, 78 student portfolios (six per teacher); categorized for focus of feedback	Percentages not reported, but most of the teacher feedback was on form rather than content
Ferris et al. (2011)	23 teachers, 3–5 student papers each; comments analyzed following Ferris et al. (1997)	A range of behaviors; some teachers had high percentages of grammar comments

FIGURE 4.1 Studies examining the focus of teacher feedback

Overall, this body of studies suggests that previous expert indictments of teacher feedback (e.g., Brannon & Knoblauch, 1982; Knoblauch & Brannon, 1981, 2006a; Sommers, 1982; see also discussion in Chapter 2) as being overly controlling, directive, and excessively focused on form may no longer accurately describe the practices of modern composition instructors. While even the most expert, enlightened responders still provide written CF in some proportion (e.g., Straub & Lunsford's experts in their 1995 study), they balance grammar comments and corrections with feedback on other, more global, concerns. However, it is important to qualify these statements by observing that in many of the studies in Figure 4.1, the teacher-participants were experienced instructors, chosen for analysis because they were perceived as knowledgeable and dedicated enough to provide high-quality feedback on a range of concerns to their students. It is possible that a broader range of real-world composition instructors may focus on grammar feedback to a much greater degree than some of the statistics in the chart above would suggest (Ferris et al., 2011; Lunsford & Lunsford, 2008). In short, while it is unlikely that many writing instructors today give *only* written CF to the complete exclusion of responding to other writing issues, there is most likely quite a diversity of classroom responding practices with regard to the amount of attention given to written CF in teacher feedback.

Types of Errors Marked by Teachers

In the previous section, we looked at studies that assessed the relative proportions of written CF given by teachers compared with feedback on other writing issues such as content or arrangement of ideas. Here, we examine the handful of composition studies in which the *types* of errors made by student writers and marked by teachers were the subject of scrutiny. These studies are summarized in Figure 4.2.

The Connors/Lunsford and Lunsford/Lunsford studies vary from that of Ferris (2006) in several notable ways. Ferris' study was situated in a local context: six classes taught by three university-level ESL instructors in the same program (and teaching at the same class level) were studied, while the other two studies gathered writing/commentary samples from thousands of writing instructors from around the US. Ferris' study also focused specifically on ESL classes, while the other studies assumed a mainstream composition population (which undoubtedly also included multilingual writers in many contexts). An important methodological difference was that Connors and Lunsford (1988), and later Lunsford and Lunsford (2008), read portions of their samples inductively to arrive at the "Top Twenty" error lists later examined by raters on the larger sample of papers. One of the goals of their studies was to assess whether and how student error patterns had increased and/or changed between the two studies (1988 and 2008) and between the earlier study and previous descriptive work done decades

80 Analysis of Research on Written CF

Study	Description	Major findings	Errors per 100 words of text
Connors and Lunsford (1988)	3,000 marked student papers from college teachers around the US were analyzed for 20 error types	28,571 errors in the 20 error categories were found by raters; 11,607 were marked by the teachers (41 percent); percentages of errors marked varied by category, ranging from 24–64 percent	2.26
Ferris (2006)[1]	146 marked essays written by 92 ESL college students; 5,707 errors marked by three classroom teachers were analyzed for 16 error types	83 percent of the errors marked by the researchers were also marked by the teachers; there was variation across the three teachers and across error types as to error-marking strategies	2.38
Lunsford and Lunsford (2008)	Replication of Connors and Lunsford (1988) with 877 student papers, again analyzed for 20 error types	22,202 errors were marked by the researchers; 8,711 (39 percent) were marked by the teachers; percentages of errors marked varied by category, ranging from 27–54 percent	2.45

1. The analysis described here was taken, in part, from an M.A. thesis (Chaney, 1999).

FIGURE 4.2 Studies of student errors marked by writing instructors

earlier. Because student error patterns did indeed change somewhat over time, the two Top Twenty lists are different from one another (see Appendix 4.1).

In contrast, Ferris' classroom study was designed primarily to assess the short- and long-term effects of written CF in ESL writing courses; the descriptive information shown in Figure 4.2 and Appendix 4.1 was a by-product of the analysis rather than its primary goal. In that study, Ferris and her colleagues began with a pre-selected list of 15 error categories (also shown in Appendix 4.1) chosen by the course supervisor with input from veteran instructors. This list was used by the three instructors to mark student papers during the term and also by the researchers to assess the accuracy, consistency, and effectiveness of the teacher feedback.

With these methodological differences in mind, we can look at the findings of the three studies more carefully. Of particular interest is the final column in

Figure 4.2; this demonstrates that, despite the differences in the ways the samples were gathered and marked—and, in particular, despite the fact that the students in Ferris' study were all ESL writers in a developmental writing course—the rate of errors per 100 words in the student texts was remarkably similar across the three studies. As shown by Lunsford and Lunsford (2008), this error rate has also not increased much over time (Figure 8, p. 800). The authors noted that, "contrary to what the doomsayers would have us believe, this study confirms that the rate of student error is not increasing precipitously but, in fact, *has stayed stable for nearly one hundred years*" (Lunsford & Lunsford, 2008, p. 801, emphasis added). While the types of errors students make may change over time and may vary across diverse student populations, it is not necessarily the case that the errors themselves are more prevalent than in the past or even in the case of L2 student writers.

While this similarity across studies as to student error rates is striking, there are also important differences across the findings of these studies. Most notably, while the teachers in Connors and Lunsford (1988) and Lunsford and Lunsford (2008) marked around 40 percent of the errors found by the researchers in the student papers, the instructors in Ferris' (2006) study marked 83 percent of the errors found independently by the researchers. The difference here is most likely contextual. The three instructors in Ferris' study had been asked to mark the papers comprehensively, labeling with predetermined codes all instances of errors they found in the 15 categories. These were second drafts of a three-draft sequence, and the first drafts had previously received content-focused teacher feedback. We do not have similar information available about the teachers in the other two studies about which draft(s) were being considered or whether the teachers intended to mark the student papers comprehensively or selectively.

Also of interest in the Connors/Lunsford and Lunsford/Lunsford studies is the differences in rankings between frequency of errors *made* by the students and those *marked* by the teachers (see Connors & Lunsford, 1998, Figure 1, p. 403; Lunsford & Lunsford, 2008, Figure 7, p. 795). For instance, in Connors and Lunsford's study, the most frequently marked error, "wrong word," was only the fourth most frequent error actually observed by researchers in the sample—and, even then, only 50 percent of the wrong-word errors were marked by the teachers. There are many other examples of such mismatches in the two studies, and they suggest that the teachers had some kind of filter operating such that they perhaps noticed certain errors more than others (see Williams, 1981) and/or they were bothered enough by particular errors to call the student writers' attention to them through their feedback. However, because the study design did not include asking teachers about their marking strategies, we can only speculate as to the reasons behind their written CF choices. Similarly, because in Ferris' study the teachers were asked to mark certain error categories predetermined for them as being most salient to L2 writers at this level, it is impossible to know whether they would have marked the same errors in the same proportions had they been operating

82 Analysis of Research on Written CF

independently, as were the teachers in the Connors/Lunsford and Lunsford/Lunsford studies.

With those limitations noted, the three lists of errors shown in Appendix 4.1 at least provide an indication of the types of errors made by the student writers represented in the studies and noticed by the teachers and researchers in those investigations. While there are certainly areas of overlap, it is easy to notice immediately that the ESL list (from Ferris, 2006) is more concerned with lexical, morphological, and syntactic errors, while the two lists from the 1988/2008 studies focus more heavily on various mechanical issues such as comma use and citation. If we assume that the lists are reasonably accurate in reflecting current/recent reality (as to college-level writers in the US),[2] it is clear that L2 writers and their instructors have unique issues/challenges on which to focus when compared with mainstream/L1 student populations. We will talk further about the implications of this observation for instruction in Chapter 7 and for teacher preparation in Chapter 8.

Effects of Written CF on Short-term Revision

Having examined research on the types of errors marked by instructors, we turn now to studies on the effects of written CF on student writing. One of the biggest challenges or issues raised in reviews of written CF studies has been whether or not the findings of studies on student revision after receiving written CF are useful to understanding both the process of written CF and student writing development (Ferris, 2004, 2010; Sachs & Polio, 2007; Truscott, 1996, 2007; Truscott & Hsu, 2008). In this section, we review written CF studies that focus on immediate revision of existing texts in composition class settings. We follow this by discussing the critiques that have been made of this segment of the written CF research. An overview of these studies is shown in Figure 4.3. They are again presented chronologically and include one L1 study (Haswell) along with a number of L2 studies.

The evidence in Figure 4.3 makes clear what even Truscott, the most vocal critic of revision studies in written CF, acknowledged: "[O]ur findings confirm once again that correction does help students reduce their errors on the writing on which they receive the corrections, and that the effect is substantial" (Truscott & Hsu, 2008, p. 299). This finding is remarkably consistent across a range of differences in the studies—between "minimal marking" with checkmarks in the margin (Haswell, 1983), simple underlining of errors (Fathman & Whalley, 1990; Ferris & Roberts, 2001, Truscott & Hsu, 2008), and more elaborate coding of specific error types (Ferris, 2006; Ferris & Roberts, 2001); across a broad range of error types; under different conditions for writing and revising; and across different student populations and learning contexts (Haswell's US college freshmen, ESL writers in developmental courses, EFL graduate students in Taiwan). With the exception of Haswell's study and the classroom study in Ferris

Study	Description	Findings
Haswell (1983)	24 students in a freshman composition course self-edited errors marked by checkmarks in the margins	Students were able to quickly correct (in 15 minutes or fewer) over 61 percent of the marked errors, regardless of error type
Fathman and Whalley (1990)	72 ESL students at two US colleges were divided into four treatment groups; two of the four received comprehensive, indirect, uncoded grammar feedback (all errors underlined); they had 30 minutes in class to revise their marked errors	Students who received grammar feedback significantly reduced their number of errors; the two groups not receiving grammar feedback did not
Ashwell (2000)	50 Japanese university students (EFL context) in four treatment groups; three of the four received form-based feedback before revising their texts	Students who received form-based feedback wrote significantly more accurate revised drafts than a control group receiving no feedback
Ferris and Roberts (2001)	72 ESL students were divided into three treatment groups; two of the three received error feedback on five major error types; they had 30 minutes in class to revise their marked errors.	Students who received error feedback successfully revised 60–64 percent of their total errors; their correction ratio was significantly higher than a control group's ratio
Ferris (2006)	92 ESL college students had second drafts of their essays marked by their teachers in 16 error categories; their papers were revised at home; 146 pairs of second and third drafts (two different assignments) were analyzed for self-editing success	Students successfully revised over 81 percent of the errors marked by their teachers; success ratios varied across error categories and teacher correction techniques
Truscott and Hsu (2008)	47 EFL graduate students were divided into two treatment groups; the experimental group received underlined, uncoded feedback on errors; texts and revisions were written in class	Students in the experimental group significantly outperformed the control group in self-correcting errors during revision

FIGURE 4.3 Studies on the effects of written CF on short-term revision

84 Analysis of Research on Written CF

(2006), all of the research designs reported in Figure 4.3 included control groups of students who received no error feedback. In short, when students receive written CF on a text and are then asked to revise that text, they do so successfully, with "success" defined as a statistically significant reduction in the number of errors from one draft to the next. When they do not receive written CF, they are much less able and likely to correct errors on their own.

While these findings are clear and consistent, the bigger and more controversial question is, "Does ability to self-correct errors after receiving written CF matter in the long run?" To put it another way, if students receive feedback and use that feedback to improve an existing text, will that process of receiving and applying written CF make them more successful writers in the future, as to linguistic accuracy? This is an important question both for SLA researchers and for classroom teachers. SLA experts are interested in instructional interventions that help learners acquire language forms over time. Classroom instructors are concerned with ways to help their students become better writers, and teachers (as discussed above in this chapter and in Chapter 2) tend to spend a lot of time and energy on written CF. So, from both a theoretical and practical perspective, the influence of written CF on short-term revision is an interesting and relevant issue.

Truscott (1996, 2007; Truscott & Hsu, 2008) has consistently argued that revision studies such as those reported in Figure 4.3 are essentially meaningless and theoretically uninteresting.[3] In his first major piece on written CF, a 1996 review essay published in *Language Learning*, Truscott made the following comments on Fathman and Whalley (1990), the only L2 study shown in Figure 4.3 that had been published at that point:

> The result . . . does not address the question: Does grammar correction make students better writers? Fathman and Whalley have shown that students can produce better compositions when teachers help them with those particular compositions. But will students be better writers in the future because of this help?
>
> *(Truscott, 1996, p. 339)*

In a 2007 review, Truscott continued in the same vein, citing additional revision studies that had been published since his earlier piece:

> A writing task that students do with help from the teacher (the revision) is obviously not comparable to one they do on their own (the original essay), and so a study with this design does not yield any measure of learning, short-term or otherwise.
>
> *(p. 257)*

Truscott shortly thereafter conducted a revision study of his own (Truscott & Hsu, 2008), to investigate whether learning could occur as a result of written CF provided in the revision process. Though a brief summary of this study is provided above in Figure 4.3, there is a more detailed discussion in Chapter 3. Truscott and Hsu's paper concluded with the following statements:

> The revision studies reviewed offer no evidence regarding the effect of correction on learning. The debate over the effectiveness of error correction should thus be carried on either without reference to such studies or with a sharp distinction maintained between the value of correction for learning on the one hand and for improving a particular piece of writing on the other.
>
> *(p. 300)*

In short, Truscott's latest word on written CF during the revision process is that, while it is clearly (even from Truscott's own data) useful for helping students improve the particular written product under consideration, there is no evidence that such intervention helps students either to acquire particular linguistic forms or to improve the overall linguistic accuracy of their writing on future pieces of writing.

Other researchers have mounted counter-arguments in defense of the role of written CF in revision to facilitate longer-term acquisition. For example, Sachs and Polio (2007), writing from an SLA perspective, stressed the role of feedback (of various types) in raising learners' noticing of non-target, interlanguage forms (or errors) in their spoken or written output. As to the specific issue of written CF and revision, they noted:

> . . . the term *acquired* might refer to various sorts of *gradual and nonlinear changes in both linguistic and metalinguistic behavior*, which include not only the appropriate use of linguistic forms but also, for example, the constructs of emergence, detection, restructuring, and awareness. If we can consider this line of thinking to be relevant to studies of written feedback as well, then a range of psychological processes might be seen as constituting steps toward L2 development, and it might be possible to talk about the process of acquiring L2 forms based on learners' . . . revision changes.
>
> *(p. 75, emphases added)*

In other words, the cognitive processes involved in receiving and applying written CF in the revision of an existing text might yield the sorts of "gradual and nonlinear changes" in students' long-term language and writing ability that could also be hard to measure in short-term experimental studies of the "learning" facilitated by written CF, such as the one conducted by Truscott and Hsu (2008). In an extended discussion, Sachs and Polio noted that various strands of SLA evidence point to two conclusions: (1) feedback of various types (oral/written, more/less explicit) helps learners to notice gaps between the target language and

86 Analysis of Research on Written CF

their own output, to analyze those mismatches, and to make repairs not only to their immediate output but to their still-developing language knowledge; and (2) if evidence suggests that oral corrective feedback can yield these types of benefits for SLA, it makes sense that written CF would do so also, and perhaps even more so because learners have more processing and reflection time in writing tasks than in oral production.

Ferris (2004) similarly focused arguments for written CF and revision on evidence from SLA research: "It can be argued that the cognitive investment of editing one's text after receiving error feedback is likely a necessary, or at least helpful, step on the road to longer term improvement in accuracy" (p. 54). Again drawing a parallel with SLA research on oral CF, Ferris suggested that studies examining both short-term or immediate learner uptake (attention, understanding, application) of written CF (i.e., the types of results reported in the revision studies) and long-term development are important. In a later article (Ferris, 2010), she suggested a possible research design that would combine the short-term approach of the revision studies with the longitudinal approach of SLA studies with their pre-test/post-test/delayed post-test structure (see Ferris, 2010, Figure 1, p. 195).[4]

Ferris (2010) made a different argument for written CF in revision based on strategic pedagogical grounds:

> there is widespread agreement in composition studies concerning the centrality of revision in the development of students' writing abilities and processes. L2 writing researchers and teachers thus have a keen interest in identifying strategies to help students more successfully revise and edit their work . . . Second language writing researchers thus see the development of effective strategies and writing processes that can impact students' subsequent writing as the primary goal of writing instruction. Thus, . . . revision studies are not only interesting but provide important evidence that helps teachers refine their practice.
>
> *(p. 189)*

In other words, written CF may serve as a tool (one of several) in teaching students strategies for self-editing their future texts more effectively, and this strategic awareness may develop over time in ways that are hard to measure in quasi-experimental research designs.

To summarize this section, the revision studies on the short-term effects of written CF on student writers' ability to use feedback to revise their own texts successfully provide clear evidence in favor of written CF under those conditions. The practical and theoretical issue under debate is whether such short-term interventions truly help students become better writers in the long run, when "better" is defined as "fewer errors/more linguistically accurate texts." With the exception of two small studies by Chandler (2003) and Ferris, Liu, Senna, & Sinha (2010), discussed further in the next section, there have been, to date, no research designs in composition settings that have intentionally combined written CF followed by revision with longitudinal measures of development (i.e., the model suggested in Ferris, 2010, and discussed further in Chapter 5). The long-term efficacy of written CF on intermediate drafts of a student text is a question that still needs to be explored (if not resolved) through future research. In the next section, we turn our attention to longitudinal studies of the effects of written CF in the writing classroom.

Effects of Written CF on Long-term Improvement

As discussed in the previous section, reviewers of written CF research have questioned whether evidence about the benefits of written CF on students' revisions (from one draft of a text to the next) really matters very much. We agree with Truscott and others that studies of written CF that are longitudinal and include learners' production of new texts after receiving feedback are extremely important. It is to these longitudinal studies that we turn our attention in this section. Readers will note that two of the studies (Ferris, 2006; Haswell, 1983) discussed in the previous section and shown in Figure 4.3 are also included here; this is because those articles reported on both short-term and long-term effects of written CF. The studies discussed below are summarized in Figure 4.4.

Examination of Figure 4.4 suggests that this set of studies is messier, more problematic, and more difficult to interpret than the revision studies discussed in the previous section. All of the studies show that the students who received error feedback made at least some progress in written accuracy over time. However, several important qualifications must be made about that statement. First, in most of the studies, no control group was included in the design. Even in the case of Chandler (2003), the "control group" was not a "no-feedback" group but rather one that received feedback and made corrections to their texts some weeks later than did the treatment group. As has been repeatedly pointed out in previous critiques of this research, the absence of a control group makes it difficult to argue that written CF alone caused any measurable improvements (see Truscott, 2007; see also many of the written CF studies reviewed in Chapter 3).

In several instances, the researchers in the above group of studies acknowledge and explain this limitation. For example, Haswell (1983) noted, "I have not had the heart to set up a control group to isolate this marking technique" (p. 603). Chandler explained that results of a questionnaire had demonstrated "that the vast majority of students wanted the teacher to mark every error. Since the students felt so strongly about this, the teacher could only justify the treatment of the control group by offering them the same treatment as the experimental group later in the semester" (2003, p. 273). Ferris has described the issue as a "methodological Catch-22" (2004, p. 56): writing researchers (who are almost always also teachers) feel ethically constrained from withholding written CF from students for any substantial period of time by using a subset of student writers as

Study	Description	Findings
Haswell (1983)	Three freshman composition sections; Haswell compared error ratios on essays written at the beginning and ending of a semester after Haswell's minimal marking technique was used; no control group	All three groups substantially reduced their error ratios over the semester; fluency also improved, as the final essays were 23 percent longer (and written under the same timed conditions)
Ferris (1995a)	30 ESL freshman composition students at a US university followed over a 15-week semester; each student had individual error patterns identified at the beginning of the course, and written CF throughout the term focused specifically on those patterns; no control group	All but two of the students showed improvement on at least some of the individually targeted error patterns over the semester; results varied as to error type and writing task
Chandler (2003)	31 international students at a US music conservatory wrote five papers; treatment group was required to correct marked errors after every first draft	Experimental group significantly decreased its overall error ratios between Paper 1 and Paper 5; this was also significantly better than a control group's ratios
Ferris (2006)	55 ESL students in six sections of a developmental writing course at a US university; errors made on Paper 1 and Paper 4 (end of semester) were compared across five error categories after students received systematic written CF all semester	Students significantly reduced their total error ratios and their verb errors; changes in other categories were non-significant; tremendous individual variation as to long-term improvement
Foin and Lange (2007)	58 students in an advanced ESL composition class at a US university; errors made on an early draft and a final draft were compared across eight categories	"Treated" (marked) errors were successfully corrected in 77–81 percent of the cases; unmarked errors were corrected 32 percent of the time
Ferris et al. (2010)	10 ESL students in a developmental writing course at a US university, studied with qualitative case study methodology; students received written CF on up to four error patterns on four texts apiece, were given time to revise those texts, and then were each interviewed three times about their strategies and understanding of the feedback	Students all showed improvement in at least some error categories over time and all felt that the combination of individually targeted written CF and in-person discussion of errors was very helpful on both in-class and especially out-of-class writing

FIGURE 4.4 Studies of long-term effects of written CF

controls, but if they do not do so, they are criticized for lack of empirical rigor. These are substantial barriers to future progress and discussion of research in this area, and we discuss them (and some possible solutions) at some length in Chapter 5. At this point, we simply observe that the studies in Figure 4.4 have been (and will continue to be) criticized for their lack of controls.

A second way in which this set of studies is "messy" is that student progress in reducing errors over time was not always consistent or linear. In several instances, it was possible to observe tremendous individual variation across students. The qualitative multiple-case study analysis of Ferris et al. (2010) suggested a number of reasons why:

1. students came into the course with different knowledge bases and intuitions about formal language conventions;
2. they had different attitudes and motivations toward the course they were taking and their own writing;
3. they had a number of other distractions outside the course, such as course loads, off-campus employment, and family obligations; and
4. nearly all noted that they could not do their best writing under timed conditions (and all of the texts collected, marked, revised, and discussed for this study were produced in class and under time pressure).

In short, in any group of student writers, there is a complicated set of interrelated factors that influence the degree to which a given student benefits from written CF.

Other types of student variation were observed in this set of studies. For instance, students clearly made more progress with some error types and categories than others; this likely relates to several complex factors such as prior instruction and experience; relative difficulty of the language form or structure for L2 acquirers; and, possibly, types of language elicited by certain writing tasks, giving students more practice with some forms than with others in a given writing course. Similarly, there were differences across task types in some of these studies, and it has been suggested that students may regress in ratios of formal error when the writing task is cognitively more difficult (Ferris, 1995a; Lunsford & Lunsford, 2008).

What *can* be reasonably said is that there is no evidence to suggest that students who received written CF over time either regressed or failed to make at least some progress in overall written accuracy. As noted by Ferris, "if the existing longitudinal studies do not reliably demonstrate the *efficacy* of error feedback, they certainly do not prove its *uselessness*, either" (2004, p. 55, original emphases). Further, in several of these studies (Chandler, 2003; Ferris, 2006; Haswell, 1983), students' longitudinal improvements were statistically robust enough to suggest that there may be value both in teachers' continuing to provide written CF (if it is done carefully; see Chapter 7) and especially in making further efforts to

90 Analysis of Research on Written CF

design studies that address some of the unresolved questions and methodological problems (see Chapter 5). In addition, the findings of the recent qualitative study by Ferris et al. (2010) suggest some additional avenues for controlled quasi-experimental classroom research as well.

Studies of Different Approaches to Written CF

The studies reviewed in the previous two sections primarily focus on what Ferris (2004) has called "'the big question'—whether or not error feedback helps students to improve in written accuracy over time" (p. 56). However, some researchers, operating under the assumption that the important questions surrounding written CF are not *if* but *how* teachers should provide it (cf., Hartshorn et al., 2010), have examined specific sub-questions surrounding written CF in writing classes. These questions and studies are summarized in Figure 4.5 and discussed below.

The studies in Figure 4.5 are important because they begin to address the "how" of written CF—the question that is likely of the most interest to practitioners. As discussed in Chapter 2, most writing instructors believe in and practice written CF and are unlikely to stop doing it regardless of the pronouncements of either composition theorists or applied linguists conducting experimental research. Thus, issues of when to provide written CF, how much to provide, the level of explicitness required, what types of errors to mark, and what related instructional interventions (required revisions, etc.) might be helpful are important and productive areas for researchers to consider.

Figure 4.5 suggests that, while there are a variety of questions that have been investigated, in most cases there have been relatively few studies that have looked at a particular issue. This leads to the obvious conclusion that researchers in the future should also take up these questions and provide more evidence to confirm, refine, or rebut the fairly limited findings that exist (see Chapter 5). However, the picture is more complicated than the usual "further research is necessary" statement. While the studies in Figure 4.5 do indeed touch on these issues, in many instances, they do so indirectly as a by-product of other types of analyses rather than having been explicitly designed to look at the particular phenomena identified here. For instance, Ferris (2006) found that students seemed to benefit more long-term from indirect feedback (an indication that an error has been made) than from direct correction (teacher provision of the correct form). This was an accidental finding, however, as the study was designed only to look at the effects of indirect feedback, and some of the teacher feedback (mostly from one particular teacher) deviated from the agreed-upon procedure. Thus, it would be an overstatement to say that the findings of this study prove that indirect feedback is more beneficial than direct feedback for long-term student improvement. Similarly, though Haswell's (1983) data on the effects of his "minimal marking" method are robust, he did not actually compare students' performance based on

Written CF question	Study/studies that address it	Findings
Should content- and form-based feedback be provided on separate student drafts?	Ashwell (2000); Fathman and Whalley (1990)	In both cases, researchers found that students could attend to both types of feedback in the same draft to make successful revisions
Does revision after written CF help long-term improvement?	Haswell (1983); Chandler (2003); Truscott and Hsu (2008)	**Haswell:** Students who corrected their texts after receiving "minimal marking" improved their written accuracy over time **Chandler:** Students who did immediate rewriting after written CF reduced their error ratios significantly more than those who did not make corrections until weeks later **Truscott & Hsu:** Students wrote new texts one week after revising a previously corrected text; they found no improvement in accuracy on the second text
Is direct or indirect feedback more beneficial?	Chandler (2003); Ferris (2006)	In both studies, researchers reported that direct feedback led to more accurate revisions. In Chandler's study, direct correction also led to greater accuracy on the next paper. In Ferris' study, data suggest that indirect feedback had a greater long-term effect
Should indirect feedback be more or less explicit?	Haswell (1983); Chandler (2003); Ferris and Roberts (2001); Ferris (2006)	All studies suggest that even minimally explicit indirect feedback is helpful. In Chandler's study, one of the less explicit marking methods (underlining) proved more effective over time than the more explicit "underlining with description" method. In Ferris and Roberts' revision study, there was no significant difference in short-term correction rates between underlined errors and those labeled with an error code
Does selective, individualized written CF feedback help student writers to improve in targeted areas of weakness?	Ferris (1995a); Ferris et al. (2010)	In both studies, individual students demonstrated improvement over time in targeted areas. However, progress was variable across different students, across error types, and at different points in the term (and/or different types of writing tasks)
Does written CF help students to improve on some types of errors more than others?	Ferris (1995a); Ferris and Roberts (2001); Ferris (2006); Ferris et al. (2010)	Certain types of errors definitely seemed more responsive to written CF than others in all studies. However, again, there was individual student variation

FIGURE 4.5 Studies of different approaches to written CF

92 Analysis of Research on Written CF

this written CF technique with other types of written CF. All we can really say is that Haswell's paper provides interesting potential evidence that extremely implicit feedback (checkmarks in the margins) followed by required rewriting might help students to reduce their own written errors over time.[5] Thus, much of the information in Figure 4.5 should be examined carefully and used as suggestions to inform new research designs, not as the final word on any of these specific practical sub-questions.

Besides the rather incidental, even anecdotal nature of many of these findings, another problem with this set of studies is the important questions that have *not* yet been carefully investigated. Though there are doubtless a number of these, two in particular are worth mentioning here. First is the question of whether it is better for a teacher to identify specific types of errors to mark or to simply underline or correct all the errors he/she sees in a student paper without any predetermined categories in mind. Though both intuition and the existing research evidence (much of which is discussed in Chapter 3 rather than this chapter, because it is focused on language teaching contexts rather than writing instruction) would suggest that focused feedback is better than unfocused feedback, there are no studies in the writing/composition literature that explicitly contrast these two general approaches to written CF.

A related and unexplored question about written CF is about whether it is better for teachers to mark papers comprehensively (i.e., mark everything that is wrong, even if it is fairly minor) or selectively (mark only the most serious/ frequent/ stigmatizing errors). Though there have been arguments made in favor of selective written CF (see Ferris, 2002, 2003 for reviews; see Chapter 7), in fact, there are no studies that compare the impact of comprehensive versus selective feedback on student writers. A sub-question to both of the above major issues (focused versus unfocused; selective versus comprehensive) is how many errors or error types in a given paper can productively be marked without overwhelming the students and diluting their attention to and the impact of written CF. Possible research questions on these topics and others are listed in Ferris (2004, 2010) and discussed in more detail in Chapter 5. To summarize this section, for those researchers/teachers who are ready to move on from the question of whether written CF should be provided at all, there are a number of inadequately answered questions that could be extremely relevant to the success or failure of teachers' approaches to written CF in their writing courses.

Student Views of Written CF

We close this chapter with a brief review of studies that have examined student preferences regarding written CF. We follow the summary in Figure 4.6 with a discussion of whether or not student preferences should concern teachers and researchers.

Type	Study/studies	Findings
Student perceptions about what teacher feedback covers	Cohen (1987) Cohen and Cavalcanti (1990); Enginarlar (1993); Ferris (1995b); Hedgcock and Lefkowitz (1994, 1996); Montgomery and Baker (2007); Radecki and Swales (1988)	Earliest studies (Cohen, 1987; Radecki & Swales, 1988) reported that teachers focused heavily on grammar; later studies reported a balance of teacher concerns in feedback
Student preferences about written CF	Enginarlar (1993); Ferris (2006); Ferris and Roberts (2001); Ferris et al. (2010) Leki (1991); Radecki and Swales (1988); Saito (1994)	Students believe strongly in the value of written CF; some prefer direct feedback but believe that indirect feedback (ideally coded and with explanations) is most helpful for long-term improvement
Student preferences about written CF versus content feedback	Cohen (1987); Cohen and Cavalcanti (1990); Ferris (1995b); Hedgcock and Lefkowitz (1994, 1996); Radecki and Swales (1988)	Students want feedback both on ideas and on grammar; in some cases they thought grammar feedback was more important

FIGURE 4.6 Student views of written CF

Student survey (and sometimes interview) research on written CF or teacher feedback in general has covered three areas: (1) On what issues do students *perceive* their teachers focus when providing feedback? (2) On what issues do students think their teachers *should* focus when providing feedback? (3) What are students' *specific preferences* with regard to the form and scope of teacher-provided written CF? Early studies on student perceptions of teacher feedback suggested that (at least in the students' eyes) writing teachers focused their feedback heavily on grammar and mechanics concerns. As process-based pedagogy, with its attendant focus on formative feedback (see Brannon & Knoblauch, 1982; Sommers, 1982), began to permeate composition classes in general and L2 writing courses in particular, students began reporting that their teachers' feedback covered a range of concerns, from content to organization to mechanics and vocabulary. As this approach to pedagogy and feedback took hold, students also seemed to react positively to feedback that covered all aspects of writing—as long as it continued to give them adequate input about grammar. There is no indication in any of the studies that students wish their teachers would not provide written CF or would provide less of it. On the contrary, it is fair to say that while students appreciate teacher feedback on other writing issues, they insist upon language-focused feedback and in fact would be bitterly frustrated by its absence.

94 Analysis of Research on Written CF

In several studies, students have also been asked fairly detailed questions about the type of written CF they prefer—do they want all of their errors marked, or only the most important ones? Do they like their teacher to correct all of their errors (direct correction), or do they think it is better for the teacher to indicate where an error has been made and ask the student to make the correction (indirect feedback)? When these questions have been asked, the answers are remarkably consistent across a range of student populations: students generally prefer comprehensive rather than selective correction, worrying that errors left unmarked might hurt their grades later. They prefer direct feedback on their errors because it requires less effort for them to deal with it, but they believe that, in the long run, indirect feedback—especially if errors are located and labeled with some kind of explanation or at least error code—will help them most in improving their writing. In short, despite the fears of some theorists (e.g., Krashen, 1982; Truscott, 1996) that written CF is harmful and may discourage learners, students themselves have strong opinions not only about written CF's value but about the optimal forms it should take.

The question that has been raised, primarily by Truscott (1996, 1999) is whether these student preferences should be considered in making decisions about written CF. As Truscott noted in his 1996 essay:

> Abundant evidence shows that students believe in correction . . . but this does not mean that teachers should give it to them. The obligation teachers have to students is not to use whatever form of instruction the students think is best, but rather to help them learn . . . When students hold a demonstrably false belief about learning, the proper response is not to encourage that belief, but rather to show them that it is false.
>
> *(p. 359)*

Truscott claimed that teachers' beliefs and practices have influenced student attitudes about written CF, leading to a vicious circle: "By using correction, teachers encourage students to believe in it; because students believe in it, teachers must continue using it" (1999, p. 116). Truscott went on to acknowledge that changing students' attitudes about correction is not likely to be an easy task, but argued that it is teachers' responsibility to "help learners adjust to its absence." In his 1999 piece, he cited anecdotal evidence that students in his own classes adapted nicely to his correction-free pedagogy, showing neither frustration nor a decrease in motivation.

Truscott's injunction to dismiss students' preferences in favor of written CF makes sense only if one also accepts his larger argument—that written CF is without value and should be abandoned. Of course, if a teacher is convinced that a particular pedagogical approach is not only useless but may actually be harmful to students, that teacher should not follow that approach, regardless of what the students might think about it. Absent that sort of certainty, however, a consideration of student desires is a variable that should be in the mix, along with others, in teachers' decision-making. Further, Truscott's assertion that teachers have actually created the desire in students for written CF is reminiscent of Williams' (1981) claim that teachers, in a sense, create error by looking for it when they read student papers (see Chapter 2)—both authors have a legitimate point, but their claims also do not tell the whole story. Perhaps some students have indeed become overly dependent upon teacher written CF because they have been conditioned to need/expect it, but others clearly have concrete experiences of expert feedback helping them to notice gaps in their language production, analyze the sources of the gaps, and avoid those problems in later iterations or new products. There simply is too much individual variation in how people learn, how they are motivated, and what they already know to attach a "one-size-fits-all" label to the question of written CF in writing courses—and, if this statement is true, then writing instructors should be collaborating with their students to discover which feedback approaches serve them best rather than imperiously deciding what is or is not good for them. This cooperative spirit should apply not only to the larger question of whether or not to provide their students with written CF but how to do so (i.e., selectively, indirectly, explicitly, etc.). In short, student survey research about written CF has, to date, given us some fairly clear answers about what students think and prefer, and we should carefully consider their opinions and desires.

Summary

In this chapter, we reviewed six major themes in written CF research conducted in writing/composition class contexts. Based on this review, we can make the following generalizations.

1. Though writing teachers believe in providing feedback across a range of writing issues, even the most progressive composition experts still provide written CF on student errors (Figure 4.1 and discussion).
2. Students make—and teachers mark—a wide range of error types (Figure 4.2, Appendix 4.1, and discussion). These error types and proportions have changed over time and are somewhat different when L1 and L2 student populations are considered.
3. Studies of the effects of written CF on short-term revisions of the same text demonstrate consistently that this feedback helps students to edit their texts more successfully (Figure 4.3 and discussion). However, scholars disagree as to whether student success in self-editing drafts of their papers translates into longer-term learning or improvement in writing.

96 Analysis of Research on Written CF

4. Longitudinal studies of the influence of written CF on student improvement over time have shown that in most cases, students receiving written CF do improve in written accuracy, though there is variation across individual students and error types (Figure 4.4 and discussion). However, this body of work has been consistently questioned because of the absence of control (uncorrected) groups in the research designs, and this is a methodological problem that is hard to solve.
5. Researchers have also looked at several sub-questions about the most optimal ways to provide written CF (Figure 4.5 and discussion), but for most of these questions, there are only a handful of studies available, and there are other important questions that have not been investigated at all.
6. Student survey research has consistently demonstrated that student writers want, expect, and value written CF and have strong opinions about how their teachers should provide it. Research on teacher views of written CF suggests that writing instructors may be somewhat conflicted—they believe that its role should be limited and that it should be subordinate to feedback on higher-order concerns, but in practice, they provide a great deal of written CF and do not always do so in ways consistent with their stated philosophies (Figure 4.6 and discussion).

Concluding Remarks

So where are we with regard to the issue of written CF in the writing classroom and especially for L2 writers? The research discussed in this chapter presents several arguments in favor of continuing the practice: (1) written CF clearly helps students to revise and edit their texts more successfully, and these are important skills and strategies for student writers to develop; (2) longitudinal evidence, while somewhat problematic as to design, also indicates that correction can have a positive influence on student accuracy over time—at least for some students on some types of errors; and (3) both students and instructors believe in written CF, so they may be motivated to apply it (as to students) and to implement it (as to teachers) as effectively as possible. None of the studies discussed in this chapter provide any evidence that written CF is harmful or even neutral to the development of student writers. There is a good deal more to say about how written CF can and should be implemented most successfully in writing classes (the topic of Chapter 7) and about ways in which the limited and somewhat flawed research base can and should be improved in the future (the topic of Chapter 5)—but what we have examined in this chapter, at minimum, supports continuing the conversation.

Appendix 4.1: Student Error Types in L1 and L2 Composition Studies Listed in Order of Frequency

Connors & Lunsford (1998, (US college students)	*Lunsford & Lunsford (2008) (US college students)*	*Ferris (2006) (ESL university students in California)*
1. No comma after introductory element	1. Wrong word	1. Sentence structure
2. Vague pronoun reference	2. Missing comma after an introductory element	2. Word choice
3. No comma in compound sentence	3. Incomplete or missing documentation	3. Verb tense
4. Wrong word	4. Vague pronoun reference	4. Noun endings (singular/plural)
5. No comma in non-restrictive element	5. Spelling error (including homonyms)	5. Verb form
6. Wrong/missing inflected endings	6. Mechanical error with a quotation	6. Punctuation
7. Wrong or missing preposition	7. Unnecessary comma	7. Articles/determiners
8. Comma splice	8. Unnecessary or missing capitalization	8. Word form
9. Possessive apostrophe error	9. Missing word	9. Spelling
10. Tense shift	10. Faulty sentence structure	10. Run-ons
11. Unnecessary shift in person	11. Missing comma with a non-restrictive element	11. Pronouns
12. Sentence fragment	12. Unnecessary shift in verb tense	12. Subject-verb agreement
13. Wrong tense or verb form	13. Missing comma in a compound sentence	13. Fragments
14. Subject-verb agreement	14. Unnecessary or missing apostrophe (including its/it's)	14. Idiom
15. Lack of comma in series	15. Fused (run-on) sentence	15. Informal
16. Pronoun agreement error	16. Comma splice	
17. Unnecessary comma with restrictive element	17. Lack of pronoun-antecedent agreement	
18. Run-on or fused sentence	18. Poorly integrated quotation	
19. Dangling or misplaced modifier	19. Unnecessary or missing hyphen	
20. Its/it's error	20. Sentence fragment	
(Figure 1, p. 403)	*(Figure 7, p. 795)*	*(Appendix, p. 103; from Chaney, 1999, p. 20)*

98 Analysis of Research on Written CF

Notes

1. Exact comparisons across studies are difficult because different terminology was used by various authors. For instance, the term "local" was sometimes used as being synonymous with grammar or mechanics feedback—but not always.
2. Because of the different ways in which the data were collected, it seems more likely that the Connors/Lunsford and Lunsford/Lunsford studies reflect errors made by college student writers across the US and that Ferris' findings are more specific to the local/regional demographics. For example, in an ESL context in the US where there are more international students than resident immigrants or Generation 1.5 students (Ferris, 2009; Harklau et al., 1999; Roberge et al., 2009), a researcher might find more verb errors or more plural or article errors—and, again, this might vary across contexts depending upon the student L1s represented. That said, the general statement—the L2 writers' errors differ in substance from those of a largely L1 population—likely still holds true.
3. For instance, in his 2007 meta-analysis of written CF studies, Truscott specifically excluded this type of study, saying that "the revision studies do not address the question in which I am interested" (p. 257), namely, whether "learning" occurs as a result of written CF.
4. Truscott and Hsu might counter that their 2008 study does indeed follow this model. However, we would argue that a one-week delay between a written CF-aided revision and a new text (especially when the written CF consists of simple underlining of undefined error types) does not constitute the type of effective longitudinal design we are suggesting here. See Chapter 3 for more discussion of this study; see Chapter 5 for our suggestions for future research investigations of written CF.
5. It is important here to restate that Haswell's study was conducted in freshman composition classes in 1983; most likely, few, if any, of his students were L2 writers. It would be a mistake to assume that checkmarks in the margins would be as helpful to L2 students as they might be for L1 students—but that is another reason why more studies along these lines could be useful.

5
FUTURE DIRECTIONS IN SLA AND COMPOSITION RESEARCH

In Chapters 3 and 4, we reviewed the written CF research that has been conducted in language learning and composition contexts and, in doing so, pointed to (1) conclusions that can be drawn from the findings of some studies, (2) shortcomings with the design and execution of some studies that may, to some extent, have compromised the robustness of their findings, and (3) areas in which further research needs to be carried out so that firmer conclusions can be reached. In this chapter, we identify areas that we believe should be investigated, starting with those related to the role of written CF in the language learning context and moving on to consider those related to the composition or writing context. As far as possible, we have grouped our recommendations in these two sections under the same or similar subsections so that readers can make comparisons when desired.

Written CF in SLA Research

In Chapter 1, we reviewed the literature on the role of error and corrective feedback in SLA, pointing out the different theoretical positions and the limited attention that has been given to the specific role it might play in the SLA process. In this chapter, then, we suggest ways in which this theoretical work might be developed. In Chapter 3, we reviewed the research that has investigated a number of key theoretical and pedagogical questions and, in doing so, identified some of the shortcomings in the research and suggested that clear answers to the questions being investigated would likely be more forthcoming if these were addressed in further research. Therefore, in this chapter, we also outline what we consider to be key areas for ongoing research into the role of written CF in SLA.

100 Analysis of Research on Written CF

Development of a Theoretical Basis for Written CF in SLA

In Chapter 1, we pointed out how recent theoretical perspectives on the role of learner error in the acquisition or learning process place importance on understanding the underlying processes involved in acquiring a second language and how this includes an understanding of the role of error and its treatment. In terms of the role that negative evidence (including corrective feedback) has been shown to have in the acquisition process, the literature (and, in particular, the research) has tended to focus on the role of oral corrective feedback rather than written corrective feedback. In fact, it was only as a result of Truscott's 1996 paper, in which he debunked the practice of providing learners with written CF on selected theoretical and pedagogical grounds, that the question of its efficacy gained attention. Prior to this, most teachers and researchers had assumed that the practice was beneficial to learners and proceeded to ask more pedagogically driven questions about the most effective ways of providing it. For theoretical reasons, Truscott (1996), following Krashen (1982), claimed that teachers were not only wasting their time providing written CF but also that of their students because, as he put it, there was enough SLA evidence about why it is unlikely to be effective. The main theoretical reasons for this position were identified and discussed in Chapter 1. Recent critiques of his case against the practice, provided by Bitchener and Knoch (2010a) and van Beuningen et al. (2012), have explained that they are not necessarily valid on theoretical or pedagogical grounds but, as these commentators also explain, the rebuttal has been rather piecemeal. Thus, there is a need for a more fully developed theoretical consideration of how written CF might contribute to SLA. A model that comprehensively identifies the various theoretical components should include not only cognitive components but socio-cultural components as well.

Cognitively based empirical studies have shown that, even when there are positive group effects for written CF, there are always learners within these groups who fail to benefit from the feedback they are given. The existing research base has touched on some of the possible reasons for this but there is a need to explore the extent to which more socially mediated and context-motivated factors can enhance our understanding of why some learners benefit from written CF and others fail to. Recent thinking and research within a socio-cultural perspective has made a number of interesting proposals (see Chapter 1), and these are worth considering when proposing what a comprehensive model of the role of written CF in SLA might include. A comprehensive theoretical model is needed if empirical research is to be more focused on testing factors that ultimately determine the effectiveness of written CF for L2 development.

Development of Current Research Questions

In Chapter 3, we discussed the key written CF research questions that have been investigated over the last 30 years and, in doing so, reflected on why we have so few clear answers about the role of written CF in the acquisition process. One reason that we identified for this is the conflicting findings of earlier studies. Another reason for not being able to make more definite conclusions about some of the findings is the presence of intervening variables within a study that might have had a mediating effect on the reported findings. For instance, while there is no problem with one study employing a particular testing instrument (e.g., journal entries) and another study employing a different testing instrument (e.g., essay), there is a problem if one wants to draw conclusions from studies with different instruments. It would seem, therefore, that future research should not only look at main effects but at the interactional effect of other variables as well. For instance, as we explain below, studies that look at the interaction of different types of written CF on different linguistic error categories are more likely to produce clear, robust, meaningful findings and conclusions than studies that look only at the main effect of each of these two variables. Furthermore, if we add another variable (e.g., proficiency level) to this example, the findings might change again when the interactional effect of the three variables is considered. With these thoughts in mind, we reflect in this section on what the available research has revealed about each of the key research questions discussed in Chapter 3, outline what we believe should be the focus of further research on each of these questions, and suggest other areas of research that should be undertaken in order to give us a more complete understanding of why some learners benefit from written CF and others find it less helpful.

Can written CF facilitate the acquisition of L2 forms and structures? In response to the theoretical debate, initiated by Truscott (1996) and Ferris (1999), about whether written CF can be expected to be beneficial to L2 learners, a number of studies have been designed to investigate its potential. As we saw in Chapter 3, there is growing evidence that written CF is effective in targeting some linguistic forms and structures, but the extent to which it is helpful in treating others is still unknown. Across these studies, the effectiveness of written CF for treating discrete, rule-based linguistic form in both the short-term and long-term is clear, but the *extent* to which it can play a role in successfully targeting other discrete rule-based categories and more complex, idiosyncratic linguistic forms and structures is unknown. We think it is likely that further research will find that written CF is also effective in treating other discrete, rule-based categories, but its potential for treating more complex, idiosyncratic structures (e.g., syntactic structures) requires investigation. This, then, is the second main research area to be investigated. It is one that could be guided by the following research question that focuses on the interaction of written CF with different L2 forms and structures:

- To what extent can written CF facilitate the acquisition of different L2 forms and structures?

102 Analysis of Research on Written CF

In Chapter 3, we also showed that, in seeking an answer to the question of efficacy, it was necessary to investigate a number of related questions including the short-term and long-term benefits of written CF. Studies of the short-term benefits have most often examined whether or not it is effective in helping learners improve the accuracy of an original piece of writing (i.e., by means of a text revision). These studies, conducted mainly in composition class settings (see Chapter 4), have shown that learners can and do respond positively to the feedback they receive and are able to use it to accurately when revising linguistic errors made in the first version of a text. From a language learning/acquisition point of view, where the goal is to help learners acquire over time target-like accuracy in the use of forms and structures, the research evidence on the benefits of text revisions are less conclusive. As we have seen in Chapter 3, the research findings on the extent to which improved accuracy in text revisions is a predictor of long-term retention are conflicting, meaning, therefore, that further research is required to resolve this issue. To guide this research, we suggest the following research question:

- To what extent can accurate text revisions, as a result of written CF, facilitate accuracy in the writing of new texts over time?

In order to answer this question, studies will need to be designed with at least four or more writing tasks: a pre-test piece of writing, a revision of this pre-test text immediately after written CF has been provided, an immediate post-test piece of writing (i.e., involving the writing of a new text), and one or more delayed post-test pieces of writing (Ferris, 2010). Additionally, the accuracy with which learners use different linguistic forms and structures (i.e., the different linguistic error categories being investigated) in each of the writing tasks will need to be compared. If future research continues to investigate broad categories of error, we will never know which specific forms or structures within these categories are the reasons for observed improvement or lack of improvement.

The more long-term studies discussed in Chapter 3 reveal a consistent pattern of effectiveness, but most were conducted over a relatively short period of time (e.g., a few weeks or one to two months). The enduring effect of written CF, targeting a discrete, rule-based linguistic form, over a more extensive period of time (i.e., 10 months) has so far been revealed in only one study (Bitchener & Knoch, 2010a). Further research on a range of linguistic error domains and categories over extended periods of time is therefore required to test the truly longitudinal effectiveness of written CF. This research focus should also investigate, for example, whether a single treatment (as in the 10-month study mentioned above) is sufficient for retained accuracy or whether multiple feedback treatments are required for certain types of error. The following research question could therefore guide this recommendation:

- Over what periods of time are single and multiple provisions of written CF effective in targeting different types of linguistic form and structure?

Is focused written CF more effective in treating L2 errors than unfocused written CF? Most of the early studies on the efficacy of written CF investigated the effectiveness of providing learners with unfocused feedback (i.e., feedback on a wide range of different types of error). Early studies, as we saw in Chapter 3, reported that written CF was not effective in helping learners improve the accuracy of their writing, but, as we also explained, the design and methodological flaws of these studies meant that the findings should not necessarily be taken as definitive and that further well-designed research should be conducted to confirm the findings one way or other. One such recent study (van Beuningen et al., 2012) has found that unfocused feedback can be effective in treating a range of error categories. With conflicting findings on this issue, we suggest the following research question be investigated so that we can understand which particular error categories within a range of error types can be effectively treated with unfocused feedback:

- How effective is unfocused written CF in treating specific types of L2 error?

In Chapter 3, we explained that most of the studies on the efficacy of written CF examined the effectiveness of providing learners with focused feedback (i.e., intensive feedback on one or a few linguistic error categories). In each study, a single feedback treatment was given. The findings across the studies were consistent in showing that written CF, when focused in this way, is effective in treating the targeted form or structure and that the levels of improved accuracy are retained over time. We would expect to see similar results from studies that target other discrete, rule-based forms but, as we explained above, the jury is still out on whether focused or unfocused feedback is effective in treating more complex forms and structures. The following research question would therefore be useful in guiding further investigations:

- To what extent is focused written CF effective in treating different categories of linguistic error?

In light of the positive findings from the group of focused written CF studies and the one recent unfocused written CF study, it is clear that further research is needed to examine the relative effectiveness of the two types. It is particularly important that this question be investigated given the design flaws of the two studies that sought to compare these two types and from which no definitive answer could be made. Again, it is important that the question be considered in relation to other variables that might be expected to have a mediating effect. For instance, the interaction of focused and unfocused feedback with different types

104 Analysis of Research on Written CF

of direct and indirect feedback, proficiency levels, age groups, and target language backgrounds might reveal different effects. Thus, we would suggest the following general research question be investigated with respect to different variables:

- To what extent is focused or unfocused written CF effective in treating L2 errors when compared with the interactional effect of other variables?

Is written CF more effective in targeting some linguistic error domains and specific error categories than others? In Chapters 1 and 3, we referred to the suggestion in the literature that written CF may not necessarily be effective for all types of linguistic error. So far, studies reported in Chapter 3 have shown that written CF is effective in targeting some discrete, rule-based forms (e.g., some functional uses of the English article system and the use of the simple past tense). However, it has shown that learners find written CF less helpful in overcoming errors in the use of prepositions. This said, it should be noted that the study investigating preposition use did not target specific uses of prepositions in the same way that recent studies have targeted specific functional uses of the English article system. Consequently, we would suggest that, in targeting any linguistic category, specific functional uses of the linguistic item be examined. It might also be the case that forms or structures that fail to respond to a single written CF treatment require additional feedback. This is an area of research that needs to be more fully explored if single treatments fail to produce significant accuracy improvements. A case has also been made in the literature that more complex and idiosyncratic forms and structures may be resistant to the effect of written CF. This is an area of research that has not been investigated. One reason for the delay might be the difficulty of identifying sufficient examples of the targeted error from the types of writing instrument typically used in quantitative group-based studies. A more longitudinal, qualitative case study approach may be one way of launching this type of investigation if researchers find it difficult to access sufficient "obligatory" uses of a targeted error category. The following research questions might be helpful in guiding this research:

- To what extent are single and multiple treatments of written CF effective in treating errors arising from different functional uses of simple and complex linguistic forms and structures?

Are some types of written CF more effective in treating L2 errors than others? Over the years, the more pedagogically driven question about whether some types of written CF are more effective than others has received more research attention than any other question. This is understandable given the tendency among teachers and researchers to assume that written CF is, to some extent, effective in treating learners' errors and the desire of teachers to know whether they might more profitably spend their time providing one type of feedback rather than another type. Making a distinction between feedback that is direct or indirect (defined in Chapter 3), the earlier research, comparing the relative effectiveness of these two types, concluded that there was no significant difference in their effectiveness. But, again, caution has been advised in taking this conclusion too seriously because of the design and methodological flaws of the studies. Recently, the work of van Beuningen and colleagues (2008, 2011) (see Chapter 3) has found that direct error correction is more effective over time even though short term benefits for both direct and indirect feedback were also noted. Confirming these results, Bitchener and Knoch (2010b) also found direct error correction was more effective than indirect feedback over time. Other studies reviewed in Chapter 3 that compared the relative effectiveness of different types of direct feedback reported conflicting results. The studies by Bitchener and Knoch found no difference in effect between different types of direct feedback, but Bitchener et al. (2005) and Sheen (2007) reported an advantage for direct feedback including meta-linguistic explanation. The reason the first group of studies by Bitchener and Knoch did not find an advantage for the inclusion of meta-linguistic feedback whereas those by Bitchener et al. and Sheen found an advantage might lie in the nature of the meta-linguistic explanation provided. Thus, we would suggest that further research investigating the relative effectiveness of direct types of feedback alone and/or with indirect types of feedback compare the nature and amount of written meta-linguistic feedback provided. It might be that more detailed explanations and examples yield more gains for some types of error category and for certain types of learner. Additionally, we would suggest that single feedback variables (e.g., written meta-linguistic feedback without direct error correction) be compared rather than variable groupings (e.g., combining written meta-linguistic feedback with direct error correction) so that the specific reason for effects can be identified.

The theoretical arguments in support of a direct or indirect approach, outlined in Chapter 3, were often related to the proficiency level of learners or to different types of linguistic error. Intuitively, it seems reasonable to suggest that indirect feedback might be more effective if given to more advanced learners rather than lower proficiency learners because they would be expected to have a larger linguistic repertoire to draw on. However, arguments such as this need to be tested empirically. It would also seem reasonable to suggest that more complex structures might be more easily treated with one of the more explicit direct feedback approaches (e.g., with written meta-linguistic feedback). If we consider the potential interactional effect of these variables, it would seem that clearer conclusions might be reached on the relative effectiveness of different feedback types. Thus, we would suggest that the following research question might be useful in reaching more pedagogically applicable conclusions:

- To what extent do the interactional effects of different types of direct and indirect written CF with other variables influence the effectiveness of written CF?

106 Analysis of Research on Written CF

Does the educational and L2 learning background of learners determine the extent to which they benefit from written CF? Over the years, attention has been drawn to the potential effect of a learner's educational background (both L1 and L2 learning experiences) and reasons for studying a second language on the level of motivation they bring to writing tasks in the L2 classroom. As we pointed out in Chapter 3, suggestions have been made that learners who come from a background where formal and systematic approaches to language learning in the classroom have been their experience may be more likely to respond positively to written CF. However, only one study has specifically investigated this possibility, and, with no indication of significant difference between the two groups of learners in the study (international students who were thought to have been exposed to the importance of linguistic accuracy and migrant students who were thought to have not had the same type of L2 learning background), it is unclear whether learners with different background experiences might respond differently to the provision of written CF. The authors of the study pointed to the need for future researchers to more carefully define the groups of learners being compared and to consider whether or not a different approach might yield clearer results, namely, one that compares learners who self report (1) that they have been exposed to written CF in their earlier L2 classroom learning and those who say they have not had this experience and (2) the extent to which they see formal accuracy, as opposed to communicative fluency, as an important part of their classroom lessons. We suggest, therefore, that the following research question might be effective in teasing out whether these variables might be expected to impact upon the way in which learners respond to written CF:

- To what extent do different goals, different prior L1 and L2 learning experiences, and different motivations have on the way learners respond to and benefit from written CF?

To what extent can the proposals of socio-cultural theory and activity theory enhance our understanding of the effectiveness of written CF? In Chapters 1 and 3, we reported on the contribution that socio-cultural theory and empirical studies of its claims are beginning to make in the written context. Studies have shown how socially mediated learning, as a result of teachers scaffolding their learners' linguistic performance with less and less explicit feedback, can enable learners to become more independent, accurate users of targeted L2 forms and structures. However, the effectiveness of this research, in the written context in particular, is in the very early stages of development. As yet, we do not have causal explanations for the observed improvements in accuracy or indications from more quantitative studies of the extent to which the findings can be generalized. Consequently, we would suggest that further research of this type be undertaken, using the following research question as a guide to focusing the investigations:

Current research questions	Future research questions
Can written CF facilitate the acquisition of L2 forms and structures?	To what extent can written CF facilitate the acquisition of different L2 forms and structures? To what extent can accurate text revisions, as a result of written CF, facilitate accuracy in the writing of new texts over time? Over what periods of time are single and multiple provisions of written CF effective in targeting different types of linguistic form and structure?
Is focused written CF more effective in treating L2 errors than unfocused written CF?	How effective is unfocused written CF in treating specific types of L2 error? To what extent is focused written CF effective in treating different categories of linguistic error? To what extent is focused or unfocused written CF effective in treating L2 errors when compared with the interactional effect of other variables?
Is written CF more effective in targeting some linguistic error domains and specific error categories than others?	To what extent are single and multiple treatments of written CF effective in treating errors arising from different functional uses of simple and complex linguistic forms and structures?
Are some types of written CF more effective in treating L2 errors than others?	To what extent do the interactional effects of different types of direct and indirect written CF with other variables influence the effectiveness of written CF?
Does the educational and L2 learning background of learners determine the extent to which they benefit from written CF?	To what extent do different goals, different prior L1 and L2 learning experiences, and different motivations, have on the way learners respond to and benefit from written CF?
To what extent can the proposals of socio-cultural theory and activity theory enhance our understanding of the effectiveness of written CF?	To what extent can written CF, employing the regulatory scale, enable learners to improve over time the accuracy with which they use forms and structures (1) within and (2) outside the learner's ZPD?
To what extent can written CF, employing the regulatory scale, enable learners to improve over time the accuracy with which they use forms and structures (1) within and (2) outside the learner's ZPD?	Are some individuals and contextual factors more likely than others to reduce the engagement a learner might have with writing tasks that focus on an effective use of written CF?

FIGURE 5.1 Summary of research questions for written CF in language learning contexts

108 Analysis of Research on Written CF

- To what extent can written CF, employing the regulatory scale, enable learners to improve over time the accuracy with which they use forms and structures (1) within and (2) outside the learner's ZPD?

We have also noted in Chapters 1 and 3 how activity theory provides a compelling justification for investigating individual and contextual factors outside the learner's cognitive "black box." Claims have been made in the wider SLA literature about the effects that a learner's goals and motivations can have on the extent to which they develop in their knowledge and use of the target language. The claims would seem to be equally applicable to the way in which learners respond to and benefit from written CF. Activity theory also draws our attention to the way in which these individual factors can (1) interact with other task-based, activity-oriented factors, (2) determine how a learner approaches oral and written activities, and (3) influence the extent to which he/she engages in an activity. For instance, with regard to writing tasks, which provide learners with opportunities to make use of written CF provided by a teacher or peer, some learners may make full use of the feedback because they want to engage with it whereas others may not be motivated to engage with it in the same way. The presence of individual and context factors (including these and others identified in the literature) might therefore mean that cognitive variables, with the potential to impact on the effectiveness of written CF, are of little or no consequence. In other words, learners' uptake and retention may be mediated by any of these factors. The question that arises from this, then, is which of these factors or combination of factors is likely to exert the strongest influence and have the most inhibitive effect. If we are able to find clear answers to this question, we may gain a clearer understanding of why some learners respond better to written CF than others. Thus, we suggest that the following research question be investigated:

- Are some individual and contextual factors more likely than others to reduce the engagement a learner might have with writing tasks that focus on an effective use of written CF?

Summary

The first half of this chapter has focused on research issues relevant to written CF in the language learning context. Figure 5.1 summarizes the questions we have recommended for further research.

Written CF in Composition Research

As discussed in Chapter 2, mainstream (L1) composition researchers, for the most part, lost interest in studying error or written CF by the end of the 1980s, and nearly all of the written CF research activity for the past 20 years has been undertaken by L2 writing specialists, other applied linguists, and foreign language researchers. This mixture of pedagogical contexts, goals, and perspectives, has, as we have previously noted, muddied the waters as to research designs, findings, and their implications. We attempted to sort through some of this confusion by separating our discussion of studies in Chapters 3–4. In the second half of this chapter, we focus attention on what future written CF research can do to improve both knowledge and practice in composition teaching (whether in L1, L2, or mixed settings).

Continuing with the themes raised in previous chapters and in Ferris (2010), we discuss first the methodological difficulties that have plagued researchers who have conducted earlier studies in this vein and suggest some possible perspectives toward those issues. Then, we look at important questions that have been inadequately explored or neglected entirely and discuss possible research questions and designs that could be utilized to investigate them. An overview of the issues to be discussed in the two following sections is provided in Figure 5.2.

Subtopic	Issue(s) or question(s)
Research problems to resolve	
Control groups in classroom studies	Are there practical and ethical ways to incorporate control groups into longitudinal, contextualized designs?
Role of the classroom teacher	How can teachers' knowledge, perspectives, and practices be better incorporated into written CF research designs?
Unexplored or under-explored questions	
Content of written CF	What error types should be focused upon in studies of *writing classes*?
Form of written CF	How can research questions of direct versus indirect written CF and focused versus unfocused written CF be appropriately situated within the larger goals of a writing course?
Amount of written CF	What helps students develop better writing skills: selective feedback that trains them to focus on error patterns or comprehensive feedback that trains them to carefully edit entire texts?
Going beyond written CF	Do classroom activities such as revision, strategy training, and grammar instruction, in conjunction with written CF, lead to greater progess in written accuracy?
Individual student differences	How do differences in student background knowledge, knowledge, education, motivation, and learning styles impact writers' ability to benefit from written CF?

FIGURE 5.2 Summary of research issues for written CF in L2 writing contexts

110 Analysis of Research on Written CF

Resolving Methodological Problems

Control Groups in Longitudinal Designs. As we discussed in Chapter 4 and as Ferris has noted elsewhere (2004, 2010), the largest methodological conundrum facing writing researchers is how to incorporate a no-feedback control group into a study of the long-term impact of written CF on student writing. (We distinguish here between such studies conducted in experimental settings and those contextualized within the day-to-day activities of a writing class. It is the latter setting that raises methodological and even ethical questions.) Previous L2 writing researchers have utilized control groups for short-term "one-shot" treatments (e.g., Fathman & Whalley, 1990; Ferris & Roberts, 2001), but as previous reviewers have rightly noted, demonstrating that students' ability to successfully revise a text does not prove that the feedback and revision cycle will lead to long-term improvement in written accuracy or in writing quality. On the other hand, longitudinal studies are usually situated in natural classroom settings, and instructors and researchers do not feel comfortable with substantial long-term interventions such as withholding written CF from one subgroup of students for an extended period of time. (In contrast, researchers feel they can justify such differential treatment for a short-term period—or for a laboratory-type study conducted outside of regular class activities—because students will have other opportunities during the term to receive feedback, so they will not be excessively disadvantaged.)

Some might argue that medical or pharmaceutical researchers conduct such studies all the time (e.g., dividing subject groups between treatment groups who receive a new experimental drug and control groups who receive a placebo). However, teachers (and their supervisors) who may already believe in the need for and value of written CF would not consider it an "experimental" drug, and subjects in such medical research studies typically do not even know which treatment they are receiving. It would be impossible to replicate such conditions in a classroom—not only would students know what kind of treatment they are receiving (or not receiving), but they would be able to compare notes with other students in the class, possibly leading to resentment or charges of unequal treatment. One way to get around this limitation would be to compare two or more intact classes taught by the same instructor that are otherwise identical (classes taught by different instructors raise other issues, as discussed below).

In short, the interacting problems of teacher ethics or feelings of guilt, possible repercussions from supervisors, and potential resistance from students make it difficult to design and execute longitudinal written CF studies in writing classrooms that include control groups of students receiving no language-focused feedback. We do not really see a "solution" to this dilemma, but we can suggest two general approaches that researchers could consider.

Redefine What "Control Group" Means. Chandler (2003) included a "control group" in her study, but this did not mean that students received no feedback. Rather, they were not asked to apply the feedback through revision until weeks later, in contrast to a treatment group that revised immediately after receiving written CF. Thus, the contrast set up was between "written CF followed by immediate revision" and "written CF followed by delayed revision." While not the same as "students who received written CF regularly for 15 weeks versus students who received no written CF at all," Chandler's contrast is a legitimate one to examine. Other such contrasts could include students who received written CF at the specific point of error in the text versus those who received only a summary end note advising them to attend to certain patterns of error in their future writing; while the latter "control" group would be getting some generalized feedback, it would be of a very different nature than the text/error-specific feedback given by the treatment group. A variation on this design could be contrasting the use of Haswell's (1983) "minimal marking" (checkmarks in the margins) technique with more detailed feedback at the exact point of error.

Other approaches to this problem could include students receiving focused, selective feedback on certain error types and no feedback on other errors; their progress on marked and unmarked error categories could be measured over time. Alternatively, students in the same class could be in different treatment groups for different writing tasks, perhaps with one group getting written CF on the first paper but not the second and vice versa for a second group. One could question, however, whether this is really a "longitudinal" treatment or rather a variation on early short-term studies; the problem of different tasks and student progress over time could also confound interpretation of the findings. The larger point here is that, for researchers who cannot bring themselves to identify a control group of student writers who will not receive any written CF over an extended period of time, there may be other ways to isolate written CF's effects in ways that are less intrusive. That said, none of these possible variations truly "solve" the problem of controls in a longitudinal study.

Just Do the Research Anyway. There may be teachers or researchers who do not feel the same ethical constraints about giving (or not) students written CF (see Truscott, 1999), and if those individuals have the freedom to conduct longitudinal classroom studies in which some students receive written CF and others do not, they could do so. Perhaps students could be persuaded to volunteer for such studies in the same way that subjects are recruited for medical research; if the students themselves know that they may be in a control group receiving no written CF, many of the ethical issues are less troubling. If Truscott (1996, 1999) is right that students, with some explanation, can adjust to the absence of written CF, finding such volunteer participants may not be as difficult as it might sound. In fact, there may be students who would enjoy the freedom of not receiving text-specific feedback about their errors.

Addressing the "Teacher Variable"

Another issue that is inadequately addressed in research reviews of written CF is the differential treatment that students receive because of variation across classroom

112 Analysis of Research on Written CF

instructors. In most of the recent written CF studies, error feedback has been provided by the researchers conducting the study, ensuring that student participants received feedback that was similar in quantity, quality, and approach. In contrast, written CF studies examining the feedback provided by classroom instructors have painted a different picture. For example, the studies by Connors and Lunsford (1988) and Lunsford and Lunsford (2008), in which feedback provided by a large cross section of writing instructors was analyzed, demonstrated that teachers mark different types of errors in varying proportions. A recent study of the response practices of 129 college writing instructors further suggested widely diverse instructor approaches to error feedback (Ferris et al., 2011). A more focused semester-long analysis of the error feedback of three classroom instructors (Ferris, 2006) yielded several dramatic insights: (1) even though the teachers had all agreed to give comprehensive indirect feedback using standard error codes, in practice none of them followed the plan; (2) when the teachers' specific feedback strategies were compared, there were substantial differences among them; and (3) the differences in written CF approach could be directly connected to student outcomes or progress. Similarly, two recent studies of the feedback practices of L2 writing instructors (Lee, 2009; Montgomery & Baker, 2007) suggested that teachers did not always follow their own stated beliefs when providing feedback to their students. This is all to say that there are differences across writing instructors in both feedback philosophy and practice, and these variations impact students and should be accounted for more carefully in written CF research.

Instructor Versus Researcher Feedback. As already noted, most written CF studies feature feedback provided by researchers rather than classroom instructors. The reasons for this are likely practical ones. First, writing teachers are busy and already spend a lot of time providing feedback; they might not be especially receptive to researchers' requests to give feedback in a particular way and/or to have their actual feedback collected and studied. Second, if the purpose of the study is to examine the effects of specifically focused feedback delivered in precise ways, it is easier to guarantee a consistent approach if the researchers give the feedback, as they (a) know exactly what they are trying to do; and (b) are obviously primarily committed to the goals of the research, whereas these goals are likely only of secondary importance to classroom writing instructors (as seen in Ferris' 2006 study, in which even "cooperating" teachers proved to be either unwilling or unable to stick to a particular feedback approach). Third, there might be other confounding variables that could muddy the design or the results: (a) teacher competence or knowledge about language structures and how to mark them; (b) the amount of time, energy, and focused attention each teacher could or would devote to written CF; and (c) other aspects of the classroom setting, including the content and structure of lessons and the relationship between teacher and students. With all of these issues in mind, it is not surprising that researchers often choose the neater, cleaner, and easier path of providing written CF themselves.

Nonetheless, if continued research on this issue is going to be truly helpful to classroom writing instructors, it is imperative that at least some of the studies be designed to include the teachers. We can offer a few practical suggestions or approaches along these lines. One option is for the researcher(s) and the classroom teacher(s) to be the same. If this option is pursued, there should be independent researchers or assistants as part of the project so that the teachers' efforts and the effects of written CF can be analyzed objectively. Another possibility is to conduct descriptive studies that examine what teachers actually do and why, rather than focusing solely on quasi-experimental pre-test/treatment/post-test/delayed post-test designs. A third approach is to ask and train teachers to provide various written CF treatments but then carefully assess not only the effects of the treatments on student writers but ways in which the individual teachers actually delivered the feedback, rather than simply assuming that the teachers gave the written CF as planned and in the same way that the researchers would have. For the third option, of course, researchers will have to think of ways to either make the written CF treatments minimally intrusive on the teachers' time (and on their students' progress) or to compensate the teachers for their cooperation. While involving the classroom writing instructors will be challenging and will change the nature of the research questions and the designs employed to explore them, such contextualized, non-experimental efforts are the only way to examine many issues of great practical interest to writing teachers and their students.

Types of Teacher-specific Questions to Consider. Before we move on from the "teacher variable," we want to suggest some possible avenues for exploration. While this list is certainly not exhaustive, it should give researchers some food for thought.

1. *What preparation do writing instructors receive for providing written CF?* This question is especially relevant in composition/writing settings, as opposed to language teaching contexts. Most language teachers have had some formal training that included linguistics, grammar, and even pedagogy of grammar. In contrast, many teachers of L2 writers may have had composition training, but this often does not include either linguistics or grammar coursework, let alone focused preparation on how to work effectively with language issues facing L2 writers (see Ferris, Brown, Liu, & Stine, in press). Truscott (1996) rightly noted that teachers' inability to provide accurate or effective written CF was a "practical problem" that predicted the ultimate failure of written CF. In short, any examination of how writing instructors deliver written CF should include consideration of those teachers' background knowledge, training, and experience. Nor should it be assumed that veteran writing instructors are necessarily effective in their provision of written CF; the studies

114 Analysis of Research on Written CF

by Ferris and colleagues (Ferris et al., 2011; Ferris et al., in press) suggested a wide range of instructor abilities, even among very experienced teachers.

2. *What are writing instructors' philosophies toward written CF, and to what degree do their practices mirror their beliefs?* As already noted, several recent studies have suggested that teachers may often say one thing but do another when it comes to written CF (Ferris et al., 2011; Lee, 2009; Montgomery & Baker, 2007). Research designs to investigate this question could include mixed-method approaches of surveys, interviews, and analyses of student texts with teacher corrections.

3. *How do teachers' written CF practices intersect with their other response practices and their overall approach to the writing class (syllabus, assignments, lessons, materials, grading scheme, etc.)?* Written CF has usually been studied as an isolated phenomenon, but in reality it occurs alongside many other interacting elements of a writing course. Studies in which teachers' written feedback is simply collected and analyzed may fall short of seeing the big picture: how much does error factor in how student papers are graded? Does the teacher design and deliver lessons that teach editing strategies and/or problematic grammar/usage points? How are such lessons delivered—through interactive, hands-on application activities or through eye-glazing teacher lectures?[1] What kinds of supporting materials (handouts, textbooks, websites) are provided for the student writers so that they can consult them outside of class while working on papers? What is the relationship between teacher and students like?[2] Examining this question will likely involve some ethnographic techniques such as classroom observation, interviews of teachers and students, and collection of classroom artifacts such as the syllabus, grading rubric, and class handouts.

Readers who have followed us through the reviews in Chapters 3–4 and/or who have read the primary sources discussed in those chapters will again note that the types of questions and research designs suggested here are quite different from those in most of the studies conducted about written CF in L2 writing thus far. While the above suggestions might cause some discomfort for researchers who prefer experimental quantitative research approaches, we believe that broadening the methodological scope of the research base can only benefit the discussion and especially the teachers and students it might potentially serve.

Investigating Unexplored or Under-explored Questions

As we noted in Chapter 4, besides the investigations of "The Big Question" (Does written CF help student writers to improve in accuracy?), there have been various examinations of specific types of written CF. These have largely been conducted by researchers who were ready to move beyond the "if" question of written CF to the "how" question. However, all of these questions need further exploration. They can be subdivided into five larger themes: (1) content of written CF; (2) form of written CF; (3) amount of written CF; (4) other activities that support written CF; and (5) individual differences in student writers' progress after receiving written CF.

The Content of Written CF: Error Types. A difficult but important sub-question to consider in written CF research is what types of errors should be treated with expert feedback. Truscott (1996) raised this issue in noting that previous research had ignored insights of second language acquisition studies about the ways in which different language domains (lexical, morphological, syntactic) are mastered, instead lumping all "writing error" into one large amorphous category in which a missing plural ending is the same as wrong-word preposition error or an incomprehensible sentence. Ferris (1999, 2002, 2006; Ferris & Roberts, 2001) suggested that errors could be divided into "treatable" (rule-governed) issues and "untreatable" (idiosyncratic or idiomatic) difficulties, and that different written CF approaches might be beneficial for various error types.

The recent SLA-based studies discussed in Chapter 3 have focused on discrete categories of language such as definite and indefinite articles and have yielded robust findings in favor of written CF. However, writing researchers and especially classroom practitioners would note that, in real writing classes, students make a variety of errors in language and usage, and that these errors differ from student to student and from text to text (Ferris, 2010). While giving feedback on a handful of easily defined and explained language features might indeed lead to increased student control over those features, such interventions might do little to improve the overall quality and accuracy of student writing over time. Instead, L2 writing specialists have suggested that teachers focus their attention on errors that are *frequent or systematic, serious, and stigmatizing* (Bates et al., 1993; Ferris, 1995a, 1995c, 2002; Hendrickson, 1978, 1980). A "serious" error has also been termed a "global" error (contrasted with "local"); it simply means an error that interferes with the comprehensibility of the text's message. A "stigmatizing" error is one that identifies the writer as coming from an L2 background and which might cause a reader/rater/evaluator to have a negative impression of the student's ability. In short, when considering research on *writing* classes rather than *language* classes, there is a range of issues to consider. Merely isolating error types as being "lexical" or "treatable" and so forth may miss the big picture of how student errors may impact their progress as successful writers and communicators.

Researchers interested in questions of error type for writing contexts could approach them in several ways. First, they can use lists from descriptive studies (such as the ones shown in Appendix 4.1) as starting points to select error types for written CF treatment. Second, they could conduct more "error gravity" studies (see Chapter 2) to assess whether certain errors are indeed serious and stigmatizing in the minds of real-world readers such as instructors across the disciplines or

116 Analysis of Research on Written CF

potential employers. Third, having generated ideas about errors that are frequent, serious, and stigmatizing for a target group of student writers, they can design written CF treatment studies that assess whether those errors can indeed be addressed through written CF and/or supplementary activities. Again, the point of these suggestions is that L2 writing researchers should study errors that are actually important for L2 writers, not simply those that are easy to study or represent a particular linguistic domain.

The Form of Written CF: How It Is Delivered. As noted elsewhere in this book (see especially Chapters 3–4), previous researchers have examined various discrete issues: should written CF be *direct*, providing the correct form to the student writer, or *indirect*, giving feedback that an error has been made but leaving it to the writer to solve the problem? Should it be *explicit*, telling the student what the problem is (with an error code, a rule reminder, or a brief explanation), or *implicit*, simply making the student aware of an unspecified error via an underlined or highlighted text portion or a check mark in the margin? Should written CF be *focused* (or "selective"), providing feedback only about specific predetermined errors, or should it be *unfocused*, responding to a variety of error types comprehensively as they are encountered in the text?

Various studies and researchers have posited different answers to these questions; our point in mentioning them here is that all of them require further examination, especially in the specific context of a writing class. For instance, while there might be good philosophical and practical arguments in favor of selective/focused written CF, it has also been noted that student writers in the real world need to learn to edit their texts for *all* types of errors (Evans, Hartshorn, McCollum, & Wolfersberger, 2010; Hartshorn et al., 2010), so providing feedback on only a few specific errors might neglect their long-term needs and mislead them about the amount of effort and attention it takes to self-edit an important piece of writing before it goes to an audience (an employer, a professor, a graduate school admissions committee). This is but one example of how an issue (focused versus unfocused feedback) might appear in a particular light when SLA issues are at the forefront but have different implications when students' progress as effective writers is the goal.

Amount of Written CF: Is Less Really More? The discussion in the previous section raised the issue of *how much* written CF should be provided to student writers and whether written CF should be comprehensive or selective. The arguments around this question have been reviewed previously and elsewhere in this book, so we will simply make two comments here. First, the question of whether comprehensive or selective written CF is better for students in a writing class may depend upon the teacher's immediate goals for the written CF with that group of students at a particular point in time. For instance, if the teacher is strategically using selective written CF as a way to teach students how to self-edit their own work, focusing on a few discernable patterns of error might be most effective. However, if the teacher's goal in giving written CF is to help students produce high-quality final products (such as a final portfolio to be read by a committee), comprehensive feedback might be needed. Second, the effectiveness of comprehensive versus selective written CF has not been compared in any kind of controlled or longitudinal research study. It could be useful to compare two equivalent groups of writers over time—one receiving unfocused, comprehensive feedback, and the other focused, selective feedback—to see whether one approach benefits student writers more than the other over an extended period of time.

A related quantity issue arises if a focused/selective approach is chosen: on how many error types can written CF productively focus on a given paper or over an extended period of time? As noted previously and in Ferris (2010), one or two error categories for written CF is probably too few to help student writers make adequate progress, but too many error types may be confusing or overwhelming for teachers to mark and students to process. Studies of focused written CF that compared, for instance, groups of students who received feedback on two error categories at a time versus five or ten could yield some information of specific practical use to writing instructors.

Beyond Written CF: Support Activities to Build Written Accuracy. As argued by Ferris (1995c, 2002), research on the "treatment of error" should go beyond expert written CF and also examine other types of classroom activities that can support students' language and writing development. Support activities could include required revision after written CF, strategy training, and classroom language instruction focused on structures either problematic for students in the class and/or that will be needed by the students to successfully accomplish specific writing tasks (such as the passive voice for scientific writing or verb tense sequences in narratives). Though such supplementary interventions have been recommended for years in publications for teachers, with a few minor exceptions,[3] there has been no focused research on the effects of these treatments.

Compared with major methodological problems discussed previously, such as how to add no-written CF control groups to longitudinal classroom designs and how to study "the teacher variable," it should be fairly easy to design studies that isolate these ancillary activities. For example, two groups of students could receive equivalent amounts/types of written CF, but one group would be asked to immediately revise their texts based on the feedback while the other would simply be asked to note it for their future writing. Similarly, one student group could receive in-class instruction about specific error types, could be taught a specific editing strategy such as reading texts aloud or monitoring for specific patterns of error, or could be asked to chart their own marked errors over a period of time while another group does not receive such instruction. It could be very useful to teachers to know if such activities are or are not helpful to students; follow-up studies could investigate the best ways to deliver such instruction

118 Analysis of Research on Written CF

(traditional grammar lecture versus application activities; reading aloud versus reading for specific error patterns; error logs that track five categories of error versus ten or twenty, etc.).

Does One Size Fit All? Individual Student Differences. As noted in Chapter 4, one of the most glaring gaps in the written CF research base to date has been the lack of consideration of individual student differences—in L1, in L2 education, in L1/L2 literacy, in motivation, learning style, personality, and so forth. Rather, statistics are calculated about groups of students as if their unique characteristics were irrelevant. However, any experienced writing teacher knows that some students appear to benefit greatly from feedback (of any type) while it seems to have little or no effect on others. As discussed in Ferris (2006), while statistical comparison of group means showed relevant differences in student progress in written accuracy over time, the standard deviations for individual students were enormous—in some cases, more than three times larger than the means. In short, some students made substantial progress in accuracy over a semester, others made minimal progress, and others actually regressed. All of these students were taking the same writing course, so their L2 writing proficiency level was not a major issue. What accounts for these dramatic differences?

Though the possible variables listed above—background, education, motivation, etc.—seem reasonable ones to examine, the fact is that they have not been examined in written CF research thus far.[4] These variables could be (and should be) examined in various quantitative, qualitative, and mixed-methods designs. A few questions that could guide such studies might include the following:

- (How) does previous formal L2 instruction (i.e., classroom grammar teaching) impact students' ability to benefit from written CF in their writing?
- How do student attitudes (toward the writing class, toward writing accuracy, toward written CF itself) correlate with progress in accuracy after receiving written CF?
- According to student writers themselves, why do they utilize (or not) expert written CF in revising their texts or writing new ones?
- What strategies do individual students identify for understanding and applying written CF from their teachers, and how successful do those strategies appear to be?
- What opinions do students have about the best ways for teachers to give written CF, and, if feedback were tailored to their individual preferences, would it be more effective for them?

A program of research that investigated the above set of questions would add considerably to our practical knowledge about this still-controversial pedagogical topic.

Summary

The latter half of this chapter has focused on research issues relevant specifically to written CF in writing/composition class settings. Though some of the questions and suggestions should be familiar to followers of this literature, we also highlight some important new directions and recommend some different approaches from what has gone before. Specifically, we note that:

1. Studies examining written CF in writing class contexts need to be intentionally embedded in the larger goals of a composition course. Focusing exclusively on learners' acquisition of a few discrete language structures may provide useful insights for research into SLA processes, but given the bigger picture concerns of the writing course, such designs alone will not be adequate, though they do, in our view, serve as a useful starting point.
2. Writing-based studies of written CF should employ a broader variety of research designs than have been utilized in the past, adding qualitative and mixed-methods approaches to the previous emphases on quantitative studies.
3. Future research on written CF in composition courses should focus more intentionally on *teachers and their classrooms* and on *differences across individual students*. Prior research has focused heavily on groups of students, as if they were all alike and would all respond to feedback in the same ways, and it has reduced the individual knowledge, beliefs, and preferences of classroom instructors to virtual irrelevance. These are both large gaps in the research and in our knowledge that should be addressed.

Concluding Remarks

Written CF in L2 writing and in SLA is a topic that has received considerable exposure in journals and at conferences over the past 15 years. It is tempting to think that we are finished investigating it and should move on to other issues. In our view, however, that would be a mistake. We hope that the discussion in Chapters 3–4, and particularly in this chapter, clarifies the state of the research base on written CF at this point in time as well as some future directions for researchers who continue to be interested in this topic.

Notes

1. Ferris recently observed the classroom of a teacher who took great pride in her ability to deliver grammar lessons to her students. However, this "delivery" consisted of over an hour of the teacher reading aloud to the students from the assigned handbook. The teacher's course evaluations included many complaints from students about this stultifying approach to grammar "instruction."
2. It could be assumed that if the teacher's classroom persona is harsh, intimidating, boring, etc., students' feelings about the instructor might impact their response to written CF and thus its overall effects on student progress.

120 Analysis of Research on Written CF

3. For instance, in the study by Ellis et al. (2008), one treatment group was given "metalinguistic explanation" in addition to written CF. The study by Ferris (2006) was designed originally to investigate the effects of student maintenance of error logs on their progress in written accuracy.
4. A new study (Ferris et al., 2010) was a longitudinal multiple-case study of ten student writers over the course of a semester and was designed to begin addressing such individual difference questions. However, this is barely a start.

PART III

Practical Applications of Written CF Theory and Research

6

FROM THEORY TO PRACTICE

Written CF for Language Learners

In this section, we discuss practical applications of the theory and research on written CF for the classroom. This chapter focuses, in particular, on how second and foreign language teachers can integrate written CF effectively into their language learning programs. In many respects, the language courses for second and foreign language learners are similar because instruction focuses on teaching the forms and structures of the target language irrespective of whether it is offered in a L2 or FLL context. However, uses of the language in these two contexts may be different to some extent, reflecting a difference in the overall goals or reasons for learning the language and reflecting the extent to which the language is being learned for use in a native-speaking environment. For example, international visa learners of ESL, studying English in a native-speaking environment, are likely to leave that environment at the conclusion of their course of study, so their focus and motivation may be different to that of migrant learners of ESL, studying the language so that they can become active members of the English-speaking community they have chosen to settle in. Consequently, language learning activities for the latter group may be more communicatively oriented than for the former group, who may be less concerned with developing their communication skills. Also, the types of tasks that the two groups of learners engage in may differ in terms of their relevance and appropriateness to real-world uses of the target language. These differences may be even more noticeable if learners are studying the target language as a foreign language in a non-native speaking environment. Irrespective of the teaching/learning context and the reasons for learning the target language, language teachers will always be committed to the teaching of language form and structure. In doing so, attention will always be given to the development of linguistic accuracy. This means,

124 Practical Applications

therefore, that there are a number of issues about the provision of written CF in the L2 classroom that teachers should be aware of.

The issues we focus on in this chapter arise from the theoretical, empirical, and pedagogical literature, so, in discussing what we consider to be elements of effective practice, we draw upon insights from this literature as well as from our years of language teaching experience. The content of this chapter is organized around the following subtopics:

1. Purpose and goals of providing written CF in a language learning program.
2. The timing and frequency of giving learners written CF.
3. The amount of written CF to provide.
4. The types of linguistic form and structure to focus on.
5. Options in the delivery of written CF.
6. The providers of written CF.
7. How written CF can be supported with other approaches to accuracy.
8. How learners can be actively involved in accuracy-oriented learning.

Purpose and Goals of Providing Written CF in a Language Learning Program

To understand the purpose and goals of providing written CF in a language learning program, it is necessary to start with a consideration of the wider purpose and goals of learning a second or foreign language and to then consider where written CF fits into the language learning process. Understanding its place in this process is a prerequisite to understanding its purpose and goals.

Learners of another language may have a variety of reasons for doing so, but, whatever their reasons, they expect to be taught the essential linguistic elements of the target language and, to some extent at least, pragmatic and idiosyncratic uses of the language for different purposes and contexts/occasions. This being the case, teachers should design language learning programs to help their learners achieve these goals. In determining what to teach in these programs, they should take into account the goals that are common to all language learners as well as the specific goals of each cohort of learners. One of the general needs of all learners is knowledge of the forms and structures of the target language. Specific goals of learners are likely to vary with some more focused on general communicative competence (including a focus on pragmatic and idiosyncratic uses of the language), so they can interact successfully with native speakers in a native-speaking environment. Others may be satisfied with achieving a more declarative knowledge about the language rather than a procedural knowledge. Irrespective of the specific foci of language learning programs, all courses of instruction should seek to help learners develop their knowledge and use of linguistic forms and structures.

In Chapter 1, we provided an overview of what we consider to be the key theoretical perspectives on how a second or foreign language is learned. In our discussion of the cognitive process, we explained that feedback is an important part of the learning process and that written CF is provided as a response to errors that learners have made in their written output. As a form of instruction, written CF is understood to be effective because it is provided at a time when learners are most likely to notice it, understand it, and internalize (uptake) it. Thus, its role is to help learners identify where their errors have been made and to provide them with information about why their output was incorrect and on how they can correct it. Other theoretical issues (discussed in Chapter 1), for example, the role of practice in converting declarative knowledge to procedural knowledge, will be referred to at an appropriate time in subsequent sections of this chapter.

Understanding the role of written CF in the language learning process is a prerequisite to understanding the pedagogical considerations we discuss in this chapter. For example, if the goal of providing written CF is to help learners understand and use the target language with accuracy, then the types of error that are most likely to be treated effectively with written CF are those whose form or structure lie within the learner's zone of "readiness" (see discussion of Pienemann in Chapter 1) or within their ZPD (see socio-cultural theory discussion in Chapter 1). Similarly, decisions about the way in which the feedback is provided might be determined by the linguistic proficiency level of learners. It may be that more advanced learners benefit from written CF targeting a range of linguistic errors whereas lower proficiency learners may only be able to focus their attention on one targeted category at a time. Thus, an understanding of how written CF fits within the overall language learning process should inform the pedagogical decisions made by teachers.

Other factors that teachers should also consider when making decisions about written CF are based on the findings of empirical research. In Chapter 3, we provided an overview of these findings, noting that they were sometimes conflicting but, at other times, clear and corroborated by those of other studies. One clear finding was the role that written CF can play in helping learners develop mastery and control over the use of two key functional uses of the English article system and the past simple tense. Although the research has only examined the effectiveness of written CF in treating a few linguistic forms/structures, it seems that it might also be effective in targeting other discrete, rule-based forms/ structures that learners are "ready" to acquire. Being aware of these findings should therefore help teachers understand which types of error are most likely to benefit from their written CF. Other findings from the research will be discussed in the following sections of this chapter.

The Timing and Frequency of Giving Learners Written CF

In many respects, the question of when to give written CF may be easier to answer for learners in language learning classes than for those in composition classes.

126 Practical Applications

Although composition class teachers do provide written CF to their students at certain times during the writing process, they emphasize that their responsibilities go well beyond the provision of feedback at the sentence level. As we explain in Chapter 7, attention in these classes must also be given to the construction of the wider discourse, the development of critical thinking skills, rhetorical awareness, argumentation, and so on. However, this does not mean that language class teachers are not also concerned with the development of these skills. Rather, it is a matter of degree and this, in turn, is very much determined by the proficiency level of the learners and the type of program or course they are taking. For example, more advanced language learners, while still receiving instruction on elements of the target language such as grammatical form and structure, are often taking classes to prepare them for further academic study. This means that attention is also given to the skill areas identified above for composition classes. These skills, together with language instruction (including, for example, rhetorical features of academic discourse) are often considered in relation to the writing genres that are taught. Thus, attention may be given to more complex grammatical structures (e.g., the coordination and subordination of different clause patterns, including embedded clauses, and the word order of qualifying statements/ propositions). While language teachers of advanced learners may provide written CF on these structures, they often find it necessary to provide feedback on other earlier taught forms and structures that have yet to be fully acquired. In other words, feedback on any category of error could be given to learners of any proficiency level and at any time. Nevertheless, there are several key factors that teachers will want to consider when deciding if one particular occasion is more appropriate than another.

Perhaps the first factor to consider is the proficiency level of the learner. Typically in language classes, more corrective feedback (both oral and written) is given to lower proficiency learners than higher proficiency learners. Lower proficiency learners expect their teachers to provide regular feedback on the accuracy of their writing but, in doing this, teachers need to be sensitive to the amount of corrective feedback they provide at any one time. Failure to do so could be discouraging, detrimental to self-esteem and de-motivating for those who experience difficulty in making progress and it could also be counter-productive if their attentional capacity is overloaded. Higher proficiency learners, on the other hand, may need less corrective feedback but more feedback on other aspects of their writing.

Another factor in deciding whether or not to give written CF on a particular piece of writing is the teacher's aim or purpose in assigning the task. Sometimes, the piece of writing may be a short exercise that focuses the learner's attention on a particular linguistic form or structure. The following example is a typical writing exercise given to learners after instruction has been provided.

Sample Feedback Exercise

Each of the following sentences has at least one error. Underline each error and write the correction above it.

1. This is the story about James Cash.
2. He is a boss of the large company.
3. He does same activities everyday.
4. In the morning, he reads a newspaper in the bed.
5. He always has meeting with his team in the morning.
6. He is a head of meeting.
7. Later, he looks at a sales report.
8. In an evening, he goes to the party with friends.
9. Sometimes, he goes to restaurant or to hotel.
10. He likes to drink the wine until 2 a.m. in the morning.

Exercises such as this are typically given to language learners to see if they can make accurate use of a targeted form or structure. Feedback on the accuracy with which learners have used the targeted form or structure is sometimes given orally to the whole class because it is more immediate than written feedback.

Writing tasks, on the other hand, are often characterized by a particular communicative purpose and, as such, often provide learners with opportunities to use targeted forms and structures. For example, if the task involves the writing of a narrative (e.g., about a series of events that happened last week), it is likely that the teacher is targeting the use of the past simple tense and maybe the use of adverbs and their placement. Additionally, the teacher may want to see if his/her learners can produce a fluent piece of narrative writing, or if they can clearly and effectively create a narrative structure. If the teacher's main focus is on fluency and narrative structure, it would not be appropriate for the learner's attention to be given to issues of accuracy. On the other hand, if the main focus is on the accurate use of the past simple tense and/or the accurate placement of adverbs of time, written CF would be appropriate. Then again, if all three foci were important aims, the teacher might be inclined to respond first to the fluency with which the text had been written or to the narrative construction of the storyline and then to respond to the accuracy of the writing with written CF. In other words, teachers in language classes, as well as those in composition classes, need to make these decisions in accordance with the aims of their lessons. Sometimes, it may be more appropriate for teachers to focus on content before form and, at other times, to focus on form before or instead of content. At the same time,

128 Practical Applications

a decision needs to be made about whether or not it is appropriate to tell learners the aim(s) of the writing exercise or task. Most often, one would expect learners to be told, but there may be times when writing tasks are given as assessment tools, and the teacher does not want to alert them to what is being targeted in the writing assessment.

Another decision that teachers need to make is the frequency with which written CF is to be given. Assuming that it is being provided on partially acquired linguistic forms and structures, some learners may increase the accuracy with which they use them after receiving only one feedback treatment. Recent research targeting specific linguistic forms (see Chapter 3) has shown that this is possible for many learners. However, the extent to which this occurs is likely to depend on how well the targeted form has been acquired. Other learners may require more regular feedback, especially on recurrent error categories. Short writing exercises and tasks could be given on a daily basis for a certain period of time (e.g., a week) to see if intensive feedback is helpful. In Chapter 1, we referred to the explicit/implicit interface position which hypothesized that practice (including further writing once written CF has been received) can enable learners to develop a automatized, procedural use of targeted forms and structures. Some of the factors or variables that might determine whether a learner benefits sufficiently from a single feedback session might include his/her proficiency level, the type of linguistic error category being targeted, and the type of feedback provided. These and other factors are discussed in the following sections of this chapter.

The Amount of Written CF to Provide

As we have already mentioned, some learners might be more sensitive than others about the amount of feedback they receive from their teacher. It is a well-established fact that most learners want and expect clear and regular feedback on their writing, but there is always the possibility that too much feedback at any one time might be de-motivating or too burdensome for cognitive processing. Thus, careful consideration needs to be given to the amount of feedback that learners are given. In deciding how much to provide, two questions need to be considered. First, there is the question of whether feedback should be focused on certain targeted categories of error or whether it should be more unfocused and therefore more comprehensive. If the decision is to provide targeted or focused feedback, the next question to consider is the number of targeted categories to focus on at any one time. If the decision is to provide unfocused feedback, the second question about the number of error categories to focus on becomes less important. In making their decisions, teachers should reflect on the theoretical arguments that support both focused and unfocused feedback and on the extent to which research findings support the two approaches (see Chapter 3). One of the main reasons for a focused approach targeting specific error categories and only one or a few of these at a time is the processing capacity of learners.

At lower proficiency levels, learners can easily be overwhelmed with too much information to process, even when they are not given much corrective feedback. We pointed out in Chapter 1 that advanced learners are more likely to have a larger attentional capacity than lower proficiency learners and so are more likely to be able to cope with a greater amount of corrective feedback. On the other hand, an argument can also be given for unfocused, comprehensive feedback. Learners at an advanced level of proficiency may be able to benefit from this type of feedback if they have already developed a high level of accuracy in using the items that are responded to. It may be that a greater range of advanced learner errors can be treated in a short period of time.

A number of empirical investigations into the effectiveness of providing learners with focused and unfocused written CF have been reported in recent years and these were discussed in Chapter 3. It will be remembered that the focused targeting of one or two discrete, rule-based linguistic items (e.g., two key functional uses of the English article and the use of the past simple tense) produced positive gains for learners at both advanced and lower proficiency levels. It is likely, we believe, that further research will show that focused written CF can also treat other discrete, rule-based error categories. For some forms and structures, learners may need more than one feedback session. At this point in time, it is not possible to predict how effective written CF is in targeting more complex, idiosyncratic forms and structures. For this type of error, it may be that a targeted focus is more effective than an unfocused approach. Many of the early studies on the effectiveness of unfocused written CF for composition students (reviewed in Chapter 4) and for language learning students (reviewed in Chapter 3) failed to produce evidence of the effectiveness of this approach over time but, as we reported in Chapter 3, one recent study found that unfocused written CF in content-oriented classes in the Netherlands enabled secondary school learners to improve the accuracy of their writing. However, the research base is too limited at this stage for us to conclude that an unfocused approach is generally effective. On the other hand, we know, from a growing range of studies on written CF (see Chapter 3) and on oral CF that targeted feedback is effective in treating some discrete, rule-based error categories at least.

It is sometimes said that the targeted approach is a slow way of treating the many types of error that learners make. However, this does not have to be the case. It is important to understand, when reading the literature, that the targeting of one or two linguistic error categories over a number of months is necessary in empirical research to determine whether or not written CF is effective over time. It does not mean that teachers should only start treating new linguistic error categories after learners have demonstrated significant levels of improvement over months of accurate use. As we have shown in Chapter 3, learners often demonstrate a high level of improved accuracy after only one feedback session. When this is also seen in the classroom, teachers should immediately introduce a new targeted form/structure but continue from time to time to monitor the

130 Practical Applications

ongoing accuracy with which earlier targeted forms are continuing to be used. Depending on the proficiency level and the simplicity or complexity of the targeted linguistic form/structure, teachers may decide to provide written CF on more than one or two items in each feedback session. For example, if teachers were to provide written CF on three targeted items in session one and found that their learners achieved a high level of accuracy in using two of these three items in a new piece of writing, it would be the time to introduce two new targeted items to replace the two that had been effectively treated as a result of the first feedback session. Over a semester, this targeted approach could well enable learners to increase their levels of accuracy in using a wide range of forms and structures. The number of categories that could be treated effectively in this way might also depend on the presence of other variables (e.g., proficiency level of learners; simplicity or complexity of linguistic form or structure being targeted; and others discussed throughout this chapter).

The Types of Linguistic Form and Structure to Focus On

Before teachers decide which linguistic forms or errors to focus on, they should determine first of all whether, in fact, an observed error is an error and not just a mistake. If there are a number of instances in a single text of what appears to be an error, it is likely that they are errors. Another way of determining whether an error has been made is to provide indirect feedback on such instances and see if learners can correct them without feedback. If they are accurately used in a new piece of writing, the original instances are likely to have been mistakes and are therefore not in need of written CF.

Once errors have been identified, teachers need to decide whether to provide focused or unfocused feedback. If the decision is to provide unfocused feedback, the teacher would be wise to think about whether in fact all errors should be treated in this way. As we mentioned before, it may be unwise to adopt this approach if it is likely to de-motivate the learner or create too much of a demand on his/her attentional capacity and therefore not produce lasting gains. If the decision is to provide focused feedback, the teacher will then need to decide which error categories to target. In doing this, a number of options might be considered. It may be best to target, first of all, the most frequently made types of error (e.g., past simple tense; noun-verb agreements) and then to introduce, over time, the less frequent types. This was the approach used in Bitchener et al. (2005) when they identified, first, which errors from an extensive list were the most frequently occurring. The same approach could be adopted through the use of a needs analysis. An advantage of the focused approach is that it may help the learner reduce a large number of frequently occurring errors within a particular category. Another option might be to target errors that have recently been taught in grammar lessons. The combination of explicit instruction and written CF is likely to focus the learner's attention more acutely than if only one of these forms of input is provided.

Another decision that teachers will need to make is whether to target only discrete, rule-based forms/structures or to also treat more complex and idiosyncratic forms and structures. While this is less likely to be a decision that needs to be made with lower proficiency learners, it is certainly one that teachers will need to make with their advanced learners. In doing so, teachers would need to also consider the type of written feedback that is most appropriate. For example, more complex items might be more effectively treated with meta-linguistic feedback than with direct error correction.

Options in the Delivery of Written CF

In discussing the ways in which written CF may be provided, the literature has tended to separate the discussion and research into two main types of delivery: direct and indirect. This might seem like a very straightforward and useful way to answer the question about what works best, but, unfortunately, the literature is sometimes unclear and inconsistent in the way it characterizes each of these approaches. In the early literature, *direct* feedback has been defined as the provision of a correction that identifies where an error has occurred and provides a specific solution to the problem. While there is nothing wrong with this definition, it fails to explain what "specific solution" means. Early studies of written CF, in both composition and language classes, tended to offer specific solutions in the form of either (1) a presentation of the correct linguistic form or structure, (2) a crossing out of erroneous forms or structures, or (3) an addition of items that had been omitted. More recent written CF studies, conducted in language classes, have included written meta-linguistic explanation (with or without examples) as another form of direct feedback. The following example of direct feedback, employed in several recent studies (Bitchener, 2008; Bitchener & Knoch, 2008, 2009a, 2009b, 2010a, 2010b), illustrates how meta-linguistic explanation and examples for two functional uses of the English article system can be provided:

Explanation

- Use "a" when referring to something for the first time.
- Use "the" when referring to something that has already been mentioned.

Examples

- **A** man and **a** woman were sitting opposite me.
- **The** man was British but I think **the** woman was Australian.

132 Practical Applications

Each of these types of feedback are categorized as *direct* because they provide a specific solution to the problem in the form of either a target-like correction or linguistic information about the cause of the error and about how it can be corrected. *Indirect* feedback, on the other hand, identifies where an error has been made in a text but it does not provide a solution; rather, the learner is left to make the necessary correction. A number of ways of indicating that an error has been made can be adopted (e.g., underlining, circling, highlighting). Occasionally, teachers may even list in the margin of a text the number of errors that have been made in each line. In some of the early studies, coded versions of meta-linguistic explanation were also classified as indirect types of feedback. Examples of these indirect options are presented in Chapter 7.

In defining these *direct* and *indirect* approaches, it can be seen that some are more explicit than others. Direct error correction is clearly the most explicit form of direct feedback insofar as it tells the learner what the correction is. On the other hand, providing the learner with grammatical information about what is wrong with his/her use of a form or structure and providing an example of target-like use is likely to be more useful if the learner has not fully understood why his/her usage is erroneous. Meta-linguistic information can be provided in one of two ways. When an error has been made, an asterisk or similar can be inserted above or after the error to refer the learner to the explanation and example(s) given at the end of his/her text. Alternatively, the teacher may want to provide the learner with a correction above or after the error as well as referring him/her to the meta-linguistic explanation and example(s) at the end of the text. This alternative approach is clearly a more explicit form of direct feedback than the first option. Considering the extent to which different *indirect* feedback options are explicit or implicit, the three most frequently used methods—underlining, circling, and highlighting—are more explicit than the marginal tally of errors because they identify where an error has occurred.

From a classroom teacher's perspective, differences of opinion about how various types of feedback are classified are probably unimportant. What is likely to be of greater interest and concern to teachers is whether any one of these types of feedback is more effective than another in helping learners understand where their errors have occurred, why they have occurred, and how they can be corrected. These issues have also been of considerable interest to researchers. As we reported in Chapter 3, many of the early studies found no difference in effect for direct and indirect types of feedback, but recent studies comparing the two approaches have found that direct feedback is more effective for SLA purposes over time even though there may be short-term benefits for both. We explained in Chapter 5 that further research is needed in this area before any firm conclusions can be made. If further research does confirm that direct feedback options have a long-term advantage over indirect options, the next question that would need to be answered would be which types of direct feedback are the most effective over time. In recent years, a number of researchers have begun looking at the relative effectiveness of different types of direct feedback but, unfortunately, firm conclusions on this issue are also unclear. Some studies (e.g., Bitchener & Knoch, 2008; 2010a) have found no difference in effect between the different direct feedback options while others (e.g., Bitchener et al., 2005; Sheen, 2007) have reported a longitudinal advantage for meta-linguistic explanation over direct error correction. Intuitively, it would seem that the provision of direct error correction with written meta-linguistic explanation would be more effective because, as we explained above, it not only tells the learner what the correction is but explains the cause of the error in grammatical terms. One way of giving written meta-linguistic feedback is to provide the rule(s) and example(s) for each targeted form or structure once (e.g., at the end of a learner's text) and asterisk instances of the error in the text so that the learner can consult the information provided in the meta-linguistic explanation. Further discussion of this approach can be found in Chapter 8. However, some teachers might consider this to be a very time-consuming way of providing written CF.

Other approaches might also be considered effective. Teachers may find, for example, that a mixture of direct and indirect feedback options are the best way to scaffold learners who fail to benefit immediately from a single feedback session. This approach has been referred to in Chapter 3 where we discussed the use of the regulatory scale (implicit to explicit) by Aljaafreh and Lantolf (1994) and Nassaji and Swain (2000). This approach could be used with lower proficiency learners as well as advanced learners. It might involve (1) the provision of indirect feedback to see if an error is able to be corrected by the learner; (2) follow-up sessions with direct feedback (maybe with direct error correction first and, if this is not immediately effective, with direct error correction and meta-linguistic explanation/example); and (3) indirect feedback once there are signs that the learner is less in need of more direct feedback. However, it is questionable in terms of the time involved whether this approach would be feasible for groups. Certainly, individuals would stand to gain much from this closely monitored approach.

In the process of deciding which type of feedback to give learners at any one time, teachers should also reflect upon the other factors we have been discussing in this chapter. It is likely that the greatest benefits will occur if they think carefully about the interaction of these factors. For example, it might be that lower proficiency learners benefit most from direct forms of feedback whereas advanced learners benefit as much from indirect forms of feedback. Even though proficiency level and types of feedback might be regarded as the two most important factors to be considered, this does not mean that the other factors discussed here can be ignored. Rather, it means that these two factors may be the first ones that need to be considered.

So far, we have been discussing these feedback options from only the teacher's perspective. Although it is often reported that students prefer direct, explicit feedback, this is not necessarily always the case. Many keen language learners want to try to self-correct their errors before the teacher provides them with a

134 Practical Applications

correction. Indirect options are not only preferred by many advanced learners but also by some lower proficiency learners. Some of the factors that might determine whether a learner prefers direct or indirect feedback include prior language learning experience, confidence or apprehension, commitment to the task of learning the language, contextual and situational variables, and nature of the writing task. Language learning in the classroom needs to be seen as a two-way process between teacher and learner. Thus, it would seem reasonable to suggest that decision-making be a two-way process and that any decision about giving written CF should consider what the learners expect. If learners buy into an approach that teachers have negotiated with them, they may be more likely to engage in the feedback process and, as a result, be more effective users of the feedback they receive.

In deciding what type(s) of written CF to provide, teachers may also find it useful to think about the tools they can use when giving feedback. Apart from the obvious need to provide legible feedback, abbreviations also need to be clearly and easily understood by learners and notes (as opposed to grammatically complete statements) need to be sufficiently full to have clear meaning. If writing tasks or exercises have been produced with a word processor, teachers may find it better to provide feedback online, using *comments* or *track changes*. These and other mechanical options for giving feedback are discussed and illustrated in Chapter 7.

The Providers of Written CF

From what we have been saying in this chapter, as well as in other chapters, classroom teachers are typically the key provider of written CF. It is generally assumed that teachers have the required knowledge to (1) identify where errors have occurred, (2) provide effective feedback on linguistic errors, and (3) deliver it in a clear and meaningful manner. It is also assumed that teachers have had sufficient training and experience to know what works best for individual learners, as well as for groups or classes of learners. However, this may not always be the case. Some teachers are well trained while others are less well trained or, in fact, not trained at all. The linguistic knowledge base of teachers can sometimes be less than adequate, meaning that some teachers may not be able to provide accurate feedback on a range of error types.

The learners themselves certainly expect their teachers to have the level and depth of knowledge required to give them appropriate feedback. Some learners may have higher expectations of their teachers than others and expect them to provide written CF on all of their written errors. Nevertheless, most learners understand that there are times when written CF is appropriate and times when it is not because attention needs to be given to other aspects of their writing. The amount of written CF and the frequency with which learners expect their teachers to provide such feedback may vary from learner to learner, and this may be the result of their prior learning experiences.

In language learning classrooms, the teacher is not always at the center of classroom activities. Language learning programs that are communicatively focused provide opportunities for learners to interact not only with the teacher but also with other members of the class. These activities often involve pair work and group work. While they are frequently used for oral interaction, they may also be used in combination with written activities, including peer feedback. There are a number of advantages that can be gained from this type of feedback. In pair work, for example, learners can gain experience in identifying where linguistic errors have occurred and this may mean that they will be more likely to read their own texts with a keen eye and self-correct them before their teacher or partner does. Whether learners should be encouraged to then correct their partner's errors is an issue that not everyone will agree with. Some may think this practice is like inviting "the blind to lead the blind." They may or may not be right. It may be that advanced learners are better placed to provide direct form of feedback. However, we would suggest that all learners can play a role by at least identifying where they think an error has occurred. Having done this, the text could be returned to the writer in order to see if he/she is able to self-correct those that have been identified by the partner. At this stage, it may be appropriate for the teacher to review what has been done and make any necessary corrections. Similar approaches could also be used for groups of learners who make the same types of error.

Written CF, together with other forms of instruction, can also be provided by tutors at the learner's institution or by those a learner chooses to employ outside his/her school. The latter is a popular option for those who have recently migrated to a country where the target language is the native language of citizens in that country. Learners of the target language as a foreign language might also employ the services of a tutor, particularly if the language is a subject taken for high-stakes examinations. Most often, learners make their own choice about who a suitable tutor might be but often this is based on the advice of friends, peers, and sometimes their classroom teacher. Advice from teachers should always be the preferred option because they are more likely to know who is sufficiently qualified and experienced to provide a reliable service. Without this, any written CF provided by someone without sound linguistic knowledge and teaching experience may be little better than receiving feedback from a classroom peer.

How Written CF Can Be Supported with Other Approaches to Accuracy

Explicit instruction is the primary means of developing a learner's knowledge and accurate use of target language forms and structures. At lower proficiency levels, plenary instruction is the main approach of language teachers, and these sessions typically precede written tasks and written CF on the accuracy with which

136 Practical Applications

learners have used the taught items. Plenary instruction is usually followed with some kind of short written exercise, designed to give learners the opportunity to practice the taught linguistic form or structure. Feedback on the level of accuracy achieved by the learner may be immediate if delivered orally in class or it may be provided at a later stage as written CF. Once the teacher is satisfied that learners have understood their instruction, they typically present their learners with longer oral and written tasks in order to see if they are able to accurately use the targeted linguistic features in more natural, everyday situations where they are not specifically primed to focus on particular forms and structures. It may be that other recently taught grammatical items are also tested for accuracy when tasks such as these are given by the teacher. This is an effective way of testing the extent to which learners have acquired what they have been taught. Writing tasks that are popular in language classes are those that provide learners with a stimulus for their writing (e.g., a single picture, a series of pictures, the opening section of a narrative, or a simple rubric that invites learners to describe or explain something). The picture description task used by Bitchener and Knoch (2010a), for example, is effective for targeting learners' use of the definite and indefinite articles, the past simple tense, or the present progressive tense (depending on whether the learners are asked to describe what happened or what is happening in the picture).

Instruction can also be provided to groups of learners who show, as a result of written CF, that they are producing the same types of errors as other learners in their writing. For example, the teacher may provide a mini-lesson on the use of the simple past tense to those whose written texts contain errors in the use of this linguistic form. Other learners in the class may also be placed in groups according to the types of errors they are making. There may also be times when one-on-one (teacher and learner) conferences are more effective for helping learners develop their understanding of and accuracy in the use of recurrent errors. Bitchener et al. (2005) reported effective gains in the use of this individualized approach. They found that learners who were given a short five-minute conference session (including clarification of where errors had occurred, the cause of the errors, rules, and examples of correct usage) outperformed those in other treatment groups. Teachers may find the individualized and focused nature of conference sessions particularly effective for helping learners overcome more persistent errors.

We have seen in recent studies that some types of error can be treated effectively when written CF is given on just one occasion. It may be that other types of error require written CF on more than one occasion as well as additional plenary or group instruction and individualized conference sessions. Each of these approaches should be implemented when teachers believe their learners are "ready" to acquire the category of error being targeted. It may become clear to the teacher, after a number of approaches have been tried, that learners are not "ready" and that their time would be better spent on other categories of error.

How Learners Can Be Actively Involved in Accuracy-oriented Learning Outside the Classroom

Most language learners expect to be asked to do some form of homework on a regular basis. There are a number of written tasks that can be given as homework in order to engage them in accuracy-oriented learning. One task that learners find interesting and helpful is identifying errors that have been made in someone else's writing. Learners can be asked, first of all, to identify as many errors as they can before attempting to provide a target-like correction and an explanation about why the error is an error or provide a rule for correct usage. Teachers can then respond to these efforts by either having a plenary class discussion of their findings the next day and/or by providing feedback on an individual learner's work. The advantage of the first approach is that it saves time, enables learners to hear what others think, and enables the teacher to provide clarification and additional examples of correct usage. The disadvantage of the second approach is the amount of time it takes for a teacher to review everyone's work.

Self-study books and websites are always popular with language learners, so this is another option for out-of-class learning. Most commercially produced books provide answers so that learners can receive immediate feedback on their work. While these materials focus on a range of language learning activities, teachers can direct their learners to sections that provide feedback activities and those that provide support activities such as grammar practice exercises on targeted items.

Concluding Remarks

In this chapter, we have explored a range of practical suggestions and recommendations based on our years of teaching experience. Underpinning each of these has been our understanding of the theory and research presented in earlier chapters and, therefore, our understanding of the purpose and goals of providing written CF for language learning/acquisition. The task of providing written CF to all individuals in a class on a regular basis and in a consistent and accurate manner can sometimes be seen as an idealistic dream. Knowing that this is the reality for many teachers, we hope that the ideas and advice given in this chapter will help them see a variety of ways of meeting a particular goal. Feedback to pairs and groups from the teacher and classmates may often be just as effective as one-on-one conference feedback provided by the teacher. As we have shown, it is sometimes possible to use one-on-one approaches with pairs and groups. In fact, a variety of approaches can often be more interesting and engaging for learners and teachers than just one well-trodden approach. Time that is spent thinking about the most interesting and effective approach for individuals, pairs, groups, and whole classes might be time well spent.

7

FROM THEORY TO PRACTICE

Written CF for L2 Student Writers

In this section, we discuss practical applications of the theory and research on written CF for the classroom. This chapter focuses, in particular, on how composition instructors who work with L2 writers might integrate written CF effectively into their writing course syllabus. By "composition instructors," we mean two distinct groups: (1) L2 specialists who teach writing courses specifically designed for L2 learners; and (2) composition instructors who might teach for mixed audiences of students who are clearly L1, those who are clearly L2, and those who fall somewhere in between, such as Generation 1.5 learners who learned their parents' L1 in the home as young children but who have been primarily or entirely educated and literate in the L2 (see Ferris, 2009; Harklau et al., 1999; Reid, 1998; Roberge, 2002; 2009; Roberge et al., 2009; Valdés, 1992). As we will discuss, some of the specific issues and suggestions we explore in this chapter may vary slightly depending upon which group of writing instructors is being addressed. Further, of course, in many local contexts, the two groups may overlap: the same instructors may teach both specially designated L2 writing courses and "mainstream" composition courses, depending upon their training, interests, and upon programmatic needs.[1]

It is in this section and chapter in particular where the need for separate discussions of written CF for language acquisition purposes and for the development of writing skills becomes especially apparent. As discussed earlier in this book, one of the problems with the mixing of studies conducted in language learning contexts and those undertaken in writing classrooms is that the narrowly focused approach of the SLA-focused studies of written CF (i.e., those reviewed in Chapter 3) can yield findings that seem unrealistic to writing instructors: "Although the clear and empirically sound designs of recent SLA studies of written CF are indeed impressive, L2 writing specialists might wonder if applying their findings to composition instruction could be difficult" (Ferris, 2010, pp. 191–192). This chapter thus focuses in very precise ways on how written CF might be utilized given the larger goals of composition instruction. We approach this by dividing the remainder of the chapter according to the subtopics shown in Figure 7.1.

Purpose and Goals of Written CF

While writing is definitely a productive language sub-skill that demonstrates whether SLA has occurred, the study and teaching of composition is influenced by a wide range of scholarly and philosophical paradigms that go well beyond applied linguistics and SLA studies. Second language writing is a sub-discipline that has been influenced by linguistics, rhetoric and composition, literary studies, cultural studies, foreign language studies, anthropology, and psychology, to name but a few (Ferris, 2010, 2011; Kaplan & Grabe, 2002; Matsuda, 2003b). The multidisciplinary nature of L2 writing impacts the research paradigms that are used to investigate it (Silva & Matsuda, 2005, 2010) and especially the ways in which composition is taught (Tate, Rupiper, & Schick, 2001).

Subtopic	Related question(s)
Purpose and goals	*Why* give written CF in a writing course?
Timing and frequency	*When*—at what stage of the writing process and on what types of texts—should written CF be provided?
Amount	*How much* written CF should a teacher provide on a particular text?
Focus	*On what types* of errors or language issues should written CF focus?
Form	*How* should written CF be given? Should it be direct or indirect? Explicit or implicit? How much explanation is useful/possible?
Source	*Who* should provide written CF? Should it always be the teacher? Can peers effectively provide CF? Can individuals gain autonomy in editing their own work?
Support	*What else* can writing instructors do in addition to written CF to help students develop self-editing strategies? What is the role of classroom grammar instruction in the writing course?
Follow-up	*What can students be asked to do* to analyze and apply written CF they have received?

FIGURE 7.1 Subtopics and questions on written CF in the writing classroom

140 Practical Applications

Therefore, a discussion of written CF in the writing class must begin with an understanding of larger purposes and goals of composition instruction. Considering such instruction at advanced levels (i.e., secondary and post-secondary contexts), the goals of composition programs and courses go well beyond a focus on language acquisition. They also include the development of critical thinking skills, of rhetorical awareness, of effective writing processes and strategies, and of specific sub-skills in argumentation and research.[2] Accurate and effective language use is seen as a means for clear and successful communication of one's ideas to a target audience, not as an end in itself. A well-edited text with shallow content, weak argumentation, or confusing arrangement would not be considered effective. In short, for a writing class, while control of language is a valuable tool for meeting the larger course goals, it is certainly not the only purpose of instruction, nor even the most important one.

What, then, is the goal of written CF in a writing course? In most instances, it should be to help student writers build awareness, knowledge, and strategic competence so that they can develop skills to better monitor their own writing in the future. Writing courses cannot, and should not, be about helping or requiring students to produce ideal or perfect, error-free texts (Brannon & Knoblauch, 1982; Ferris, 2008b). Not only are such goals unrealistic—language and literacy development take time—but they are beside the larger point of the writing course. Texts produced by students in the course are simply the means to the end of facilitating long-term student writing development. Ultimately, it is not that important what a written end product looks like but rather what the student learns from the process of developing that text, and especially lessons that are transferable beyond the immediate context of the course (to other academic or professional writing tasks). The only times that "perfect" (or as near-perfect as possible) student end products are important are when accuracy is an important criterion for final assessment (such as a well-edited final essay examination or course portfolio) or when students are writing texts that will be judged by real-world audiences (such as personal statements for graduate or professional degree programs).

This larger perspective informs our discussion of every one of the remaining subtopics in this chapter. For example, if the goal of teacher-provided written CF is to help students improve their self-editing strategies, then selective feedback that helps writers understand and make progress with their individual error patterns is likely the most effective approach (see "Amount," in Figure 7.1). In contrast, if a teacher is focused on getting students to produce final versions of texts that are as error-free as humanly feasible, then comprehensive direct feedback which the student merely has to transcribe as he/she rewrites the paper is the most efficient, reliable means to that end (see "Amount" and "Form" in Figure 7.1, and below). A similar analysis could be applied to all of the other specific questions in Figure 7.1: the purposes and goals of the writing class in general and how written CF fits into those larger aims should direct all of the decisions made by writing instructors.

Timing and Frequency of Written CF

Timing of Written CF

Content-Before-Form Arguments. A question that arises in discussions of written CF in writing classrooms in particular is how error feedback fits (or does not) into process-oriented syllabi in which students write and revise their texts several times before the paper is finalized. The process approach, at its core, stands for the principle that quality writing happens over time and with some effort—that writers need to think about, write, read and reread, obtain reader feedback on, and revise their papers before they are ready to be polished, finalized, and presented. Advocates of process teaching therefore discourage instructors from premature written CF—form-focused feedback delivered too early in the writing process— for several strong reasons. First, if a student writer will truly revise—add, delete, rearrange, and refocus text—then it is a waste of teacher time and energy to mark errors in early versions of a paper when portions of that text may disappear in later iterations. Second, excessive attention to grammatical, lexical, and mechanical errors may distract students, short-circuiting their cognitive ability to develop their content and arguments. Third, and most significantly, if a teacher focuses too much feedback on errors when the content is still being formulated, it sends the wrong message to students—they get the idea that writing is more about pristine final products than it is about engaging in the process to produce interesting and mature content. These arguments have been made repeatedly by influential process advocates in both L1 and L2 composition (e.g., Hairston, 1986; Krashen, 1984; Sommers, 1980, 1982; Zamel, 1982, 1985) and, since the 1980s, most composition instructors in the US and beyond have been specifically trained to avoid form-focused feedback on early versions of student papers, emphasizing ideas and arrangement instead, and providing written CF only at the final stages of development.

Content and Form Arguments. One of the assumptions made in the arguments outlined above is that students will be unable (and perhaps unwilling) to attend to feedback on both content and form on a particular text, or, more to the point, that they would ignore the more substantive revision-focused commentary in favor of addressing the relatively simpler feedback on language errors. However, at least in the case of L2 writers, there are two strands of evidence suggesting that these concerns are perhaps overstated. First, in studies where form- and content-based feedback were provided by teachers on the same draft of student papers, the students revised both content and form successfully (Ashwell, 2000; Fathman & Whalley, 1990; Ferris, 1997). Second, in studies of reactions to teacher feedback of various types, students indicated that they expected and valued teacher feedback on all aspects of their texts (Ferris, 1995b; Hedgcock & Lefkowitz, 1994, 1996; Montgomery & Baker, 2007). Both of these lines of research suggest that students want feedback that meets their text at its points of greatest need, whatever those may be.

142 Practical Applications

Besides the available research evidence on the separation of content- and form-focused feedback, experts on L2 writing have argued that L2 learners may require a different approach to the question than do their L1 student counterparts. For example, as the process approach took hold in L2 composition settings, several authors warned that pedagogical strategies designed for L1 students might not always be appropriate for L2 writers (e.g., Eskey, 1983; Horowitz, 1986; Leki, 1990a; Silva, 1988). A few years later, Reid (1994) argued that L2 writing instructors needed to carefully consider their feedback strategies to ensure that they were not abandoning students with their non-interventionist approaches. On the specific issue of written CF on various drafts of student papers, Ferris (2002) noted:

> One argument for providing at least some grammar feedback on all marked student drafts is that *not* doing so misses the opportunity to provide feedback at a teachable moment. Since many L2 student writers have significant accuracy problems, they arguably need all the input they can get from their teachers. By refusing to provide such feedback until the very last draft, teachers can severely limit these opportunities for needed input.
>
> *(p. 62, original emphasis)*

Due to the protracted nature of the process-based composition syllabus, students may write fewer papers with more drafts than in a writing course that is structured differently. Thus, for example, if students write four papers of three drafts each over a 15-week semester, students may only receive written CF four times, and the written CF opportunities will be weeks apart, making it difficult for students to remember and apply what they learned from previous written CF. However, if teachers provide some form of language-focused feedback at a variety of stages of the writing process, students will get more frequent and consistent opportunities to notice and analyze their written errors.

Both sets of arguments have merit: excessive attention to form can distract and de-motivate student writers, but L2 writers in particular may need more regular written CF than a typical process-oriented composition course might offer. A compromise position is offered by authors such as Frodesen and Holten (2003), who claimed that "it is in the best interest of L2 writers to attend to language issues consistently throughout the writing process" (p. 145) but also emphasized that "the teacher may wish to use a range of strategies through a multidraft process to focus students appropriately on selected forms" (Ferris & Hedgcock, 2005, p. 266; see also Ferris, 2002, p. 62). Some specific suggestions as to this "range of strategies" for different stages of the writing process are given in the sections below and in Appendix 7.1.

Frequency of Written CF

In recent work, other authors have further suggested that written CF and attention to linguistic accuracy in writing should perhaps be separated completely from the now-standard multiple-draft writing process. Hartshorn et al. (2010) argued that traditional process approaches to composition

> may be inadequate for helping students maximize their linguistic accuracy. Perhaps this is because traditional approaches lack the volume and frequency of practice and feedback needed for improvement. Thus, *efforts to improve accuracy may be more successful if separated from attempts to develop other aspects of ESL writing.*
>
> *(p. 102, emphasis added)*

As an alternative, Hartshorn et al. (2010) suggested what they called "dynamic corrective feedback," which is "meaningful, timely, constant, and manageable for both student and teacher"(p. 87) and in which "students produce new pieces of writing and receive feedback nearly every class period of the course" (p. 88). The "manageable" criterion is met by having the students frequently produce short texts to which the teacher can respond quickly.

Hartshorn et al. make useful suggestions about adding short, frequent writing tasks to the composition syllabus that could receive timely, consistent corrective feedback. Teachers should consider adding to their syllabus shorter, more regular writing tasks (whether in class or for homework) to which they and their students could give focused attention as to language problems and editing strategies.

However, it could also be argued that such short, consistent practice activities should be added to process-based written CF suggestions rather than replacing them. In real-world writing, students do have to produce longer, more complex papers, and learning to edit them successfully is an important skill for long-term proficiency. As noted in Chapter 4, research suggests that students make different kinds of language errors (and more of them) when writing tasks are more cognitively demanding, such as research papers or arguments (Lunsford & Lunsford, 2008). Thus, 10-minute in-class freewrites (the texts used in the study by Hartshorn et al., 2010) may not elicit the types of errors or writing challenges that students will encounter on other types of writing assignments. Students need to learn and practice strategies for all types of writing tasks, so helping them to edit longer texts produced over multiple drafts is also important and useful. However, to preserve teacher energy, instructors may choose to give focused written CF only on portions of longer student texts—a few paragraphs or a page or two—requiring the student writers to continue editing the rest of their papers on their own. In sum, teachers should utilize a variety of written CF strategies throughout the writing process and during the course to maximize student opportunities for learning and to build their strategies for a range of writing tasks

144 Practical Applications

and contexts. The following sections provide additional discussion and suggestions about how teachers might do so.

Amount of Teacher-provided Written CF

As already noted, one of the earliest and most important decisions a writing instructor must make (assuming that the instructor has moved from "if" to "how" in thinking about written CF) is how much written CF to give. Should the writing instructor mark or otherwise respond to *every* error observed in the entire student text (*comprehensive* correction), or should the teacher respond *selectively* to some errors while leaving others uncorrected or unmarked? There are several different issues to consider in response to this question.

Process and Product

At the beginning of this chapter, we argued that student development of strategic competence in self-editing (process) was ultimately more important than the form of the final product in addressing the goals of a writing course. If a teacher agrees with this perspective, it would argue for a selective approach to written CF rather than a comprehensive one. There are two overlapping reasons for the selective approach. First, selective correction may be less overwhelming for the student writer to process, analyze, and apply. A paper that is covered with comments and corrections can be visibly off-putting and can discourage the student writer. Second, selective correction, especially if it is focused on specific patterns of error that students can study and attend to, can actually give the students precise feedback that not only will help them to edit the current paper but ideally to avoid or reduce such errors in the future because of the detailed information such feedback provides them. Again, if the goal of written CF is to give students tools and strategies for writing more linguistically accurate texts in the future, feedback that is more cognitively and affectively appealing may actually be empowering rather than demoralizing.[3]

Counter-arguments in Favor of Comprehensive Correction

While teachers and students alike can see the benefits of selective correction when they are explained, both groups also express anxiety over the idea of leaving some errors in student texts unmarked and uncommented upon. The most basic issue is evaluation, or grading: students are afraid that (a) they will not be able to catch errors on their own if the teacher does not mark them; and (b) these uncorrected errors will hurt their grades. In studies where students have been asked for their views about comprehensive or selective error correction, a substantial percentage always say that they want *all* of their errors marked or corrected by the teacher (e.g., Ferris et al., 2010; Ferris & Roberts, 2001; Leki, 1991; see Chapter 4).

Teachers, in turn, worry that students will complain about unfair practices if errors left unmarked by the teacher are considered in the paper or course grade. Instructors may also fear that leaving errors uncorrected may reinforce those non-target patterns for students.

Real-world considerations outside of or beyond the writing course may also factor into decisions about comprehensive or selective correction. Professors in other disciplines, employers, and graduate school admissions committees may indeed care about perfect or near-perfect written texts and may negatively judge the writer for mistakes they observe. At some point, most students must learn to edit their own texts comprehensively, not simply for a few selected patterns of error (a point also made by Hartshorn et al., 2010 in their discussion of "meaningful" correction). Such self-editing involves a combination of effective proofreading strategies, awareness of individual areas of weakness, and ability to consult and use outside resources (online grammar references or dictionaries, word processor spelling and grammar checks, etc.). Selective written CF may help students to develop some of those comprehensive strategies, but not all of them.

Thus, with the larger purposes of developing students' writing strategies in mind, there may be benefits to both selective and comprehensive written CF in a writing course. A teacher may not have to choose between them, but perhaps could combine both types of correction in a syllabus. For instance, on a preliminary draft of a paper, the teacher could provide selective written CF on several prominent error patterns (see Appendix 7.1, Example A), asking the students to do what they can to address those issues on the next draft. On the penultimate or final draft, the teacher could lead students through a focused and detailed comprehensive self-editing exercise so that the finished version is as error-free as possible (Appendix 7.1, Example B). This could even be followed by comprehensive teacher-written CF for any remaining errors; students could then be asked to study the errors marked, to make corrections, and to write a brief analysis of what they learned about their own errors that they can remember for their next paper (Appendix 7.1, Example C). This is just one example of how comprehensive and selective written CF could productively be combined in an assignment sequence or course syllabus.

Focus of Written CF

If a teacher chooses to mark patterns of student error selectively, the question then arises as to *which* errors should receive attention. A common distinction made in the literature on error correction is between *global* and *local* errors (Bates et al., 1993; Corder, 1967; Hendrickson, 1978, 1980), "the former being errors that interfere with communication and the latter being more minor errors that do not obscure the comprehensibility of the text" (Ferris, 2003, p. 51). Though Ferris (2002, 2003) cautioned that the distinction between global and local errors can be more problematic than the above definition might appear, in practice, it is

146 Practical Applications

fairly easy for an experienced teacher-reader to judge particular word- and sentence-level errors as being more serious than others.[4] Examples of global or serious errors include many lexical issues and various problems with sentence structure, such as confusing word order or missing words.

Other criteria for selecting errors to mark in a particular student paper might include the *frequency* of the error (relative to other errors observed, the ratio of correct/incorrect usages in obligatory contexts, and the length of the text) and whether or not the error is especially *stigmatizing*, meaning the type of error that might label the student as a less proficient writer in the minds of real-world readers. The instructor might also prefer to devote time and energy primarily to errors that are *treatable*, or "rule-governed structures" (Ferris, 2003, p. 51) so that the teacher could send the student to the course handbook or an online writing lab site to study the rules for solving the problem. Finally, the teacher might choose not to mark errors that could be self-edited with better proofreading strategies (Haswell, 1983) and/or that a computer-based spelling or grammar checker might catch for the students, reasoning that teacher energy is best spent on errors that the students cannot find or address without some more expert assistance.

Feedback on Errors Versus Style

One philosophical decision that teachers must make is whether they will primarily focus on actual errors or problems with style in their written CF. Though there are many possible definitions for the word *error*, here we simply mean lexical, morphological, or syntactic constructions that clearly deviate from the rules of standard written English—deviations about which most literate and proficient users of the language would agree. In contrast, issues of style may reflect instructor preferences or larger concerns of register (such as informal versus formal usage), but they would not, strictly speaking, violate rules of the language. Thus, in the following simple examples, the first sentence would be an example of an error and the second a possible stylistic variation:

---

1 *Yesterday I **go** to the supermarket and **buy** food for dinner.
2 ?There are certain types of errors **that** students need to pay attention **to.**

Within a given course or in responding to a particular writing task, the teacher needs to decide if he/she will put energy into correcting students' style or whether he/she will mark only errors for which there are clear rules (such as simple past tense forms as in the above example). Such decisions rest both on the student writer's needs and abilities and on the specifications of the task. As to task-based concerns, if a student is overusing passive voice or casual language on tasks where those stylistic options would be inappropriate (e.g., a legal document as to the former or a letter of application for the latter), the teacher might want to call those issues to the writer's attention through feedback. In contrast, in some scientific writing genres, use of the passive voice is more acceptable, if not expected. It would not be helpful to tell the students to "always avoid the passive voice"; while overuse of the passive voice may lead to less effective writing in some cases, a correctly formed passive construction is not actually an *error*. Here, too, instructors need to evaluate their own biases as they decide what to mark on student papers.[5]

When L2 writers have become extremely proficient at the word- and sentence-level, there may be fewer errors (using the narrower definition above) for the instructor to give feedback about. In such instances, if there are indeed stylistic issues to point out, it might be helpful if the teacher did so—such feedback might help the writer push his/her written language to the next level of development. To list only a few common examples, the teacher might point out problems with lexical imprecision, with ineffective shifts in voice (e.g., to the second person, addressing the reader directly), with wordy sentences, with combining short, choppy sentences, and with more varied ways of achieving lexical cohesion through reference, repetition, or synonymy. The teacher may also wish to help students experiment with using more academic-sounding, sophisticated words and phrases in texts where they would be appropriate (Byrd & Bunting, 2008; Conrad, 2008; Coxhead & Byrd, 2007; Schuemann, 2008). These are all legitimate areas for written CF for student writers who are advanced in L2 acquisition and proficient in L2 writing. However, if students have serious and frequent errors that are more "basic" (such as the ones on the list in Appendix 4.1, column 3), the teacher might wish to address these problems first before attempting to improve student writers' style.

In addition to the above decision-making criteria, which are all rooted in the texts of individual student writers, the teacher may also choose to use feedback to reinforce lessons that have been taught in class. For instance, if there has been a recent mini-lesson on comma problems, the teacher may wish to refer directly to that class material the next time student papers are marked for errors. Instructors may wish to refer to lists of common student writing errors (see the lists in Appendix 4.1) as well as to their own analyses of student error patterns in a given class to make these initial decisions about what topics to cover in class and to prioritize in paper-marking. In short, the teacher has some decisions to make in approaching sets of class papers or individual student texts about what criteria to use in marking student errors selectively.

Form(s) of Written CF

Once an instructor has thought through the issue of how much written CF to give, the timing of feedback, and the amount and types of feedback to provide,

148 Practical Applications

the next question to consider is the "how" of written CF, and here the teacher has a wide range of options.

Direct Correction

Though the terms "direct" and "indirect" feedback have not always been used consistently in the literature (contrast Hendrickson, 1980 and Ferris, 2002), we define *direct correction* here as *a correction that not only calls attention to the error but also provides a specific solution to the problem.* Hendrickson (1980) suggested that this type of written CF might more properly be called "editing" (such as what a copy-editor or a proofreader might do) and observed that direct correction, if it is the sole form of written CF, may be frustrating to teachers and demoralizing to students:

> One thing is certain: providing all the correct forms in students' imperfect sentences is a time-consuming ordeal that can also be frustrating to teachers, especially when they see that identical types of errors appear repeatedly on compositions written over a period of time by the same student. Certainly, from the learner's perspective, it is disconcerting to receive a "corrected" composition with many words crossed out, new words added, and an array of marginal comments-all usually written in blood-red ink. Small wonder, indeed, that some students are embarrassed and lose confidence when they receive their written work corrected in this way.
>
> *(pp. 216–217)*

As discussed in Chapter 6, direct correction may take a variety of forms. In a writing course, the most major categories of direct corrections are cross-outs or rewrites of, or additions to, the student's original text. An example is shown in Figure 7.2; this is a short excerpt from an L2 writer's text that has been corrected using all three approaches just mentioned.

---

has   *at least*   *lives*
Everyone ~~have~~ been a liar^ once in their ~~life~~. People who lie intentionally to

harm others are bad people ^',and their lies are harmful too. However, there are lies
told
that are ~~done~~ with good intentions. So, there are times that lies are appropriate.
                                                        The only person who can
A lie is either a good or bad one based upon the liar's intention. ~~Only one person~~
~~can~~ really tell whether a lie is intended to harm or do good is the one who told
the lie.

FIGURE 7.2 Sample student text excerpt with direct corrections

Source: Complete student text originally published in Ferris (2008a).

Written CF for L2 Student Writers **149**

A careful examination of this brief text excerpt shows that the direct corrections covered a range of issues and took several different forms. This is a fairly typical example of what a comprehensively corrected text with direct feedback might look like. Hendrickson's (1980) concerns about the burdens of direct correction on writing instructors and its potentially negative affective impact on students seem legitimate. Even in the short text excerpt in Figure 7.2, quite a bit of text was marked, deleted, or added, and given how unsystematic both the error types and correction approaches are, it is difficult to see how such feedback would teach the student very much, even if he/she rewrote the text according to the suggested corrections. Hendrickson therefore advocated a "discovery" approach that involves selective correction and requires student involvement to figure out problems and suggest solutions.

However, even Hendrickson (1980) admitted that many writing instructors may, in practice, combine direct and indirect correction, depending on the nature of the error and the goals of the writing task. He also observed that some L2 students are not proficient enough to correct their own errors, even when the teacher locates them first, a point also raised by Brown (2007) and Ferris (2002). Ferris (2002) also suggested that direct correction may be appropriate for some error types (e.g., idiomatic lexical issues such as prepositions) and at some stages of the writing process (e.g., after a paper has been finalized and graded, to call students' attention to remaining errors for future reference).

Considering the larger principle discussed earlier in this chapter—that the primary purpose of written CF in the writing class is to help students learn self-editing strategies to help them in future writing tasks—it would seem that, in most instances, either indirect feedback (discussed further below) or a judicious combination of direct and indirect correction, as described above, might best meet student writers' needs. It is unlikely that a marking approach that relies entirely on direct correction would ultimately serve the larger goals of a writing course. However, in learning contexts where the focus is primarily language acquisition rather than writing skills development, selective and well-focused direct feedback may be the most effective way to help learners master specific, targeted structures over a short period of time (Bitchener, 2008; Bitchener & Knoch, 2008, 2010a, 2010b; Ellis et al., 2008; Sheen, 2007; see also Chapters 3 and 6).

Indirect Correction

While, through direct feedback, teachers provide the "correct" form to the student writer using the range of possibilities illustrated above and also discussed in Chapter 6, indirect feedback was defined by Ferris (2002) as "indicating an error through circling, underlining, highlighting, or otherwise marking it at its location in a text, with or without a verbal rule reminder or an error code, and *asking students to make corrections themselves*" (p. 63, emphasis added). Figure 7.3 shows the same text excerpt as in Figure 7.2, indirectly marked with simple underlining of

150 Practical Applications

> Everyone <u>have</u> been a liar once in their life. People who lie intentionally to harm others are bad <u>people and</u> their lies are harmful too. However, there are lies that are <u>done</u> with good <u>intention</u>. So, there are times that lies are appropriate. A lie is either a good or bad one <u>base</u> upon the liar's intention. Only one person can really tell whether a lie is intended to harm or do good.

FIGURE 7.3 Student text excerpt with indirect (underlining) correction

Source: Complete student text originally published in Ferris (2008a).

errors. Appendix 7.2 shows additional indirect correction approaches with the same excerpt.

A careful comparison of the two marking approaches illustrated in Figures 7.2 and 7.3 would quickly demonstrate that fewer errors were marked using the indirect system. Specifically, the addition of "at least" in the first sentence and the more complete rewrite of the final sentence in Figure 7.2 are absent in the indirectly marked example in Figure 7.3. It is easy to see why: in both instances, the original sentences were grammatically correct, so there was no erroneous text portion to underline. While the teacher could potentially have underscored parts of the sentence where additional text could be inserted, this feedback would not have been very clear, nor self-explanatory to the student writer. The rewrites/ additions in Figure 7.2 addressed clarity of content rather than grammatical "errors." These two simple examples demonstrate ways in which direct and indirect correction can be both quantitatively and qualitatively different, even when the text portion under consideration is identical. Again, the teacher needs to return to the initial consideration of the goals of written CF for a writing course to decide which approach is preferable in a specific instance.

Explicitness of Indirect Feedback. One issue that has been considered in a variety of studies on written CF is the amount of explanation that should accompany feedback, especially when it is indirect[6] (e.g., Ferris, 2006; Ferris & Roberts, 2001; Lalande, 1982; Robb et al., 1986). To evaluate the issue of how explicit corrective feedback should be, teachers should consider several different questions. First, *what are the goals of their written CF efforts?* If the point is to spur students on toward better proofreading and self-editing skills, perhaps simple underlining or highlighting of errors or the even less explicit approaches of Haswell's (1983) "minimal marking system" (students receive only checkmarks in the margins of lines where errors have been observed) or the end comment plus illustrative line-edits (Bean, 1996; see Appendix 7.1, Example A) will serve to meet that objective. This approach may be most appropriate for relatively advanced L2 writers who are proficient enough to self-edit substantial portions of their own texts with limited assistance.

Second, *how comfortable is the teacher with identifying error patterns in student writing and/or providing meta-linguistic explanations about them?* While trained language instructors most likely have some background in linguistics and grammar, composition instructors come from a wide range of academic backgrounds; in some settings, they may be teaching substantial percentages of L2 writers but with little or no preparation in language teaching (Ferris, 2009; Ferris et al., 2011). As we discuss in Chapter 8, the issue of teacher preparation for writing instructors delivering written CF is a challenging and important one; here, we simply note that some writing teachers may not themselves have the knowledge base to provide linguistically explicit written CF to their student writers. However, they can probably reliably recognize, in most instances, where student texts "look/sound wrong" and provide minimally explicit correction that at least gives students some input for their own further editing and analysis. It is probably better to do so than either to mismark student texts with the wrong error codes, rule reminders, or explanations, or to avoid marking errors in student texts at all.

Finally, *how explicit do students want the written CF to be*? In every study where students have been given the opportunity to express a preference, they have clearly chosen the more explicit option (e.g., "Tell me where the error is and what kind of error it is"). Students, especially L2 writers, tend to believe that they cannot possibly correct their own errors without that specific information. Teachers should take these student preferences into account along with their own answers to the previous two questions. For instance, if the teacher does not plan to tie explicit feedback into other types of instructional support (e.g., in-class mini-lessons or one-to-one error conferences), then perhaps the minimally explicit approaches might suffice. Further, if the teacher does not feel qualified to accurately and clearly provide specific linguistic information about written errors, he/she should probably not try to do so even if the students say they want it. Teachers might also experiment with providing more or less explicit information in their marking at different points in the term and with varying feedback to different students depending on those students' needs, abilities, and preferences. In short, there is no hard-and-fast rule about the level of explicitness of written CF for all writing teachers in all contexts. Rather, the teacher should evaluate the options given his/her responses to the three questions about written CF goals, teacher knowledge, and student desires.

"Mechanical" Issues in the Form of Written CF. In addition to the various options that have already been discussed and illustrated (Figures 7.2 and 7.3, Appendices 7.1 and 7.2), teachers might also consider the tools they could use to provide written CF. Studies have suggested that students dislike and are frustrated by illegible comments and confusing symbols (Ferris, 1995b; Hedgcock & Lefkowitz, 1994, 1996; Straub, 1997), which are not only unhelpful but have an unpleasant visual impact on the students when they approach their texts to revise or analyze their errors. Thus, it is important to consider whether the mechanical choices made help or hinder teachers in meeting the goals of their written CF.

Most of the issues and advice here should be obvious to a sensitive writing instructor. Massive cross-outs, circles, arrows, scrawled words and phrases, and

152 Practical Applications

so forth, while "efficient" for the teacher, may be confusing and off-putting to the receiver of the feedback. Teachers should ensure that any corrections made are legible and clear and that any codes or other shorthand are used consistently and clearly explained to the students. Teachers should also consider using technology, especially word processing tools, as a means to provide clearer and more legible feedback. For instance, portions of a sentence can be selected and tied to a verbal suggestion or error code in the margin, using the "comments" or "track changes" features (in Microsoft Word; other word processing programs have similar tools) (see Appendix 7.1, Example A). Teachers can also change font colors or use electronic highlighting options for various types of indirect corrections, and, if they insert their own suggestions into the text itself, can change the font and/or the color of their correction so that it stands out (see Figure 7.2 as an example; the font was changed to "Lucida Handwriting" to make the corrections more easily visible). While some teachers complain that using word processing tools for corrections is cumbersome, most instructors who persist find that they become quicker at it with practice, and the benefits of doing so may far outweigh any short-term annoyance. Again, the most important issue is not which tools are used but a commitment on the part of the teacher to providing corrections that are legible, clear, and not overwhelming to the students.

Two other mechanical options are worth mentioning here for teachers' consideration. It has been suggested by some researchers (e.g., Ellis et al., 2008) that teachers could more efficiently provide meta-linguistic explanations on student texts by creating macros for common errors that could be inserted into student texts with a single keystroke.[7] Assuming that a teacher has both the meta-linguistic knowledge and vocabulary and the technical proficiency to create and use such macros, the instructor should also consider whether (a) most of their students' errors are systematic and patterned enough to benefit from a preprogrammed explanation or rule reminder; and (b) their students would actually have the patience, motivation, and technical and linguistic skills to benefit from these automated corrections. These comments are not to say that creation of course-specific macros for correction might not be a useful tool if a teacher has the inclination and expertise to do so, but rather to point out that such an option might not be practical for everyone.

A technologically simpler but intriguing option was shared by Dan Brown at a recent TESOL (Teachers of English to Speakers of Other Languages) convention (Brown, 2010; Brown, personal communication). Brown selected a limited number of error categories that reflect the needs of a particular group of student writers and used highlighters to color code the error patterns when marking student papers—blue for subject-verb agreement, yellow for verb tense, orange for articles, and so forth. Brown has done some preliminary research on the effects of this approach, and he noted that students reported heightened awareness of their own predominant error patterns, which, in turn, led to motivation for improved self-monitoring. As one student noted, "after the first, second, third draft—when I saw it for a third time, *my weak points became clear to me and I remembered what they were.*" Another student added, "Before this, we were looking at the number of mistakes, 'Oh, I made 10 or 15 mistakes'—it was just a sense. But now, 'Ah! This is my weak point,' *so I would be cautious with this grammar point*" (Brown, 2010, emphases added). Brown's method is, in a sense, a hybrid between less explicit indirect feedback (underlining or highlighting errors in the text) and more explicit corrections (using colors instead of verbal/symbolic codes), with some students reporting that seeing the colors is different from (and more beneficial than) seeing the same errors coded or marked in all one color of pen or highlighter. While Brown used actual physical highlighters on student hard copies (limiting the number of error categories according to the range of highlighter colors he had available), it is worth noting that word processor highlighting offers more choices (15 shades of highlighter in Microsoft Word and dozens of options if the teacher wants to change the font color of the text rather than highlighting). In any case, it would be interesting to learn more about the effects of this technique from research.

Forms of Written CF: Summary

We close this lengthy section on the various forms of and options for written CF—direct and indirect feedback; more explicit and less explicit correction, the various mechanical issues and enhancements to consider—by observing that there are many different variables that impact teachers' choices about the forms of written CF. As veteran teachers ourselves, we can attest that our own methods have evolved and changed over time and that they continue to change depending upon the goals of the interaction and the knowledge and attitudes of the student audience(s) receiving our feedback. While the possibilities and the most effective CF methods may be more straightforward in an SLA context (see Chapter 6), in a writing/composition setting, there are many interacting issues to consider, from the larger goals of writing instruction to the diverse preparation of different writing instructors. It is not our intent in this section to argue for one "best way" to provide written CF in a writing course but rather to explain the range of possibilities and the various heuristic questions teachers might ask themselves to select from among those choices.

Source(s) of Written CF

While it is tempting to think that the "who" of written CF is obvious—the teacher—this is not always the case, nor should it be. Rather, a student writer has a range of options for receiving written CF: the instructor, classmates, a tutor or outside "peer expert," self-evaluation, and automated or electronic feedback. In this section, we briefly outline the possibilities with a few comments about benefits and drawbacks of each feedback source.

154 Practical Applications

The Instructor

In most of the earlier sections of this chapter, we have talked primarily about the "teacher" or the "instructor" as the primary, if not the only, source of written CF for the student. Indeed, in most settings, if the instructor has decided that written CF is valuable and necessary for at least some of the students, that teacher should be involved in providing at least some of the feedback; it is probably not appropriate to completely "outsource" written CF to peers, tutors, or student self-editing activities. At minimum, the teacher should start off the writing course with some kind of diagnostic analysis of student needs as observed in early pieces of writing and should convey to and model for the students what issues they should work on and how feedback might best be provided.

In-person Error Conferences. Besides the various options for written CF that have been discussed earlier in this chapter, the teacher might also consider adding in-person error conferences to the feedback repertoire, at least for some student writers. There are some written errors that are so complex and idiosyncratic that (a) the teacher may not know exactly what the problem is and/or what the student writer was trying to convey; or (b) a brief written correction may not suffice to help the student either self-edit the current text nor learn to avoid such errors in the future. In such instances, perhaps an in-person consultation is most appropriate. Error conferences can also be useful to help explain any confusion that students might have with written feedback and to help the teacher understand gaps in the students' linguistic knowledge or observe ineffective editing strategies—and these more precise observations can then inform the teacher's future in-class instruction and written CF approaches. Appendix 7.3 provides suggested procedures (from Ferris & Hedgcock, 2005) for two different types of error conference.

Classmates

Though peer review workshops have become a staple of modern composition instruction in both L1 and L2 composition courses, instructors and students continue to feel a fair amount of ambivalence about them (see Ferris, 2003, Chapter 5; Jacobs et al., 1998; Leki, 1990b; Zhang, 1995, 1999). While some can acknowledge the benefits of peer review for issues of content and organization, most observers have the greatest concerns about peer review at the editing/form-focused stage of the writing process, especially for L2 writers, who may not have either the formal knowledge or the acquired intuitions to spot classmates' errors, let alone provide accurate and clear feedback about them. As already noted at various points in this volume, L2 student writers have strong beliefs about their need for expert corrective feedback, and if the job is turned over to their peers in the classroom, they may feel anxious about not receiving adequate or accurate input.

Nonetheless, we see a possible role for peer editing workshops, even in the L2 writing classroom. Such classroom activities, if carefully designed and implemented, can have at least three distinct purposes and benefits. First, applying careful reading and proofreading skills to someone else's text can help students develop the critical analysis and reading strategies they need to later examine their own writing. As Ferris has noted elsewhere, "It seems to be true that it is easier to find errors in others' work than in one's own" (1995c, p. 19)—that is why publishers and businesses employ copy-editors and proofreaders. Second, peer review activities can be utilized to help students apply and practice specific self-editing strategies they have been taught, such as how to make focused passes through a text to look for a particular error pattern. Third, peer-editing workshops can be an appropriate follow-up to in-class grammar instruction: students can be asked to look through a partner's paper for any problems or successes with marking verb tense, making subjects and verbs agree, adding articles or noun plurals where needed, and so forth. In short, narrowly focused peer review activities can provide practice and build student confidence in self-editing skills.

The keys to realizing these possible benefits and avoiding the pitfalls of peer editing activities lie in the structure and focus of the activities, and we have several suggestions along these lines. First, early in the course, peer editing workshops should be clearly and narrowly focused and ideally should follow focused in-class instruction as application or practice activities. Second, peer editors should be carefully instructed not to make any corrections themselves but simply to review their classmate's text and note (with an underline or a question mark) any place where the author should double-check for a possible problem. Third, there should be opportunities in the classroom for the partners to consult with each other about any errors marked (to respond to questions or to brainstorm possible solutions) and to ask the teacher any questions that might arise during the activity. Finally, before doing any peer editing of texts written by students in the class, the teacher may want to model the activity first with a sample student paper written in a previous course or obtained from another teacher and to discuss the goals, limits, and possible problems with the class before the students begin working with each other's texts. Figure 7.4 shows one example of such a peer editing exercise, designed to follow a mini-lesson on the three most frequent comma errors in college student writing. The specific terms in the activity ("introductory element," "FANBOYS," the three "Comma Rules") would have been defined and illustrated during the instructional phase.

Tutors and Other Peer "Experts"

Writing instructors may sometimes feel overwhelmed by the task of responding to student errors. In some cases, they teach a number of classes and may have dozens or even hundreds of students to consider. In others, as already discussed, they may not feel competent and equipped to deal with language errors in student

156 Practical Applications

For this activity, use a paper you are working on or wrote recently. Exchange papers with a partner. Look at your partner's paper to see if he/she has used the "Big 3" comma rules correctly:

1. Look through the paper for **introductory elements**. When you find them, check to see that there is a comma between that element and the rest of the sentence (Comma Rule 1). If you see a missing comma, underline the introductory element and put a check mark in the margin.
2. Look through the paper again for uses of **FANBOY words** to join two halves of the sentence. As you did on the exercise, decide whether the sentence should follow Comma Rule 2 or Comma Rule 3. If you find any missing commas (Comma Rule 2) or unnecessary commas (Comma Rule 3), circle the FANBOY word and write CR 2 or CR 3 in the margin. When you are done with this step, return the paper to the writer.
3. When you get your own paper back, look through it at any corrections suggested by your partner. Examine them and see if you agree or disagree with the suggestions, and discuss any questions or disagreements with your partner. Consult your teacher if you have any unresolved questions. (If you have no corrections or few corrections, you might go through the previous steps yourself on your own paper to see if your partner might have missed something.)

FIGURE 7.4 Peer editing workshop activity (following a mini-lesson on frequent comma errors)

writing; this may especially be true for composition instructors who work with L2 writers but without specialized training in language pedagogy. As a result, teachers may refer their students elsewhere for additional outside help. Many colleges and universities have campus writing centers staffed by trained peer tutors where student writers can go for extra individual help. Some writing programs may even provide their own in-house support (small group workshops, individual or group tutorials) for students in their courses who may be struggling or potentially at risk (e.g., L2 writers in a mainstream composition program). In some situations, students may need to find and pay their own private tutors to obtain the assistance they need.

While sending students elsewhere for extra help can be a very valuable strategy, the classroom instructor needs to take primary responsibility for ensuring that his/her students receive appropriate outside assistance. First, instructors can familiarize themselves with the resources available and should critically evaluate them: Who are the tutors? What kinds of training and supervision do they receive? What is the philosophy of the tutoring program toward working with sentence-level issues in student writing?[8] Second, the teacher should prepare the student to work effectively with a tutor by examining the student's writing and identifying several specific issues for the student to discuss with the tutor. Third, teachers should maintain communication, where possible, with their students' tutors (e.g., providing copies of assignments, feedback rubrics, and error code keys so that the tutor can understand the larger classroom context). Finally, the teacher should evaluate with the student how effective the outside assistance has (or has not) been so that the teacher can provide any needed follow-up and can assess for the future whether to refer more students to this tutoring resource. In sum, extra assistance received outside the writing class should ideally complement but not replace the teacher's input in assessing and addressing individual students' needs with regard to written CF.

Self

This last point leads us to another observation about the source of written CF, which is that writers themselves must develop an increasingly keen ability to evaluate and edit their own work. While this may seem a self-evident statement, L2 writers in particular, lacking confidence in their own language abilities, can become very dependent on others to correct or edit their work. Students benefit from receiving tools and opportunities to self-edit their texts.

Tools for Self-editing. Teachers can provide three general types of tools for their students to develop better self-editing skills. The first, as we have been discussing, is *feedback* itself. Carefully constructed written CF can help students to edit their work in ways that not only impact the text under immediate consideration but which build skills and awareness for subsequent writing tasks. The second tool is *strategy training*, discussed further in the next section: there are specific techniques writers can use to edit their work more effectively, and teachers can help their students tremendously by presenting those techniques and giving students opportunities to practice and apply them. The third tool is *knowledge*, or, specifically, focused instruction on specific points of grammar, usage, and language. If students have access to clearly taught, formally learned rules, they can use them to edit their work. Part of this knowledge base might also include *awareness of additional sources* (handbooks, websites, other course materials) to consult for more information about the particular language point(s).

Opportunities for Self-editing. Teachers provide self-editing opportunities through the ways they construct their writing course and assignments. For example, if students are required to work through a multi-draft process during which they write, receive feedback, revise, and edit their work, they will have opportunities to self-edit before the paper is finalized. If they are allowed to further revise their texts after receiving feedback or a grade and/or to further polish a text for a final portfolio, this course structure provides self-editing opportunities. The keys here are time, structure, and the shared value that the purpose of a writing course is to develop long-term, transferable writing skills, not to produce perfect texts in one try without any help.

158 Practical Applications

Teachers also provide space for self-editing by developing in-class workshops and at-home assignments to guide students through the process of editing their almost-final texts. The last part of the activity in Figure 7.4 shows this type of self-editing activity (which, in this case, immediately follows a peer editing workshop), and Example B in Appendix 7.1 shows an at-home editing assignment for a longer research paper in its final stages of development.

Electronic Text Editors

One rarely discussed yet ubiquitous source of written CF for student writers is electronic tools, which may be part of the word processing packages on students' computers or available online (i.e., web-based editing services where students can submit a paper and get an electronically analyzed and corrected version, usually for a price). We focus here on text analysis tools readily available on commercial word processors or Internet search engines.

Spell-checker. Students should be encouraged to use a spell-checker to catch and fix typos or words that are difficult to spell. However, especially for L2 writers whose vocabulary is often more limited than that of their L1 peers, teachers might consider reminding them of two limitations to the spell-checkers. First, in many instances, the spell-checker will offer a range of alternatives. Students need to scrutinize those options carefully and ensure that the one they select is indeed the word they meant semantically and that the word form fits into the existing sentence syntactically.[9] Some students, whether because they are in a hurry or because they lack overall L2 proficiency and trust the computer more than their own judgment, will simply choose the first spell-checker alternative on the list— and that may be a sound-alike word rather than a word that fits. Second, students need to be reminded that the spell-checker will not flag "wrong" words that are in the text due to typing or homonym errors (there/their, to/too, etc.). In some contexts, it could be worth doing an in-class mini-lesson to point out the possible problems of over-relying on a spell-checker and to teach students to use it more effectively. The same holds true for other word processing features such as the dictionary or the thesaurus.

Grammar Checkers. Grammar checkers can be even more misleading for student writers, especially L2 writers, as they are typically not programmed for the types of errors that L2 learners are more likely to make. Students, therefore, might neglect to edit their papers for problematic error patterns because a grammar checker did not mark anything, or, as with the spell-checker, they may uncritically accept confusing or inaccurate advice. Again, for some student writers, this topic might justify an in-class mini-lesson. There are examples of mini-lessons on understanding the problems with and potential of spelling and grammar checkers in Ferris and Hedgcock (2005).

Other Text Analyzers. We do not mean to be entirely negative here. Used thoughtfully, word processors' text analysis features can be useful for student

Written CF for L2 Student Writers **159**

writers. For instance, "statistics" features can let students know if they have very long or very short sentences. If students know they have particular error patterns, they may benefit from setting the "find" function for specific forms such as commas, articles, coordinating conjunctions, and so forth, allowing them to quickly analyze those structures in context and to look for errors. Beyond the word processor, Google searches on specific words or phrases can help students to address idiosyncratic lexical errors that can plague L2 writers.

The key to effective use of all of these electronic tools is *informed, thoughtful use*, rather than automatic acceptance—writers need to utilize them in conjunction with—not instead of—their own self-editing skills. Teachers can be certain, however, that today's student writers in many settings are indeed using computer-based tools as a "source" of written CF, so they need to help students use them as appropriately and effectively as possible. To sum up this whole section, writing instructors, as they consider the pedagogical implications of our discussions of written CF, should bear in mind that there are many possible sources of feedback and that any of them can be either misused or under-utilized—so teachers need to give careful consideration as to how they can integrate these sources of information most effectively so that students can benefit from their potential to facilitate long-term development in written accuracy.

Support Beyond Written CF

At many points in this chapter thus far, we have mentioned strategy training and in-class instruction as possible supplements to written CF. "Treatment of error" (Ferris, 2002; Hendrickson, 1980) should go beyond teacher-provided feedback. It should be supplemented by intentional instruction that helps students learn to understand the issues and to avoid making the same errors in the future. This instruction can take at least two distinct yet related forms: building self-editing skills (strategy training) and building linguistic knowledge (grammar instruction).

Strategy Training. As we have already noted, research demonstrates that students, even L2 writers, are capable of editing a substantial portion of their own errors with limited or no assistance when they are given guidance and motivation for doing so. A number of self-editing strategies that can productively be taught to and practiced with student writers have been presented elsewhere in our work (e.g., Ferris, 1995c, 2002, 2003, 2008b; Ferris & Hedgcock, 2005), so we briefly summarize them here and add a couple of ideas to the previous lists (Figure 7.5).

The strategies below are straightforward enough, but writing instructors might want to go beyond simply presenting these in a list and asking students to consider them. For instance, rather than just urging students to read their texts aloud as an editing strategy, teachers could give a homework assignment in which students take a current paper draft, read it aloud, mark on the paper errors they found and corrected, and write a brief analysis of what they learned from the exercise

160 Practical Applications

---

1. **Allowing adequate time:** Leave time in the process to put the text away and come back to it with fresh eyes.
2. **Breaking up the task:** It can be hard to maintain focus and attention when editing a longer text. It may be best to break the text into chunks, edit a chunk carefully and take a break before editing the next chunk.
3. **Reading the text aloud:** Reading aloud can help writers notice when a word or word part is missing or unnecessary, when a word doesn't sound or look right, and when sentences are long or choppy or repetitive. Some writers find it helpful to read the text "backwards," meaning to start with the last sentence, then read the next-to-last sentence, and so forth.
4. **Focused editing on specific error patterns:** Some L2 writers make systematic errors, say with verb tense or form, noun plurals, articles, etc. It can be helpful to read through a text focusing only on one issue at a time, for instance identifying all the verbs and analyzing which ones need tense markings.
5. **Studying rules:** While not all errors of grammar or usage have systematic rules behind them, some do, and writers can study those in a handbook or website to understand the terms, the rules, and their exceptions. This knowledge can help writers to make good decisions when editing their own work.
6. **Using electronic tools effectively:** Word processor or online text-editing tools can be a writer's friend or enemy depending on how they are used.
7. **Another pair of eyes:** Asking a trusted friend or classmate to read over a paper might help writers identify issues that are hard to find in their own writing. However, this person should not replace a writer as the primary editor of his/her work.

FIGURE 7.5 Self-editing strategies for student writers

Source: See also Ferris (2002, 2008b); Ferris and Hedgcock (2005)

(see Appendix 7.1, Example B). Similarly, students could be asked to run a text through the spelling and grammar checker and to write an analysis of what the checkers marked, the suggestions given, and how helpful and accurate the student thought the advice was. The point here is that strategy training should go further than simply naming the strategy and hoping students will apply it: teachers should model it and even consider requiring students to practice it so that they can experience the strategy's usefulness.

Grammar Instruction. The topic of grammar instruction in a writing course is a controversial one (Hartwell, 1985; MacDonald, 2007). Composition instructors, out of concern for accuracy issues in student writing, may inappropriately privilege grammar teaching in the classroom, taking focus away from other important course goals. They may also focus on fairly obscure and minor issues that rarely impact the quality of student writing. Finally, many students find grammar lessons boring and de-motivating, and as already noted, some writing instructors may not be especially well equipped to provide them.

With these concerns in mind, we simply note that the occasional well-placed mini-lesson on issues that are problematic for many/most of the students in a writing class can be useful when it follows these guidelines:

- It is brief.
- It is narrowly focused.
- Explanations and examples are clear and accurate.
- It is relevant to the problems of student writers in *that particular class*.
- It includes specific practice opportunities that involve *direct application to the students' own writing*.

Sample mini-lessons designed for L2 writers can be found in Ferris (2002) and Ferris and Hedgcock (2005) as well as in student grammar/editing textbooks such as Lane and Lange (1999). In Chapter 8, we offer suggestions for preparing teachers to analyze their students' needs to identify possible topics for mini-lessons and to develop their own mini-lessons.

As noted by Hartshorn et al. (2010), it can be easy in a busy composition syllabus for accuracy issues to be pushed aside and addressed haphazardly, if at all. A teacher concerned with developing student writers' linguistic expression should design a plan for written CF, strategy training, and language instruction that can be integrated within a larger course syllabus. Ideally, written CF would reinforce language instruction, and strategy training would ensure that students analyze and apply what they have learned from feedback and from instruction. However, it is unlikely that such synergy will occur naturally without thoughtful planning by the instructor.

Follow-up to Written CF

L2 writing teachers and their students share a problem: deep down, many of them believe that the student writers are simply not capable of producing well-edited, linguistically effective work. Thus, teachers often do not require students to produce such high-quality work, and students understandably do not put forth the effort required to do so. This is why teachers, having provided the tools, the time, and the opportunity for students to become independent self-editors, must take the final step of holding students accountable for the accuracy of their final products.

Instructors can do this in at least two distinct ways. First, they can construct evaluation or assessment mechanisms (grading rubrics or scoring guides) through which students are held accountable for the quality of their writing, including the accuracy and effectiveness of their language, and they can apply these mechanisms consistently. Teachers should be sure to introduce the grading criteria early and often to their students, perhaps holding a norming workshop

162 Practical Applications

in which students use the scoring guide to rate sample student essays from another class. The grading standards can also be reinforced during peer- and self-editing workshops in class. While, in a composition class, such grading criteria will cover a broad range of issues such as content, organization, and so forth, it should be clearly pointed out to students that accuracy matters, too, and that their writing will indeed be judged against grading criteria that include language issues.

Teachers can also design assignments that ask students to analyze their own errors, make revisions, and track their progress. Example C in Appendix 7.1 shows one such assignment. In Haswell's (1983) "minimal marking" approach, students receive checkmarks in the margins of lines in which there are errors, the number of checkmarks is recorded in the gradebook, and students are given time in class to try to find and correct the errors; their success in doing so impacts their grade. There is a variety of approaches for making students more responsible for editing their own errors (at least the ones they are linguistically capable of fixing), but the core element is that writers must purposefully grapple with written CF they have received and try to learn from it.[10] This is all to say that students can, indeed, become fairly accomplished editors of their own work, but only if the teacher carefully provides the conditions—tools, opportunity, responsibility—for their success.

Summary

Using the outline provided in Figure 7.1, we have explored a number of specific heuristic questions that writing instructors should consider in designing and implementing written CF processes (including the larger "treatment of error" suggestions) to provide maximum long-term benefits for their students' writing development. In discussing those questions, we have provided a range of practical suggestions. For ease of reference, we repeat here the chart in Figure 7.1 but with another column added to summarize the ideas we have shared in this chapter. This expanded chart is shown as Figure 7.6.

Concluding Remarks

Readers of this chapter may find the number of issues and suggestions presented somewhat overwhelming. If so, here is another perspective: most teachers of L2 writers will spend many, many hours during the writing course in providing written CF to their students. The question is whether that time and energy is well spent. Thoughtful consideration of the questions raised here and careful decision-making will not only help student writers but may reduce teachers' frustrations with the marking/grading process and increase their sense of satisfaction. Those are not small benefits.

Written CF for L2 Student Writers **163**

Subtopic	Related question(s)	Answers/suggestions
Purpose and goals	*Why* give written CF in a writing course?	To help students develop transferable skills and strategies for future writing tasks
Timing and frequency	*When*—at what stage of the writing process and on what types of texts—should written CF be provided?	In most instances, written CF has maximum benefit on texts that students can revise further. Teachers may wish to add short, frequent writing tasks for more intensive written CF opportunities
Amount	*How much* written CF should a teacher provide on a particular text?	There are arguments for both comprehensive and selective correction depending on the goals of the task and the stage in the writing process
Focus	*On what types* of errors or language issues should written CF focus?	Teachers may wish to focus written CF on errors before style and on issues that are serious, frequent, stigmatizing, treatable, and not easily addressed through self-editing
Form	*How* should written CF be given? Should it be direct or indirect? Explicit or implicit? How much explanation is useful/possible?	In writing classes, indirect feedback may better address the goals of the course and of written CF. The level of explicitness may vary depending upon several contextual factors
Source	*Who* should provide written CF? Should it always be the teacher? Can peers effectively provide CF? Can individuals gain autonomy in editing their own work?	A variety of interacting sources can usefully provide written CF to student writers, but teachers should help students to utilize them effectively
Support	*What else* can writing instructors do in addition to written CF to help students develop self-editing strategies? What is the role of classroom grammar instruction in the writing course?	Thoughtfully implemented strategy training and language instruction can supplement written CF and make it more useful to student writers
Follow-up	*What can students be asked to do* to analyze and apply written CF they have received?	Students should be responsible and accountable for editing their work and improving in accuracy over time. Teachers can use grading schemes and analysis activities to help students make progress and apply what they are learning

FIGURE 7.6 Summary of written CF questions and suggestions

164 Practical Applications

Appendix 7.1: Combining Selective and Comprehensive WCF at Various Stages of the Writing Process

Example A: This is an early draft of a student paper that will be revised and edited several times before it is finalized. The teacher has responded selectively to several repeated patterns of error.

How to Write a College Essay

When students first come to college writing papers is often one of the biggest challenges they will face. The step up from writing at a high school level acts as a difficult transition. In his satire, "how to write an "A" paper", Koji Frahm suggests that there are many common errors that College writers make. Frahm hints that if a writer eliminates these common errors there writing will improve significantly.

> Dana Ferris 20/5/10 10:31
> **Comment:** (1)

> Dana Ferris 20/5/10 10:31
> **Comment:** (3)

One of the first items that Frahm discusses is a papers organization. For a paper to read well each sentence has to flow seamlessly. The writer has to make an argument and then provide evidence to support his or her claims. Every essay should have a thesis and its paragraphs should support its thesis. In a well written essay the audience understands how each argument connects to the thesis. The writer often loses organization by making useless anecdotes and getting sidetracked. Stick to the point. Make your essay clear, concise, and organized.

> Dana Ferris 20/5/10 10:31
> **Comment:** (3)

> Dana Ferris 20/5/10 10:32
> **Comment:** (1)

Another mistake Frahm noted was that students try and make their essays sound fancy but end up making them confusing. Don't get caught up using the thesaurus and changing a perfectly good word to one that will only perplex the reader. A good essay is one that people understand. Using enormous confusing words destroys clarity and flow.

> Dana Ferris 20/5/10 10:32
> **Comment:** (2)

Frahm knows that everyone makes mistakes sometimes. However, a college paper is no place to make mistakes. Check your work! After you have written a paper, read it over. When I was in high-school I was always too lazy to check my work for errors, however in college this is unacceptable. Make sure that the first sentence of your paper doesn't have grammar errors. Even great papers can be ruined by grammar errors that are extremely easy to fix. Take your time writing your paper. If something doesn't sound right it's probably because it isn't. Rework sentences to improve the papers clarity and always check for grammar and spelling errors.

> Dana Ferris 20/5/10 10:32
> **Comment:** (2)

Many students find it difficult to write at the college level. Koji Frahm exposes many errors that are commonly made by college writers. Frahm Emphasizes that a college paper must be well organized, use proper grammar, and be clearly written.

Dear Student,

Before you finalize this essay, I would like you to go over it carefully and pay attention to several specific error patterns I noticed. I have marked two examples of each type in your text (labeled by number in the margins), but you will need to go through the whole paper carefully to find others.

Error Types (the numbers match the ones in the margins of your paper):

1. **Missing commas after introductory elements:** When you begin a sentence with an introductory phrase, you need a comma to set it off from the main body of the sentence.

2. **Addressing the reader directly instead of using the third person.** You were not asked in this assignment to "talk" directly to the reader. You will need to rewrite those sentences into the third person. For example, instead of saying "Don't...," you could say "A student should not..."

3. **Proofreading mistakes:** I saw errors in spelling, punctuation, and capitalization that more carefully rereading and/or using the computer spell-check might catch. Poor proofreading weakens the overall impact of your writing: Even if your ideas are good, small mistakes can distract the reader.

Please let me know if you have any questions or problems as you edit your paper. Good luck!

Best wishes,
Your Teacher

166 Practical Applications

Example B—Student Self-editing Exercise: This is one example of an exercise that students could be asked to do in class or for homework before completing the final version of a paper. In this particular example, students were completing a research paper that involved using APA format for in-text citations and references. Note that students not only were led through editing their papers but were asked to analyze and reflect upon their understanding.

1. Look carefully at your **use of APA format** for in-text citations and in your references. Make any changes you think are necessary. Write 1-2 sentences commenting on your analysis (e.g., "I reviewed the handouts on the Smart Site and made a number of changes," "Everything seemed fine to me already").

2. Now, carefully examine your paper for specific language/editing issues (at least one and no more than three) that you are aware of—either issues I have raised in my feedback on your previous papers and/or issues you know you struggle with. Make any changes that seem necessary. Again, write a 1-2 sentence analysis that specifies what you looked for, what you found, and what you changed.

3. Divide your paper into sections (whatever division seems reasonable to you). Read each section aloud. Take notes on any changes you make while reading aloud (notes can either be on a hard copy or on screen, as you prefer). Take at least a five-minute break between reading each section aloud. Write 1-2 sentences about what you learned from doing this and the types of things you changed, if any (e.g., "I found missing words"; "I found typos"; "I realized some of my sentences were too long and wordy"; "I realized my paper is already perfect"; etc.).

4. Finally, do you have any specific questions about either language or APA format that you want to raise in class or ask me individually? List them here. If not, say "None."

Example C: For this activity, the teacher had already returned a final, graded paper with remaining errors marked comprehensively. The students were asked to analyze their errors so that they could benefit from the feedback on their next paper.

This assignment is designed to make you take an active part in correcting your own common errors. In grading your papers, I line-edited only the first paragraph and then highlighted your erroneous sentences throughout the rest of the paper. It is now your job to correct those sentences, with the following limits:

If you have 10 highlighted sentences or fewer, correct them all.
If you have more than 10 highlighted sentences, correct 15 of them.

Copy and paste the sentences onto a separate document. Provide a correct version of each sentence below the original, incorrect one (so I can see what you've changed). Please also identify the error you made; you may do so in a few words or a short sentence.

When you have completed the exercise, please write a short paragraph explaining what you learned about the types of errors you made on this paper and how this understanding might help you with your next paper. What practical steps might you need to take to reduce your errors in your future writing?

Submit one document with your incorrect sentences, your corrections with identifications, and your one-paragraph analysis. Completing this assignment successfully may raise your paper grade by up to ten percent.[11]

168 Practical Applications

Appendix 7.2: Student Text Excerpt with Alternate Indirect Correction Strategies

Example 1: Error Codes

> AGR   PRO
> Everyone <u>have</u> been a liar once in <u>their</u> life. People who lie intentionally to
>   COM
> harm others are bad <u>people and</u> their lies are harmful too. However, there are lies
>   WC
> that are <u>done</u> with good intention. So, there are times that lies are appropriate. A lie
>   VF
> is either a good or bad one <u>base</u> upon the liar's intention. Only one person can really tell whether a lie is intended to harm or do good.
>
> **KEY to Error Codes:**
> AGR = Subject-verb Agreement
> PRO = Pronoun Reference
> COM = Comma
> WC = Word Choice
> VF = Verb Form

Example 2: Verbal Rule Reminders

> agreement   pronoun reference
> Everyone <u>have</u> been a liar once in <u>their</u> life. People who lie intentionally to
>   comma
> harm others are bad <u>people and</u> their lies are harmful too. However, there are lies
>   word choice
> that are <u>done</u> with good intention. So, there are times that lies are appropriate. A lie
>   verb form
> is either a good or bad one <u>base</u> upon the liar's intention. Only one person can really tell whether a lie is intended to harm or do good.

Written CF for L2 Student Writers **169**

Example 3: Meta-linguistic Explanation

Everyone have been a liar once in their life. People who lie intentionally to harm others are bad people and their lies are harmful too. However, there are lies that are done with good intention. So, there are times that lies are appropriate. A lie is either a good or bad one base upon the liar's intention. Only one person can really tell whether a lie is intended to harm or do good.

> **Dana Ferris 27/5/10 12:05**
> **Comment:** use singular form "has" to agree with the subject "Everyone"

> **Dana Ferris 27/5/10 12:05**
> **Comment:** Use a singular pronoun form (his/her) to agree with "Everyone"

> **Dana Ferris 27/5/10 12:06**
> **Comment:** Add a comma before a coordinating conjunction

> **Dana Ferris 27/5/10 12:06**
> **Comment:** We don't "do" lies; we "tell" lies; use "told" here

> **Dana Ferris 27/5/10 12:07**
> **Comment:** Use the participle form "based" here

Example 4: End Note

Everyone <u>have</u> been a liar once in <u>their</u> life. People who lie intentionally to harm others are bad <u>people and</u> their lies are harmful too. However, there are lies that are <u>done</u> with good intention. So, there are times that lies are appropriate. A lie is either a good or bad one base upon the liar's intention. Only one person can really tell whether a lie is intended to harm or do good.

Dear Student,

I enjoyed your interesting essay about good and bad lies. As you revise your paper, you should pay attention to several language issues:

- *Be sure to check the forms of your verbs and of your pronouns to see that they agree in number (singular/plural) with the subject noun they refer to.*
- *Be sure that your word choice is accurate. You might ask someone to read your paper to let you know if any words sound wrong or are confusing.*
- *Don't forget that you need a comma before a coordinating conjunction such as "and" that connects two sentences.*

I have underlined examples of problems in these areas in the first paragraph of your essay, but you should read the whole paper carefully because there are similar errors in other paragraphs. Be sure to let me know if you have any questions!

Good luck,
Teacher

170 Practical Applications

Example 5: Minimal Marking (Following Haswell, 1983)

✓✓Everyone have been a liar once in their life. People who lie intentionally to ✓harm others are bad people and their lies are harmful too. However, there ✓are lies that are done with good intention. So, there are times that lies are ✓appropriate. A lie is either a good or bad one base upon the liar's intention. Only one person can really tell whether a lie is intended to harm or do good.

Appendix 7.3: Suggested Procedures for Error Conferences

(Adapted from Ferris & Hedgcock, 2005, Fig. 7.12, p. 285.)

Preliminary (Unmarked) Drafts

1. Ask the student to read the paper aloud while you follow along on a separate copy. Instruct the student to stop and verbalize comments about any errors or corrections s/he notices. Note the errors caught by the student and suggested corrections on your copy of the paper.
2. Then go through the paper again, this time reading it aloud yourself. For any remaining errors not caught by the student during step 1, stop and ask an indirect question ("What about this?" or simply repeat the erroneous form or phrase). See if the student can suggest a correction for errors you call to his/her attention. Take notes on your copy using a different color of ink.
3. Show the student your paper, marked with two pen colors—one representing errors s/he found and attempted to correct independently; the other representing errors you pointed out. Discuss your findings, pointing out (a) what the student did well in terms of finding and correcting errors; and (b) problematic error types that you notice (either frequent or types resistant to self-editing). Ask the student to take notes on his/her paper, including correct forms that you provide for him/her.

Revised (Marked) Drafts

1. Read and provide indirect feedback (underline or highlight all errors you notice, but do not correct them or label them according to error type) on a student's essay draft. Then ask the student, at home or during

an in-class revision session, to attempt corrections for all errors that you marked. Ask the student to number each marked error consecutively and complete an EA chart. (If you prefer, you can do the charting yourself.) Use the marked and (student-) corrected essay draft and the chart for your error conference.

2. Use the marked essay draft, the chart, and the student corrections as data sources for your conference. First, walk through the in-class corrections made by the student, discussing whether the corrections suggested by the student are accurate. Note where the student did/did not make edits and discuss why (lack of understanding, carelessness, etc.) Take notes on your discussion. Ask the student to summarize what s/he has learned about his/her patterns of error, points of confusion, and editing strategies.

Notes

1. To provide just one example, one of the authors (Ferris) used to work in a composition program where some of the instructors had training both in composition and in TESOL. There were two separate ranked lists of instructors, one for mainstream courses and one for designated ESL courses. While many of the instructors were on one list but not the other, a subset of the instructors were on both lists and regularly taught both varieties of composition courses in the department.
2. For a statement of desired outcomes for undergraduate first-year writing instruction, see, for example, Council of Writing Program Administrators (2008).
3. In a multiple-case study analysis by Ferris et al. (2010), ten students who received selective (2–4 error patterns marked per paper) individual feedback over the course of a semester not only showed greater awareness and control over specific error types but also expressed in interviews their great satisfaction with this targeted and precise approach.
4. "Experienced" may be the key adjective here. As we discuss in Chapter 8, learning how to analyze errors in student writing in order to mark error patterns selectively is a challenging skill for new writing instructors.
5. One of the authors was once told by a supervisor never to split an infinitive phrase and was so influenced by this that he/she hypercorrected his/her writing to ensure that this "error" was never committed. To his/her amusement (or chagrin), when this author began publishing, copy-editors at journals began changing sentences to split the infinitives in constructions where *not* doing so created awkwardness.
6. Direct feedback can also be accompanied by explanation, as in some of the studies reviewed in Chapter 3 and further discussed in Chapter 6. For instance, if a student wrote, "I spent my vacation last summer traveling through *a United Kingdom," the teacher could cross out "a," add "the," and add an explanatory note in the margin: "Use definite article for names of countries that are a collection of smaller entities, such as "the United States.""
7. Ferris has a colleague who has elevated this almost to an art form, having created some 50 macros that comment not only on form issues but on content and text structure— and even linking these corrective comments to online handbook pages for more in-depth explanation.

172 Practical Applications

8. Some teachers (and their students) have been taken aback to discover that their campus writing center is philosophically opposed to helping students with grammar and language issues, focusing instead on the writing process and development of content (Ferris, 2009; Leki, 2004).
9. Experienced teachers of L2 writers often have "war stories" to tell of spell-checker-induced errors in their students' texts, e.g., *defiantly* inserted when *definitely* was meant.
10. It is instructive to note that the students in Ferris and Roberts (2001) were ESL students in "remedial" writing courses—yet, when given focused feedback and time and responsibility for revising their texts, their self-editing rates were similar to those of Haswell's students, who were mostly L1 writers in a freshman writing course. This suggests that L2 writers can do a fair amount of self-correction when given some guidance, and as Haswell (1983) notes, this frees up the teacher's time and the students' attention to focus on the errors that students truly need expert assistance with.
11. You could also choose to make this a separate homework assignment or an in-class activity accompanied by some discussion with peers and with you. This activity is adapted from one provided by Blair Citron of UC Davis; we are grateful to her for permission to use it.

8

PREPARING TEACHERS FOR WRITTEN CF IN LANGUAGE LEARNING AND COMPOSITION CONTEXTS

Unlike composition instructors who may have philosophical doubts about the importance of providing their students with written CF (see the second section of this chapter), L2 teachers do not doubt the importance of providing their learners with written CF. It is considered to be as important as language instruction because it directly relates to the specific errors their learners make during the acquisition process. This does not mean, however, that all teachers necessarily provide their learners with written CF in the same way or with the same level of commitment. In many respects, the attention they give to written CF is most often determined by their academic and teacher training backgrounds and by their experience as L2 teachers.

Preparing Language Teachers for Written CF

Teachers who have a background in applied or general linguistics will usually have completed one or more degree-level papers or courses in linguistics (including grammar) and second language acquisition or learning. This background will have given them an understanding of the linguistic structures of language (including phonology, morphology, syntax, lexis, and pragmatics), an understanding of the processes involved in learning or acquiring a second language, and an understanding of how written CF might be used to help learners overcome the errors they make in using the target language. A range of academic and teacher training programs are available in countries where second languages are taught. For example, teachers may receive their education and training from a university, a teachers' college, a polytechnic, a private college, or specialized L2 teacher training institutions. While some of the courses available to teachers

174 Practical Applications

are quite extensive (e.g., those involving undergraduate degrees; Masters degrees with either or both coursework papers and thesis; Doctoral degrees in linguistics, applied linguistics, TESOL), others are more intensive and therefore of a shorter duration (e.g., Cambridge ESOL teaching awards qualifications such as CELTA and DELTA; Trinity College London Certificate and Diploma courses). Teachers with one of these backgrounds will be more likely to understand where errors have occurred in a learner's written text, why they have occurred, and how they can be corrected.

However, not all teachers will necessarily have this background. This may or may not mean that they are sufficiently equipped to provide their L2 learners with effective written CF. Some, on the other hand, through years of experience, may have developed convictions about what is effective practice and be able to provide their learners with helpful feedback. Most, however, without an academic or teacher training background, will be under-equipped to handle some of the errors that their learners make. While it is likely that most language teachers will have a clear idea about the need to provide their learners with written CF, some may not have a good understanding of what constitutes effective written CF (i.e., they may not have an understanding of the various factors and skills that contribute to effective practice). Therefore, this chapter focuses on the areas of knowledge and skill that we believe teachers should have so that the time and effort they spend on giving written CF is meaningful and helpful. But, before any training occurs, teacher trainers will need to assess the extent to which trainees already possess the knowledge and skills their training program focuses on. These areas include:

1. Identifying gaps in knowledge and preparation.
2. Understanding the role of written CF in the language learning process.
3. Identifying and understanding L2 grammar/language issues.
4. Conducting written CF needs analyses.
5. Incorporating written CF into a language learning program.
6. Providing effective written CF to individuals, groups, and classes.
7. Developing activities that support written CF.
8. Integrating a focus on accuracy into assessment activities.

The first part of this chapter discusses the needs analysis and the core competencies identified above, together with suggestions about how language teacher trainers can approach the task of helping new and experienced language teachers develop knowledge and skills to effectively meet the needs of their learners. The second part of the chapter considers the same knowledge and skill areas for those who train composition instructors.

Identifying Gaps in Knowledge or Preparation

It is likely that both new and experienced teachers will have certain beliefs about the role of written CF in the language learning process and about the role that teachers can play in helping learners overcome the errors they make in their written output. In order to identify beliefs about written CF and the extent of their knowledge, some form of needs analysis would be a useful way to start a teacher training session or program. The following self-report questionnaire shown in Figure 8.1 is one example of how this information might be elicited. If teacher trainers are interviewing teachers prior to enrolling them in their training programs, the questionnaire might be followed up with a short interview that seeks additional information on the responses given.

---

1. Have you taken any courses in English grammar, linguistics, or applied linguistics? What were they (name them)? Where were they taken (name country and institution)? How long were these courses (give months and hours per day)? Did any of them have a focus on written CF? If yes, what information on written CF was covered in the course?
2. On a scale of 1–4 (with 4 being "very knowledgeable" and 1 being "not at all knowledgeable"), how would you assess your level of knowledge of the following areas?
   a. Identifying parts of speech (in isolation and within sentences).
   b. Identifying clause structures.
   c. Identifying sentence structures/types.
   d. Identifying learners' written errors.
   e. Correcting learners' written errors.
   f. Explaining the cause of learners' written errors.
   g. Deciding on the most effective ways of giving helpful feedback on learners' written errors.
   h. Determining how effective your written CF has been.
   i. Knowing how to advise learners about their role in the correction process.
   j. Making decisions about the provision of written CF—what to give feedback on, when to give it, how to give it.
3. Have you taken any courses that wholly or partially helped you understand the processes involved in the learning and acquisition of a second language? What were they (name them)? Where were they taken (name country and institution)? What main content areas were covered in them?
4. On a scale of 1–4 (with 4 being "very comfortable" and 1 being "not at all comfortable"), how do you feel about your ability to work effectively with second language learners from a range of L1 and general educational backgrounds?
5. Considering your responses to the questions above, please list up to three specific areas or skills where you would like further input or training so that you can work successfully with the grammar issues of second language learners.

FIGURE 8.1 Questionnaire for teachers enrolled in a teacher training course or workshop

176 Practical Applications

Additionally, teacher trainers may also want to give teachers a "Grammar for Teachers Test" or similar to determine whether there are any significant gaps in their linguistic knowledge that might warrant them taking a course on general linguistics before or concurrently with the training program.

Understanding the Role of Written CF in the Language Learning Process

Depending on their academic background in general or applied linguistics, their level of teacher training and teaching experience, teachers who enroll in a teacher training course are likely to hold different beliefs about the role of written CF in language learning. Some may be dedicated to the practice but not have clear convictions about why and how they provide written CF or about its potential in the language learning process. Before they start a teacher training session or course, it may be useful for both the trainer and the teachers themselves to reflect upon these issues. The following questions shown in Figure 8.2 could be answered individually in a questionnaire, orally in an interview with the teacher trainer (if this forms part of the enrolment process), or in groups with other teachers at the beginning of the training session.

If trainers use this approach to evaluate the suitability of an applicant for their courses and find there are significant gaps in their knowledge and understanding, they may want to recommend that they do some background reading on language learning processes (e.g., Lightbown & Spada, 2008; Mitchell & Myles, 2004) or enroll themselves in a second language learning/acquisition paper or

---

1. Have you ever learned a second language? Which language(s)? Do you remember receiving written CF on the errors you made in your written texts? How did you feel about receiving it (explain)? Do you think it was effective (explain)? How was the feedback given to you? Would you be likely to follow the same approach in giving feedback to learners in your own language classes (explain)?
2. Have you ever provided written CF to learners in a language class? If yes, describe (a) what areas you tended to focus on and why, (b) how you delivered the feedback and why, (c) whether you would adopt the same approach again and why, (d) how you knew if your approach was effective or not.
3. What role do you think written CF can play in the language learning process? Do you think it is more effective with certain types of learners (explain)? Why do you think some learners appear to benefit more than other learners from written CF?

FIGURE 8.2 Questions about teachers' beliefs regarding written CF in language classes

course. The latter are offered by most university Applied Linguistics departments and may be available as on-line courses at some institutions.

Identifying and Understanding L2 Grammar/Language Issues

Most training courses are available to teachers or teachers-in-training who have, at minimum, a basic knowledge of grammar and linguistics. Most often, it is a requirement that applicants demonstrate a suitable level of knowledge before being admitted to a training course. Some institutions may offer pre-service courses in "Grammar for Teachers" if applicants have an informal, tacit knowledge and trainers believe that short courses in grammar and linguistics would be helpful to formalize their knowledge to a level that is useful for L2 teaching. In order to determine the suitability of an applicant, institutions use some form of testing to determine whether or not applicants have a suitable knowledge base. Some of the testing approaches that are used by institutions include the following:

1. Asking applicants to complete a timed or untimed grammar test. Various commercially produced tests are available. In choosing a suitable test, it is important to ensure that the test questions focus on a wide range of linguistic forms and structures.
2. Asking applicants to identify the errors that have been made in a typical piece of language learner writing. Two pieces of writing—one by a low proficiency learner and another by a high proficiency learner—might be used rather than a single text. Once the errors have been identified, applicants could be asked to explain in grammatical terms why the error is unacceptable in the target language and explain how it should be corrected.

Both of these activities can also be done by in-service trainees either as individual tasks or as group tasks. Group and plenary discussions of their findings can be an enriching follow-up activity if done as part of a training session. Additional activities targeting teachers' knowledge and understanding might also be considered by teacher trainers. Some of the options include:

1. Providing trainees with lists of errors commonly made by L2 learners, dividing the lists into linguistic categories (e.g., verb form and use), assigning one of these categories to a group of trainees, and asking them to identify occasions in which errors in the assigned category have been made and decide what grammar rule(s) and examples could be given to the learner to help him/her understand why the error occurred and how it can be corrected. The aim of this task is to see what knowledge can be pooled by trainees within the group. Once they have exhausted their combined knowledge, they could then be asked to consult a grammar handbook or reference

178 Practical Applications

grammar handbook to check the accuracy of what they have decided and to see if any additional information could be added to what they produced.
2. This task could then be extended by asking trainees to design a mini-lesson on one of the error categories. It could be designed for use in a one-on-one conference session, for use with small groups or for use in a plenary context. Trainees could be asked to consider whether or not they would provide different information to low and high proficiency learners. In doing so, they might consider information that is detailed (for low proficiency learners) and that which is less detailed (for higher proficiency learners).

The types of activities that are used to determine a trainee's understanding of grammar/language issues might vary according to their status as pre-service or in-service trainees and whether or not they are considered to have a suitable grammatical knowledge for admission to the training course.

Conducting Written CF Needs Analyses

Needs analyses are typically conducted at the beginning of a course of study, and to some extent this may also be the case when determining the language needs of L2 learners. However, language learner needs, and specifically those requiring feedback on linguistic error, can change during a course of study, so this means an ongoing approach to determining needs is also required. Teachers of language classes at particular proficiency levels will have a reasonably clear idea of the main categories of error on which many of their learners are likely to need feedback. This is because the grammatical forms and structures taught in classes at particular proficiency levels are those that learners are not yet expected to have acquired, and these are the areas that commercially produced texts and syllabi are likely to focus on.

On the other hand, there is a wide range of individual and contextual factors that can impact an L2 learner's acquisition of grammatical form and structure. So, while there will likely be a number of grammatical errors on which most learners at a particular level will need written CF, there will be others on which individual learners or small groups of learners need feedback. Some of these will become evident if teachers conduct a needs analysis at the beginning of a course of study, but many are likely to surface during the course of study. Teacher trainers would therefore be wise to make their trainees aware of the ongoing need to identify errors that are being made in their learners' written texts (both exercises and communication tasks) and of the need to think about which of these should be targeted with written CF. In talking about this issue, teacher trainers need to remind them that a decision can only be made about whether or not to focus on a particular error category if questions about what, why, when, and how (referred to earlier) are considered. Having determined what the initial and ongoing written CF needs of their learners are, teachers then need to decide whether feedback would be best provided in a plenary, group, or individual manner. How it is provided will be the subject of our next section about integrating written CF into a course syllabus.

The types of written text that teachers use for their needs analyses will vary according to when the needs analyses are conducted (i.e., at the beginning of or during a course of study) and the proficiency level of the learners. At the beginning of a course, a teacher might find that an open task, in which learners are free to choose what they write about, yields more written text and therefore more instances of grammatical error. During the course, exercises and tasks that target specific grammatical forms and structures can enable the teacher to focus written CF on the ongoing and specific needs of learners.

Incorporating Written CF into a Language-learning Program

In many respects, the integration of written CF into language class programs may be more straightforward than it is in composition courses. While decisions in both contexts need to be made about when it is appropriate or best to provide written CF, it would be true to say that language teachers, because their primary goal is to help learners acquire mastery and control over the use of target language forms and structures, can be expected to provide written CF more often than composition instructors. In both contexts, teachers need to be clear about their aims and priorities when assigning a written exercise or communication task because it may not always be appropriate for learners to have their attention directed to matters of accuracy. Language teachers are equally committed to helping their learners develop fluency in their writing and, especially at higher proficiency levels, greater levels of complexity in their writing. Therefore, if the primary aim of a particular piece of writing is fluency or complexity, it would not be helpful for learners if their attention was also directed to the grammatical errors they had made. Sometimes, of course, a teacher may have several aims. For example, it may be that a teacher wants to focus on fluency as well as accuracy. On such occasions, it may be best to focus learners' attention on fluency first and then accuracy. At lower proficiency levels, teachers are more likely to focus on accuracy and do so on a regular, daily basis. Once learners have progressed to higher proficiency levels, and as other writing skills are developed, less attention is likely to be focused on accuracy. That said, however, teachers at the higher proficiency level are more likely to provide learners with incidental feedback on errors that they think they can help them overcome recurrent errors. Frequently occurring categories of error that teachers think a learner should be able to use with accuracy are likely to be the candidates for their attention. Written CF on such forms or structures is likely to be provided as and when necessary but unlikely to be given on a daily basis.

180 Practical Applications

At the lower proficiency level, written CF will typically be provided in response to errors that are made in writing exercises and tasks that follow a period of instruction on targeted grammatical forms and structures. For example, if a teacher has been teaching a class the present progressive tense, this is likely to be followed up with a series of oral and written exercises that give learners the opportunity to practice the use of this tense. Written activities that are completed in class time can be responded to with individual or plenary, oral, or written CF. This type of exercise is often followed up with the writing of a communication task designed to make learners use this tense. Such tasks may be given soon after the lesson has been conducted and/or at a later stage during the course of study. Written CF on these tasks is typically given to individual learners. In this way, the provision of written CF complements what is being taught explicitly in class and can be seen as a mechanism for providing learners with feedback on the extent to which they have acquired the tense and as a tool for providing them with further input on the tense (especially if the feedback includes written meta-linguistic feedback). Some learners may acquire a high level of mastery and control over the use of the tense as a result of explicit instruction, while others may do so with one or two targeted and intensive written CF sessions. Then again, some learners, for any number of reasons, may not be "ready" to acquire an accurate and consistent use of the tense. Adopting this approach means that written CF plays an important and ongoing role in the language learning classroom. To some extent, then, it can be pre-planned to coincide with scheduled explicit instruction, but often teachers will want to give learners written CF on other linguistic forms and structures when they find that they are being used inaccurately.

Providing Effective Written CF to Individuals, Groups, and Classes

In Chapter 6, we discussed a number of questions that teachers need to consider before providing learners with written CF. These included when to give feedback, how much feedback to give, what errors to focus on, and how to deliver feedback. For some teachers, these decisions can be made quickly and easily, but others may find the decision-making process more difficult. To some extent, this may be the result of a teacher's inexperience, but, in other cases, it may be that the context is more complex and the written proficiency level of learners is not particularly homogeneous even though, in terms of overall proficiency across reading, writing, speaking, and listening competence, the class is considered to be homogeneous. Thus, attention needs to be given by teacher trainers to help teachers understand how to deal with both straightforward and less straightforward cases.

Attention should also be given in training courses to individual, group, and whole class feedback. The first priority in a training session might be a discussion of issues associated with when to provide feedback, how often to provide it, how to provide it and so on. Having done this, trainees might then benefit from an exercise that requires them to provide written CF on a learner's text. First, they could be asked to identify the errors that have been made. This could be done individually and then discussed as a group. Groups of trainees could then be placed into groups and each group asked to provide a different type of feedback. Then the groups could present their work to the class as a whole and have it commented on by other trainees and the trainer. Additional experience could be gained if trainees analyzed errors and gave feedback on a range of written texts from different proficiency levels.

When it comes to giving feedback to groups of learners who have yet to acquire a particular grammatical form or structure, the same approach could be adopted by teachers and trainers. Alternatively, teachers could ask pairs of learners to identify the errors that have been made in one another's texts and then to provide one or more of the different types of feedback. Learners are often more comfortable assessing the work of other learners when it can be done in pairs or as a group, so this might be a better option for lower proficiency learners or for all learners if they are giving feedback on another learner's writing for the first time. As a whole class activity, learners could first be asked to identify errors and provide feedback individually, in pairs or in small groups before the feedback is discussed as a whole class. In other words, the greatest gains may be achieved if individuals or pairs are asked to do the identification and feedback activities before any group or whole class discussion. Teacher trainers would not need to spend time on role-playing the group and whole class procedures. If training sessions are being offered to more experienced teachers as refresher courses, participants might be asked to bring sample texts that they have given feedback on and in small groups or as a whole group, be asked to describe and justify what they did. This activity could lead not only to the types of discussion already referred to here but would also provide an opportunity for participants to justify their choices with respect to the key decision-making questions discussed earlier (e.g., what to provide feedback on, how to provide it, and so on).

Developing Activities that Support Written CF

Apart from explicit instruction on targeted grammatical forms and structures, other activities that could follow on from written CF as support initiatives include one-on-one conferences and mini grammar lessons to small groups of learners. These activities could be seen as follow-up activities to what has been explicitly taught to the whole class and to the feedback that has been given on these targeted forms and structures. One-on-one conferences were given to learners in the 2005 study by Bitchener et al. and were found to produce significant improvements in accuracy when new texts were written. Details about this approach can be found in the journal article. The particular benefit of this individual oral attention was

182 Practical Applications

its focus on clarifying what learners had not fully understood. While the input that learners receive can be provided by means of written meta-linguistic explanation, the written context does not provide an opportunity for the same type of question and answer sequences. Conferences, then, might be seen as a follow-up activity if learners need more information than what can be provided by written CF alone.

Mini-lessons can be an effective approach for targeting errors that are made by groups of learners. They can be provided to small or large groups, including whole classes. In many respects, they can provide similar information to that given in one-on-one conferences. They give learners an opportunity to receive additional input on particular error categories and to discuss this and various examples of use with one another and the teacher. Again, the particular advantage of this approach is the clarification that can be achieved if learners need a more comprehensive explanation of what is incorrect with their output. If more than one type of correction is possible, these options can then be discussed in an oral context such as this.

Teacher trainers might choose to model effective types of mini-lesson for targeted forms and structures and in doing so might provide different scenarios and approaches that the trainees are asked to evaluate. A comparison of inductive and deductive approaches is one type of comparison that could be considered. As a follow-up, groups of trainees could be asked to prepare a mini-lesson on a particular form or structure, present it to the whole group of trainees and have a discussion on what the group thinks would be likely to work well with learners at different proficiency levels and what might work less well.

Integrating a Focus on Accuracy into Assessment Activities

In language classes, assessments based on errors might be more common than they are in composition classes because the focus of teaching and learning is on developing an accurate use of linguistic form and structure. That said, language classes at higher proficiency levels, including other aspects of written competence in their syllabi, may not give as much attention to the assessment of error or accuracy that teachers of lower proficiency levels do. For example, teachers of "English for Academic Purposes" classes will also want to instruct their learners about effective discourse organization, appropriate vocabulary choice, and other characteristics of particular written genres. In these classes, the weighting given to errors might be considerably less than that given to these other areas. At any level, teachers should be advised to signal to their learners if accuracy is a focus of the assessment. This might be done orally or in writing. If it is communicated in writing, an explicit statement might be given as part of the instructions accompanying a writing task. On other occasions, it might be expected that learners understand this by the wording of the rubric. These are issues that teacher trainers would do well to discuss with their trainees.

In the training session, teachers could be given a set of writing tasks for learners at different proficiency levels and asked to discuss in pairs or small groups whether an assessment of accuracy would be appropriate in light of the instructions and rubrics. Additionally, trainees could be asked to identify the errors made in one or more learner texts and then asked to identify which types of error might be likely to impede clear understanding before offering suggestions about a grade or numerical assessment to be assigned for grammatical accuracy. It may be, for example, that the maximum score for a written task is 20 points, and within that a maximum of 5 points is allocated to linguistic accuracy. Trainees could be asked to award 1–5 points and then defend their choice. Even if there is not a consensus among trainees about the number of points to award, the activity could likely be valuable if the discussion encourages trainees to think critically about their reasons for the choice that they made. Such discussion may challenge some trainees to change previously held views about what is error gravity and what is not and therefore about the relationship between it and the points to be awarded.

In Conclusion

The issues, options, and examples we have discussed in this first section of Chapter 8 should be seen as a range of areas that teacher trainers might focus on when offering seminars, workshops, or courses to pre-service and in-service teachers. It is likely that in-service trainers and teachers will be able to add to these possibilities as a result of their experience as language teachers. Pre-service trainers might find there are too many possibilities to cover in a single training session so may need to be selective. The background of pre-service teachers and the length of time available to teacher trainers might also be factors that influence the choices they need to make. We have suggested a number of examples of ways in which teachers can be encouraged to think about the issues associated with giving written CF to language learners. Trainers and teachers themselves may be able to modify these approaches and extend them in various ways that suit the specific needs of learners and teacher trainees. What matters at the end of the day is that teachers have an understanding of what contributes to effective practice and that they reflect upon the effectiveness of their approaches throughout the teaching of their courses.

Preparing Composition Instructors for Written CF

The task of preparing composition teachers not only to give written CF effectively but to design a course that successfully integrates language issues with other course goals (see Chapter 7) is a formidable one. The two most obvious roadblocks are philosophical and practical. Philosophically, as discussed in Chapter 2 and further in Chapter 7, composition scholars (especially in primarily L1 settings) have expressed dubious and even negative attitudes toward error treatment and

184 Practical Applications

grammar instruction in the writing class, dating back to Williams' (1981) landmark paper suggesting that written error existed mainly in the mind of the (teacher) reader. These doubts have manifested themselves in the ways composition instructors are prepared in graduate programs and in teacher-preparation materials. As a result, not only do many writing instructors come out of their training programs unequipped to grapple with errors and language issues in student writing, but they feel ambivalent about or even morally opposed to doing so.

As to practical barriers, due in large part to the philosophical stances already noted, unlike the language teacher-preparation programs described in the first part of this chapter, few graduate programs in teaching composition require or even offer courses in linguistics or grammar, let alone courses examining second language literacy development or the pedagogy of teacher feedback and grammar instruction. Teachers of L2 writers coming from these types of backgrounds tend to have academic backgrounds in the humanities and be strong readers and writers themselves; they often have little formal understanding of their students' struggles with language or adequate appreciation of ongoing language acquisition processes. L2 writing instructors trained in applied linguistics or TESOL programs mostly likely have a stronger background in the structure of English and in the principles of language acquisition, but again, they do not always have access to coursework on teaching second language writers.[1] As a result of these intersecting philosophical and practical constraints, many new and experienced teachers do not possess the core competences needed to effectively address accuracy issues in L2 writing in the context of a composition course. Similar to the competencies discussed in the first half of the chapter, these areas of knowledge and skill include the ability to:

- reflect upon and articulate the purposes for written CF and language instruction in the writing class;
- identify and understand grammar/language issues that are especially relevant for writers (including common errors);
- analyze the needs of a given group of student writers;
- sequence and integrate written CF with other writing class goals;
- pinpoint key issues for a given student/text and provide effective written CF responsive to individual needs and course goals;
- develop and deliver strategy training and language mini-lessons; and
- integrate language/accuracy appropriately into course and program assessment scheme(s).

For the remainder of this chapter, we will offer some brief discussion of each of these core competences along with suggestions about how teacher-educators, workshop presenters, and administrators of writing programs might approach helping new or experienced writing instructors develop these skills.

Step 0: Identifying Gaps in Knowledge or Preparation

If a teacher-educator, workshop leader, or consultant is getting ready to work with composition instructors on skills for written CF and language instruction, a preliminary step would be to find out what these teachers already know. A questionnaire such as the sample shown in Figure 8.3 could be a helpful start. Readers should note that this questionnaire, while similar to the one shown in Figure 8.1, is not identical to it, but rather focuses on the typical starting points for writing instructors.

Step 1: Reflecting Upon and Analyzing Beliefs About Written CF/Grammar

One exercise that could be helpful for all writing instructors, regardless of prior knowledge, preparation, or experience, could be asking them to articulate their own beliefs about or purposes for written CF in teaching writing. Most writing

---

1. Have you taken any courses in English grammar or linguistics?
2. On a scale of 1–4 (with 4 being "very confident" and 1 being "not at all confident"), how would you assess your confidence level about your knowledge of the following issues in language/usage?
   - Identifying parts of speech of words (in isolation and within sentences).
   - Identifying subjects and verbs in sentences.
   - Identifying major sentence patterns in English.
   - Explaining the purpose and usage rules for major punctuation marks.
   - Analyzing a student paper(s) and correctly identifying the types of language errors made by the student.
   - Giving feedback on language errors that is clear and helpful to student writers.
   - Teaching lessons to students (individuals, groups, whole class) on problematic grammar and usage points.
   - How much to weight language errors against other writing elements in assessing writing and assigning grades.
3. Have you taken any courses that wholly or partially helped you to understand the processes of second language acquisition, general literacy development, and the unique demands and parameters of academic literacy?
4. On a scale of 1–4 (with 4 being "very comfortable" and 1 being "not at all comfortable"), how do you feel about your ability to work effectively with second language writers from a range of language, literacy, and educational backgrounds?
5. Considering your responses to the questions above, please list up to three specific areas or skills where you would like further input or training so that you can work successfully with language issues of second language writers.

FIGURE 8.3 Sample intake questionnaire for a composition training course or workshop

186 Practical Applications

instructors have received and/or given written CF already—as noted in Chapter 2, despite scholars' ambivalence toward it, most teachers are nonetheless still doing it—but may never have thought explicitly about why and how they give feedback about student language issues. The questions in Figure 8.4 could be used for individual writing and/or group discussion.

Step 2: Awareness of Key Grammar/Language Issues for Written CF and Instruction

This step can be very challenging because of variation in teachers' formal knowledge of grammar and linguistics. If teachers have had this background, teacher-educators can (with some minimal review) proceed directly to pedagogical applications for composition instruction. If the teachers do not have a firm grasp on basic linguistic concepts, the training will have to start there—but it can be hard to condense a semester or more of linguistics work into a composition pre-service course or in-service workshop. Some suggestions for addressing this preparation gap include:

- Asking teachers to complete a pretest to assess their grammar/language knowledge. This could even be taken from online materials for students that accompany composition handbooks.[2]
- Asking participants to analyze a sample student paper, highlighting or circling any errors they observe. They should then number each error they marked and try to classify or describe it, using whatever everyday terminology they can, and create an EA chart. These charts should be compared with those

---

1. Do you remember receiving *corrective feedback* (on language errors) from a teacher on your own writing? (This could be an English teacher, a teacher in another subject, or even a foreign language teacher.) How did you feel about receiving it, and did you think it was effective?
2. Imagine that you have a set of student papers to respond to or grade. Would you mark or correct language errors on those papers? If yes, what would be your purpose for doing so? If no, why not?
3. If you have provided error feedback to student writers before, can you describe your approach or strategy for doing so? Be as specific as you can.
4. If you have provided error feedback to student writers before, how do you feel about your efforts? Was it time well spent? Why or why not?
5. Considering your thoughts on the above questions, is there anything you would like to change (or learn more about) to improve your response practices?

FIGURE 8.4 Sample discussion questions about teacher beliefs regarding written CF in composition teaching

of other class or workshop participants and discussed within the whole group. This exercise may help individuals notice what some of their own knowledge gaps might be.

- Asking teachers to obtain at least one current composition handbook (which addresses basic language issues and common problems in clear, brief terms) and at least one handbook, grammar book, or reference grammar focused on the specific needs of L2 writers. See Appendix 8.1 for a list of current suggestions. Teachers can then be asked to use these resources for application activities such as designing a mini-lesson on a particular language point (see discussion later in this section; see also Chapter 7).
- Introducing participants to research on common error patterns of student writers, especially L2 writers. The studies and lists shown in Appendix 4.1 would be a good start; indeed, Andrea Lunsford's handbook materials are based upon her two research studies (Connors & Lunsford, 1988; Lunsford & Lunsford, 2008). This suggestion will help "narrow the universe" of possible errors and language structures upon which to focus and can make the treatment of language and error a less overwhelming prospect to novice composition instructors.

Step 3: Learning to Conduct Class Needs Analyses

Some writing instructors, again because of lack of adequate preparation, will simply teach the grammar material in their assigned class handbook, regardless of whether that material represents an important area of need or concern for their students. For instance, one of the authors recently observed a class in which the instructor gave a lengthy lecture on the passive voice, concluding with the comment, "I haven't really seen any problems with this in your papers so far." She later spent class time on the fairly trivial issue of when/if writers should put a period at the end of abbreviated expressions such as "Mrs.," "Ms.," or "Ph.D." Most composition class syllabi are extremely full, and there is never enough time to adequately cover the many writing sub-skills that deserve attention, including language and grammar information. Thus, it is very important for teachers to take time at the beginning of a course to assess what the most critical needs and gaps are for a given group of student writers. Nor should they assume that, if they are teaching a course that they have taught before, the needs of the new class will be entirely the same as those of previous students.

There are several different ways a teacher can analyze and assess the language needs of a writing class; probably several of them in combination would yield the best results. First, the teacher can (and should) administer a background questionnaire as a way to get to know their new students. This will help the instructor to understand how many L2 writers are in a course and what the range of backgrounds is. Second, the teacher should immediately collect a short writing sample (perhaps of 30–60 minutes, depending upon proficiency level) on an

188 Practical Applications

accessible topic of general interest, either during the first class meeting or for homework before the second class meeting. Besides looking at students' ideas, fluency, and arrangement of content, the teacher can use these samples to perform a class EA, which in turn can help to generate a list of issues to focus upon in written CF and during in-class mini-lessons for the course. Procedures for class EA are described in Ferris (2002); a condensed version is provided in Appendix 8.2.

Finally, the teacher may find it useful to have the class do a language/grammar knowledge questionnaire or pre-test to assess the students' knowledge of formal grammar terms and error types. Again, this can be useful information for the teacher in constructing written CF—if, for instance, most of the students cannot identify a verb tense error on a pre-test, it would not be useful to start marking student papers with the error code "VT" without some prior explanation. For a simple example of these types of instruments, see Ferris and Roberts (2001).

The job of the teacher-educator is not only to acquaint pre-service or in-service writing instructors with the options and procedures for conducting needs analyses, but, crucially, *persuading them of the need to do so*. Some teachers, whether because of an expressed egalitarian wish to "treat all students the same" or simply because needs analyses are time-consuming, may resist such suggestions. They need to be reminded that, among student writers (especially those from linguistically diverse backgrounds), one size almost never fits all, and the teacher's feedback and classroom instruction will be much more effective and useful if it is based on specific, current knowledge of student needs rather than a vague, general, or out-of-date set of assumptions.

Step 4: Integrating Language Instruction into a Composition Syllabus

While learning more about grammar and error types and conducting needs analyses are valuable activities in and of themselves, one of the most formidable obstacles to effective written CF and its in-class support is teachers' inability to fit such activities coherently into a course syllabus or daily lesson plans. As noted in Hartshorn et al. (2010), in a typical process-oriented composition class, there are so many other things going on—discussion of readings, practice of rhetorical and research strategies, process-based activities such as drafting, peer review, and revision of content—that it can be hard to see where and how language work can most effectively be inserted. As a result, teachers may choose one of these less effective strategies:

- ignoring language work altogether because it's "less important" than other course goals;
- overwhelming the students with too much error feedback and in-class grammar instruction, neglecting other important activity types;[3] or

- haphazardly working in grammar, language, and editing strategy training here and there whenever there is a bit of time available.

There is no universal approach to designing a composition class syllabus that effectively incorporates language instruction, as different contexts and student needs will lead to various strategies. However, teachers should be encouraged to look at key points of their syllabus for several different types of instruction and feedback:

1. Students should be allowed to revise their papers at least once (or several times) after receiving corrective feedback. They should be assigned, whether as an in-class or homework activity, to analyze their own errors, and to make corrections (see Chapter 7). On the syllabus, this would be reflected through built-in time lines for drafting, response, and revision and through incorporation of the reflection and analysis activities.
2. As students reach the final stages of editing class assignments, in-class peer- and self-editing workshops can help students not only to edit the particular paper under consideration but also to learn and practice effective editing strategies for their future work. The teacher should build editing workshops into the course syllabus right before a final deadline.
3. After the teacher has responded to a set of papers, he/she might want to design a "common errors" lesson, using samples from the students' papers for in-class analysis and discussion. The teacher may want to list the "common errors" lesson on the syllabus right after a date on which papers are returned to students.
4. To address other language issues observed through the beginning-of-term needs analysis (see Step 3 above), the teacher may also want to create space in the syllabus for a certain number of language mini-lessons, topics to be determined once the class needs have been assessed. These could be prepared and delivered by the teacher or by the students themselves, and the number and frequency of such lessons may vary depending upon the length of the course and the needs of the students.
5. In addition to considering in-class activities and homework assignments that provide written CF and supplemental instruction, the teacher may also wish to create opportunities for one-to-one error conferences (see Chapter 7), whether with all students or with those most in need of them, or for small group tutorials or mini-lessons for students who share a particular error pattern or language gap that the rest of the class does not struggle with. The teacher may also find it useful as part of the regular homework load to make individualized assignments from a handbook or a website after assessing each set of student papers. This last point acknowledges that in many composition settings, L2 writers (and, where applicable, their L1 peers) do not all have the same writing problems and need for instruction.

190 Practical Applications

A useful activity type for teacher-preparation courses or workshops could be to have instructors look at a sample syllabus (or one of their own) to identify points at which written CF and support activities (conferences, mini-lessons, strategy training) could effectively and naturally be integrated.

Step 5: Providing Effective Written CF on Individual Student Papers

As discussed in some length in Chapter 7, writing teachers have a broad range of options to consider as they respond to individual student papers or to a class set of papers—when to give feedback, how much feedback to give, what errors to focus on, whether to make feedback direct or indirect, and so forth. In a teacher-training setting, the goal would be to help teachers sift productively through those options and practice applying chosen approaches to sample student papers. One of the possible activities listed in Step 2 above—having teachers mark, chart, and discuss errors in a sample student paper—could be a useful preparatory step. With this analysis in hand, teachers could then be asked to mark the paper as if they were going to return it to the student, using one of the various marking options presented to them. If there is a group of pre-service or in-service instructors, a useful variation can be to ask different subgroups of participants to use assigned marking strategies and then come together to compare outcomes and experiences. A sample version of this workshop activity is provided in Appendix 8.3.

If more training time is available, teachers should gain additional practice in analyzing errors and providing feedback on a packet of student papers (say three or five) that represent a range of error types and proficiency levels. Learning to give high-quality written CF takes some repetition and experience. Another useful type of activity is to have participants analyze one or more student papers marked for errors by teachers, ideally instructors with different approaches to the task, and to discuss which written CF approach they think would be most successful, efficient, feasible, and so forth. In-service teachers might even want to bring in samples of their own previous error feedback to discuss and compare with other experienced teachers and to candidly assess the effectiveness of their current approaches.

Step 6: Designing In-class Mini-lessons on Grammar and Editing Strategies

Chapter 7 outlined the key components of language and editing mini-lessons for writing classes. In teacher-preparation contexts, it can be very useful to (a) provide models of well-constructed mini-lessons; and (b) ask teachers to research and prepare their own mini-lessons, based on either self-selected or assigned topics. A two-step approach to this lesson development process might include first asking teachers to research a particular grammar point in several different pedagogical sources (a handbook, an online writing lab site, a reference grammar, etc.) to compare the information and choose ideas that might be helpful to their own presentation. Then, using their research and following models of good mini-lessons, they should be asked to design their own and share it with other teachers for discussion. Appendix 8.4 provides sample workshop prompts for these activities (adapted from Ferris & Hedgcock, 2005).

Step 7: Considering Language Issues in Classroom Assessment

One issue that many writing instructors struggle with is how heavily to weight language error in overall assessments of student writing quality. Questions frequently asked of us in workshops and conference presentations include whether we would advocate "ignoring" error in the writing of L2 students (because it is unfair to penalize them for being in the lengthy process of language acquisition) or "watering down" grading standards for L2 writers in composition classes. While we certainly have our own opinions on these questions, the important issue for our discussion here is how to help teachers recognize and articulate their beliefs and biases about language errors in writing assessment and to identify approaches to assessment that are fair and effective.

We can offer several specific suggestions to address what can be a delicate and even controversial issue. First, as in Step 1 above, teachers can be asked to articulate their own assumptions and views: Should language errors matter at all in assessing student writing? Should they matter more/less than strengths or weaknesses in other aspects of student texts? Should "typical" L2 errors (if indeed there really are such) be overlooked/graded more harshly? Should papers written by L2 writers be required to "sound like" those of their L1 peers, or is a nonnative "written accent" appropriate? Should L2 specialists be involved in training teachers and/or assessing student writing, or can any classroom teacher do the job equally well?

Second, teachers can be presented with one or more sample grading rubrics from various sources and of various types. These could be specific rubrics tied to a particular program or course or even a trait-based (task-specific) rubric designed for one assignment; they could also be rubrics produced as part of national or state/regional standards or by professional associations or commericial testing companies. They could be holistic (one score for the whole text), analytic (different scores for different aspects of the text), or portfolio-based (one score for several different text samples presented together). The purpose of the examination would be to look at the different ways in which language issues are represented in those assessment tools and to compare those approaches to the participants' own beliefs and assumptions.

A third activity would involve examining a packet of sample student papers, again with a range of error types (and severity) and other strengths and weaknesses. The teachers could assess them (perhaps first without a rubric and later with one) and discuss their own opinions about the impact of the language problems on

192 Practical Applications

their overall evaluations of textual quality. Having looked at approaches to assessing individual texts or portfolios, participants might also discuss how written errors might impact the students' overall course outcomes. For example, would measurable student progress in editing and accuracy over time impact the final grade? If students were diligent in obtaining extra help and completing self-study assignments on language issues, could that help raise their grades? There is not necessarily one correct answer to these questions, but it is useful for teachers to think through their own philosophies and practices. What is clear is that language errors will, in one way or another, impact teacher judgments, feedback, and course assessments, so writing instructors need to be conscious of these issues so that students can be treated fairly and served effectively.

Summary

The above seven steps may seem a daunting list to teacher-educators, especially if they attempt to incorporate all of the suggested sample activities. This is why "Step 0"—finding out what the teachers already know—and "Step 1" (examining what the teachers believe) can be so critical to designing training sequences. However, daunting or not, the fact remains that writing instructors *are* providing written CF and most also are providing in-class language and grammar instruction. The only question is whether or not they are doing so effectively. The discussion in this section reminds us that effective error feedback and supplemental instruction involves knowledge and skills that new teachers must learn and experienced teachers must evaluate and refine with practice. What is surprising is not that these seven steps would be useful and even necessary to these teaching activities but that they are not already routine parts of teacher preparation programs for composition/L2 writing instructors.

Concluding Remarks

In this chapter we have proceeded on two assumptions: (1) that language and writing instructors need to develop skills to effectively provide written CF and supplemental grammar/editing instruction to their students; and (2) that different types of teacher-preparation programs are more successful at helping teachers develop these skills than others are. In our experience, the principles, training sequences, and sample activities we have described can help provide the foundation for more effective language and writing instruction. The rest of the expertise that teachers will need can come only from practice, repetition, feedback from students, peers, and more experienced teacher-mentors, and ongoing analysis and reflection. If teacher-preparation programs and teachers themselves commit to developing and refining these skills, they will not only improve their own practices but will positively impact student progress—leading to more satisfaction for teachers and students alike. In a profession such as teaching, where the psychic rewards nearly always outweigh the financial ones, these benefits are not to be dismissed lightly.

Appendix 8.1: Useful Reference Materials for Teachers of L2 Writers

Note: These materials are currently available as of the time of writing. Readers should remember that sources can go out of print and URLs can change. This list is intended to be representative of useful reference types rather than comprehensive.

Composition Handbooks[4] (print)
Hacker, D. & Downs, D. *A writer's reference*. Boston, MA: Bedford/St. Martin's.
Lunsford, A.A. *Everyday writer*. Boston, MA: Bedford/St. Martin's.
Lunsford, A.A. *The St. Martin's handbook*. Boston, MA: Bedford/St. Martin's.
Raimes, A. & Jerskey, M. *Keys for writers*. Boston, MA: Wadsworth Publishing.

ESL Editing Handbooks[5] (print)
Ascher, A. (1996). *Think about editing*. Boston, MA: Heinle.
Folse, K., Solomon, E., & Smith-Palinkas, B. (2003). *Top 20: Great grammar for great writing*. Boston, MA: Houghton Mifflin
Lane, J. & Lange, E. (1999). *Writing Clearly* (2nd ed.). Boston, MA: Heinle.
Raimes, A. (2004). *Grammar troublespots*. Cambridge: Cambridge University Press.

Teacher Reference Grammar/Pedagogy (print)
Barry, A.K. (2002). *English grammar: Language as human behavior*. Englewood Cliffs, NJ: Prentice-Hall.
Celce-Murcia, M. & Larsen-Freeman, D. (1998). *The grammar book*. Boston, MA: Heinle.
Folse, K. & Azar, B.S. (2009). *Keys for teaching grammar to English language learners*. Ann Arbor, MI: University of Michigan Press.
Master, P. (1994). *Systems in English grammar*. Englewood Cliffs, NJ: Prentice-Hall.

Websites
A writer's reference companion website: http://bcs.bedfordstmartins.com/writers ref6e/Player/Pages/Main.aspx
Everyday writer companion website: http://bcs.bedfordstmartins.com/everyday writer4e/default.asp#t_11472_
Colorado State University OWL: http://writing.colostate.edu
Purdue University OWL: http://owl.english.purdue.edu

194 Practical Applications

Appendix 8.2: Sample Class EA Procedures

1. For each student paper, with a highlighter, mark errors in however many categories (and whichever error categories) you would like your analysis to focus.
2. In class, return the papers to the writers and briefly review the error categories you have marked.
3. Ask the students to number the highlighted errors consecutively throughout the paper. Use these numbers to complete an analysis chart. For each error the student will indicate its type. (Create a chart based on the categories you have chosen for marking.)
4. Ask the students to list their 3–4 most prevalent patterns of error and turn in their report form (with chart and list).
5. Compile the individual forms into a class chart. Go over it with the class later to explain why your in-class grammar work will focus on some error types but not others.

Appendix 8.3: Sample Error-marking Workshop Activity

Note: This activity was designed for a teacher-preparation course and assumes some prior reading.

Your Task
You have two copies of an essay by the same student. Assume that the student is going to revise and edit this paper at least one more time before it is finalized. Your job is to give the student feedback about errors that might impact his/her grade if they are not addressed. Complete the following steps to do this.

Step 1
Everyone: Read through the essay. On your first copy, mark (underline, circle, or highlight) all of the errors you see (grammar, punctuation, spelling, other mechanics).

Step 2
Group A: On your second copy of the paper, mark it as if you were going to return it to the student. Use Haswell's (1983) "minimal marking" technique.

Group B: Look through the errors you marked and identify 2–4 *patterns* of error—specific problems that are repeated that could be pointed out to the student. Similar to what Ferris and Roberts (2001) did in their study, on your second copy, underline all instances of the 2–4 patterns you want to call the student's attention to. Create an error code for each pattern and mark the underlined errors with the appropriate code.

Group C: Look through the errors you marked on the first copy. As suggested by Bean (1996, pp. 249–250), write an end comment that might help the student to revise the paper (see example in the middle of p. 250). As also suggested by Bean (bottom of p. 249, top of p. 250), line-edit at least one paragraph and ask the student to work on correcting the rest of the paper.

Step 3
Get into "mixed" groups (A, B, C) and discuss:

- Compare your findings from Step 1. Did you find pretty much the same errors?
- Talk about the method you used to mark errors in Step 2. Did you find it hard or easy to do? Could you imagine using this method with your own students' papers? Why or why not?
- As a group, compare the three approaches to marking grammar that you have tried. Which one do you think would be most helpful to students, and why?

Step 4
Individual Freewrite (5 min.): Considering the work you did on this exercise as well as the readings for this week, try to articulate a 1–3 sentence philosophy statement about responding to errors in student writing.

Appendix 8.4: Researching a Grammar Point and Preparing a Mini-lesson

Note: Activities adapted from Ferris & Hedgcock, 2005, pp. 293–294.

Part A: Imagine you are teaching a writing course and have selected a particular grammar point on which to present a 20–30 minute mini-lesson to the class. Consult several different sources (see Appendix 8.2 for ideas) on this grammar point. After you have examined the sources, consider the following questions:

- Is one source clearer or more appropriate for the group of students you are working with? Why?
- What basic information about this grammar point (terms, definitions, rules, examples) will you need to present? Which sources were the most helpful in providing these?
- What rules and strategies for avoiding errors might you include? Which sources were the most helpful in identifying these?
- Did you find any discovery activities or practice exercises that might be helpful for your lesson? How might you need to adapt these to accommodate your own students' needs?

196 Practical Applications

Part B: Now design a 20–30 minute mini-lesson on the same grammar point. Include a discovery (text analysis) activity, deductive explanations with examples of important terms and rules, and practice/application activities. You may wish to assign some activities as homework to stay within your time constraints. Begin your lesson with a brief overview of the procedures (grouping, timing, materials needed) that you would use to teach this lesson. The overview should specify any prior knowledge or previous instruction assumed as background for the lesson.

Notes

1. We should note that this has changed over the past 20 years. Far more M.A. programs in TESOL offer or require courses in second language reading and writing than before. Even so, there are many others that do not, and programs with such courses do not necessarily spend adequate time building the sub-skills of preservice teachers for working with language problems in student writing.
2. For example, the online companion to Andrea Lunsford's *Everyday Writer* handbook has a "Top Twenty" pre-test and post-test for students. Other handbook websites have similar resources.
3. In the class observation mentioned previously, about 70 of 110 minutes of the composition lesson were devoted to four distinct grammar/usage topics. Not only were the activities disconnected from one another and from other syllabus tasks, but that much grammar in one lesson was extremely unengaging to the students, whose body language reflected their boredom, and who later complained about it in their course evaluations.
4. Many of these composition handbooks have several different versions and are constantly printing new editions, so we did not include specific dates in this section.
5. The editing book by Fox (1992) noted in the References is no longer in print, but used copies can still be procured.

REFERENCES

Adams, R. (2007). Do second language learners benefit from interacting with each other? In A. Mackey (Ed.), *Conversational interaction in second language acquisition* (pp. 29–52). Oxford: Oxford University Press.

Aljaafreh, A. & Lantolf, J.P. (1994). Negative feedback as regulation and second language learning in the zone of proximal development. *Modern Language Journal, 78*, 465–483.

Ammar, A. (2008). Prompts and recasts: Differential effects on second language morphosyntax. *Language Teaching Research, 12*, 183–210.

Ammar, A. & Spada, N. (2006). One size fits all? Recasts, prompts and L2 learning. *Studies in Second Language Acquisition, 28*, 543–574.

Anderson, J. (1983). *The architecture of cognition.* Cambridge, MA: Harvard University Press.

Anderson, J. (1985). *Cognitive psychology and its implications* (2nd ed.). New York: Freeman.

Anderson, J. (1993). *Rules of the mind.* Hillsdale, NJ: Lawrence Erlbaum.

Anson, C.M. (Ed.). (1989). *Writing and response: Theory, practice, and research.* Urbana, IL: NCTE.

Anson, C.M. (2000). Response and the social construction of error. *Assessing Writing, 7*, 5–21.

Ascher, A. (1993). *Think about editing.* Boston, MA: Heinle and Heinle.

Ashwell, T. (2000). Patterns of teacher response to student writing in a multiple-draft composition classroom: Is content feedback followed by form feedback the best method? *Journal of Second Language Writing, 9*, 227–258.

Atkinson, D. (1999). Culture in TESOL. *TESOL Quarterly, 33*, 625–654.

Atkinson, D. (2003). L2 writing in the postprocess era: Introduction. *Journal of Second Language Writing, 12*, 3–15.

Bailey, N., Madden, C., & Krashen, S.D. (1974). Is there a "natural sequence" in adult second language learning? *Language Learning, 24*, 235–243.

Baldwin, R.G. (1960). Grading freshman essays. *College Composition and Communication, 11*, 110–114.

Bartholomae, D.G. (1980). The study of error. *College Composition and Communication, 31*, 253–269.

Bates, L., Lane, J., & Lange, E. (1993). *Writing clearly: Responding to student writing.* Boston, MA: Heinle & Heinle.

198 References

Bean, J.C. (1996). *Engaging ideas: The professor's guide to integrating writing, critical thinking, and active learning in the classroom.* San Francisco, CA: Jossey-Bass.

Beason, L. (2001). Ethos and error: How business people react to errors. *College Composition and Communication, 53,* 33–64.

Benesch, S. (1993). ESL, ideology, and the politics of pragmatism. *TESOL Quarterly, 27,* 705–717.

Benesch, S. (1999). Thinking critically, thinking dialogically. *TESOL Quarterly, 33,* 573–580.

Bitchener, J. (2008). Evidence in support of written corrective feedback. *Journal of Second Language Writing, 17,* 102–118.

Bitchener, J. (2009). Measuring the effectiveness of written corrective feedback: A response to "Overgeneralization from a narrow focus: A response to Bitchener (2008)." *Journal of Second Language Writing, 18*(4), 276–279.

Bitchener, J. & Knoch, U. (2008). The value of written corrective feedback for migrant and international students. *Language Teaching Research, 12,* 409–431.

Bitchener, J. & Knoch, U. (2009a). The relative effectiveness of different types of direct written corrective feedback. *System, 37*(2), 322–329.

Bitchener, J. & Knoch, U. (2009b). The value of a focused approach to written corrective feedback. *ELT Journal 63*(3), 204–211.

Bitchener, J. & Knoch, U. (2010a). The contribution of written corrective feedback to language development: A ten month investigation. *Applied Linguistics, 31,* 193–214.

Bitchener, J. & Knoch, U. (2010b). Raising the linguistic accuracy level of advanced L2 writers with written corrective feedback. *Journal of Second Language Writing,19,* 207–217.

Bitchener, J., Young, S., & Cameron, D. (2005). The effective of different types of corrective feedback on ESL student writing. *Journal of Second Language Writing, 14,* 191–205.

Bloomfield, L. (1933). *Language.* New York: Holt.

Brannon, L. & Knoblauch, C.H. (1982). On students' rights to their own texts: A model of teacher response. *College Composition and Communication, 33,* 157–166.

Brereton, J.C. (1995). *The origins of composition studies in the American college, 1875–1925.* Pittsburgh, PA: University of Pittsburgh Press.

Broad, B. (2003). *What we really value: Beyond rubrics in teaching and assessing writing.* Logan, UT: Utah State University Press.

Brooks, N. (1960). *Language and language learning.* New York: Harcourt.

Brown, D. (2010, March). *Reshaping the value of grammatical feedback on L2 writing using colors.* Paper presented at the International TESOL Convention, Boston, MA.

Brown, H.D. (2007). *Principles of language learning and teaching* (5th ed.). White Plains, NY: Pearson Education.

Brown, R. (1973). *A first language: The early stages.* Cambridge, MA: Harvard University Press.

Bruton, A. (2009). Designing research into the effect of error correction in L2 writing: Not so straightforward. *Journal of Second Language Writing, 18*(2), 136–140.

Burt, M. (1975). Error analysis in the adult ESL classroom. *TESOL Quarterly, 9*(1), 53–63.

Burt, M. & Kiparsky, C. (1972). *The gooficon: A repair manual for English.* Rowley, MA: Newbury House.

Byrd, P. & Bunting, J. (2008). Myth 3: Where grammar is concerned, one size fits all. In J. Reid (Ed.), *Writing myths: Applying second language research to classroom teaching* (pp. 42–69). Ann Arbor, MI: University of Michigan Press.

Cathcart, R. & Olsen, J. (1976). Teachers' and students' preferences for correction of classroom errors. In J. Fanselow & R. Crymes (Eds.), *On TESOL '76* (pp. 41–43). Washington DC: TESOL.

Cazden, C., John, V., & Hymes, D. (1972). *Functions of language in the classroom.* New York: Teachers College Press.

Chandler, J. (2003). The efficacy of various kinds of error feedback for improvement in the accuracy and fluency of L2 student writing. *Journal of Second Language Writing, 12,* 267–296.

Chaney, S.J. (1999). *The effect of error types on error correction and revision.* California State University, Sacramento, Department of English: M.A. thesis.

Chomsky, N. (1959). Review of verbal behavior by B.F. Skinner. *Language, 35,* 26–58.

Cohen, A. (1987). Student processing of feedback on their compositions. In A.L. Wenden & J. Rubin (Eds.), *Learner strategies in language learning* (pp. 57–69). Englewood Cliffs, NJ: Prentice-Hall.

Cohen, A. & Cavalcanti, M. (1990). Feedback on written compositions: Teacher and student verbal reports. In B. Kroll (Ed.), *Second language writing: Research insights for the classroom* (pp. 155–177). Cambridge: Cambridge University Press.

Cohen, A.D. & Robbins, M. (1976). Toward assessing interlanguage performance: The relationship between selected errors, learners' characteristics, and learners' expectations. *Language Learning, 26,* 45–66.

Connor, U. & Kaplan, R.B. (Eds.). (1987). *Writing across languages: Analysis of L2 text.* Rowley, MA: Newbury House.

Connors, R. (1985). Mechanical correctness as a focus in composition instruction. *College Composition and Communication, 36,* 61–72.

Connors, R. (1997). *Composition-Rhetoric: Backgrounds, theory, and pedagogy.* Pittsburgh, PA: University of Pittsburgh Press.

Connors, R. (2003). Grammar in American college composition: An historical overview. In L. Ede & A.A. Lunsford (Eds.), *Selected essays of Robert J. Connors* (pp. 117–138). Boston, MA: Bedford/St. Martin's.

Connors, R. & Lunsford, A.A. (1988). Frequency of formal errors in current college writing, or Ma and Pa Kettle do research. *College Composition and Communication, 39*(4), 395–409.

Connors, R. & Lunsford, A.A. (1993). Teachers' rhetorical comments on student papers. *College Composition and Communication, 44,* 200–223.

Conrad, S.M. (2008). Myth 6: Corpus-based research is too complicated to be useful for writing teachers. In J. Reid (Ed.), *Writing myths: Applying second language research to classroom teaching* (pp. 115–139). Ann Arbor, MI: University of Michigan Press.

Corder, S.P. (1967). The significance of learners' errors. *International Review of Applied Linguistics, 5,* 161–170.

Corder, S.P. (1973). *Introducing applied linguistics.* Harmondsworth, UK: Penguin.

Council of Writing Program Administrators (2008). WPA outcomes statement for first-year composition. Retrieved from www.wpacouncil.org/positions/outcomes.html (accessed December 15, 2010).

Coxhead, A. & Byrd, P. (2007). Preparing writing teachers to teach the vocabulary and grammar of academic prose. *Journal of Second Language Writing, 16*(3), 129–147.

Dabaghi, A. & Basturkmen, H. (2009). The effectiveness of implicit and explicit error correction on learners' performance. *System, 37,* 82–98.

Davis, A.L. (Ed.). (1972). *Culture, class, and language variety.* Urbana, IL: NCTE.

200 References

DeKeyser, R.M. (1997). Beyond explicit rule learning: Automatizing second language morphosyntax. *Studies in Second Language Acquisition, 19*, 195–222.

DeKeyser, R.M. (2001). Automaticity and automatization. In P. Robinson (Ed.), *Cognition and second language instruction* (pp. 125–151). Cambridge: Cambridge University Press.

DeKeyser, R.M. (2003). Implicit and explicit learning. In C. Doughty & M. Long (Eds.), *The handbook of second language acquisition* (pp. 313–348). Oxford: Blackwell Publishing.

DeKeyser, R.M. (Ed.). (2007). *Practice in a second language.* Cambridge: Cambridge University Press.

de Villiers, P.A. & de Villiers, J.G. (1973). A cross-sectional study of the development of grammatical morphemes in child speech. *Journal of Psycholinguistic Research, 1*, 299–310.

Donato, R. (1994). Collective scaffolding in second language learning. In J.P. Lantolf & G. Appel (Eds.), *Vygotskian approaches to second language research* (pp. 33–56). Norwood, NJ: Ablex Publishing Corporation.

Dulay, H. & Burt, M. (1973). Should we teach children syntax? *Language Learning, 24*, 245–258.

Dykema, K.W. (1940). Criteria of correctness. *College English, 1*(7), 616–623.

Ellis, N.C. (2005). At the interface: How explicit knowledge affects implicit language learning. *Studies in Second Language Acquisition, 27*, 305–352.

Ellis, R., Loewen, S., & Erlam, R. (2006). Implicit and explicit corrective feedback and the acquisition of L2 grammar. *Studies in Second Language Acquisition, 28*, 339–368.

Ellis, R., Sheen, Y., Murakami, M., & Takashima, H. (2008). The effects of focused and unfocused written corrective feedback in an English as a foreign language context. *System, 36*, 353–371.

Enginarlar, H. (1993). Student response to teacher feedback in EFL writing. *System, 21*, 193–204.

Ervin-Tripp, S. (1970). Structure and process in language acquisition. In J. Alatis (Ed.), *21st annual Georgetown roundtable on language and linguistics.* Washington DC: Georgetown University Press.

Eskey, D.E. (1983). Meanwhile, back in the real world . . . Accuracy and fluency in second language teaching. *TESOL Quarterly, 17*, 315–323.

Evans, N., Hartshorn, J., McCollum, R., & Wolfersberger, M. (2010). Contextualizing corrective feedback in second language writing pedagogy. *Language Teaching Research, 14*, 445–464.

Falk, J. (1968). Nominalizations in Spanish. In *Studies in Linguistics and Language Learning V.* Seattle: University of Washington Press.

Fathman, A. & Whalley, E. (1990). Teacher response to student writing: Focus on form versus content. In B. Kroll (Ed.), *Second language writing: Research insights for the classroom* (pp. 178–190). Cambridge: Cambridge University Press.

Ferris, D.R. (1994). Rhetorical strategies in student persuasive writing: Differences between native and non-native speakers. *Research in the Teaching of English, 28*, 45–65.

Ferris, D.R. (1995a). Can advanced ESL students be taught to correct their most serious and frequent errors? *CATESOL Journal, 8(1)*, 41–62.

Ferris, D.R. (1995b). Student reactions to teacher response in multiple-draft composition classrooms. *TESOL Quarterly, 29*, 33–53.

Ferris, D.R. (1995c). Teaching students to self-edit. *TESOL Journal 4*(4), 18–22.

Ferris, D.R. (1997). The influence of teacher commentary on student revision. *TESOL Quarterly, 31*, 315–339.

Ferris, D.R. (1999). The case of grammar correction in L2 writing classes: A response to Truscott (1996). *Journal of Second Language Writing 8*(1), 1–11.

References **201**

Ferris, D.R. (2002). *Treatment of error in second language student writing.* Ann Arbor, MI: University of Michigan Press.

Ferris, D.R. (2003). *Response to student writing: Research implications for second language students.* Mahwah, NJ: Lawrence Erlbaum.

Ferris, D.R. (2004). The "grammar correction" debate in L2 writing: Where are we, and where do we go from here? (and what do we do in the meantime . . .?) *Journal of Second Language Writing, 13,* 49–62.

Ferris, D.R. (2006). Does error feedback help student writers? New evidence on the short- and long-term effects of written error correction. In K. Hyland & F. Hyland (Eds.), *Feedback in second language writing: Contexts and issues* (pp. 81–104). Cambridge: Cambridge University Press.

Ferris, D.R. (2008a). Feedback: Issues and options. In P. Friedrich (Ed.), *Teaching academic writing* (pp. 93–124). London: Continuum Press.

Ferris, D.R. (2008b). Myth 5: Students must learn to correct all their writing errors. In J. Reid (Ed.), *Writing myths: Applying second language research to classroom teaching* (pp. 90–114). Ann Arbor, MI: University of Michigan Press.

Ferris, D.R. (2009). *Teaching college writing to diverse student populations.* Ann Arbor, MI: University of Michigan Press.

Ferris, D.R. (2010). Second language writing research and written corrective feedback in SLA: Intersections and practical applications. *Studies in Second Language Acquisition, 32,* 181–201.

Ferris, D.R. (2011). Written discourse analysis and L2 teaching. In E. Hinkel (Ed.), *Handbook of research in second language teaching and learning* (Vol. II) (pp. 643–662). New York: Routledge.

Ferris, D.R. & Hedgcock, J.S. (2005). *Teaching ESL composition: Purpose, process, and practice* (2nd ed.). Mahwah, NJ: Erlbaum.

Ferris, D.R. & Roberts, B.J. (2001). Error feedback in L2 writing classes: How explicit does it need to be? *Journal of Second Language Writing, 10,* 161–184.

Ferris, D.R., Brown, J., Liu, H., & Stine, M.E.A. (2011). Responding to L2 writers in college writing classes: What teachers say and what they do. *TESOL Quarterly, 45,* 207–234.

Ferris, D.R., Liu, H., & Rabie, B. (2011). "The job of teaching writing": Teacher views of responding to student writing. *Writing and Pedagogy, 3*(1), 39–77.

Ferris, D.R., Liu, H., Senna, M., & Sinha, A. (2010, April). *Written corrective feedback & individual variation in L2 writing.* Paper presented at the CATESOL State Conference, Santa Clara, CA.

Ferris, D., Pezone, S., Tade, C., & Tinti, S. (1997). Teacher commentary on student writing: Descriptions and implications. *Journal of Second Language Writing, 6,* 155–182.

Foin, A. & Lange, E. (2007). Generation 1.5 writers' success in correcting errors marked on an out-of-class paper. *CATESOL Journal, 19,* 146–163.

Fox, L. (1992). *Focus on editing.* London: Longman.

Frantzen, D. (1995). The effects of grammar supplementation on written accuracy in an intermediate Spanish content course. *The Modern Language Journal, 79*(3), 329–344.

Fries, C.C. (1940). *American English grammar.* New York: Appleton.

Frodesen, J. (1991). Grammar in writing. In M. Celce-Murcia (Ed.), *Teaching English as a second or foreign language* (2nd ed.) (pp. 274–276). Boston, MA: Heinle & Heinle.

Frodesen, J. & Holten, C. (2003). Grammar and the ESL writing class. In B. Kroll (Ed.), *Exploring the dynamics of second language writing* (pp. 141–161). Cambridge: Cambridge University Press.

202 References

George, H.V. (1972). *Common errors in language learning.* Rowley, MA: Newbury House.

Gilbert, A.H. (1922) What shall we do with freshman themes? *English Journal, 11,* 392–403.

Ginsburg, H. & Opper, S. (1969). *Piaget's theory of intellectual development: An introduction.* Englewood Cliffs, NJ: Prentice-Hall.

Glenn, C. & Goldthwaite, M.A. (2008). *The St. Martin's guide to teaching writing* (6th ed.). Boston, MA: Bedford/St. Martin's.

Gray-Rosendale, L. (1998). Inessential writings: Shaughnessy's legacy in a socially-constructed landscape. *Journal of Basic Writing, 17*(3), 43–75.

Guénette, D. (2007). Is feedback pedagogically correct? Research design issues in studies of feedback in writing. *Journal of Second Language Writing, 16*(1), 40–53.

Hairston, M. (1981). Not all errors are created equal: Nonacademic readers in the professions respond to lapses in usage. *College English, 43:* 794–806.

Hairston, M. (1986). On not being a composition slave. In C.W. Bridges (Ed.), *Training the new teacher of college composition* (pp. 117–124). Urbana, IL: NCTE.

Harap, H. (1930). The most common grammatical errors. *English Journal, 19,* 440–446.

Harklau, L., Losey, K., & Siegal, M. (Eds.). (1999). *Generation 1.5 meets college composition: Issues in the teaching of writing to U.S.-educated learners of ESL.* Mahwah, NJ: Lawrence Erlbaum Associates.

Harley, B. & Swain, M. (1984). The interlanguage of immersion students and its implications for second language teaching. In A. Davies, C. Criper & A. Howatt (Eds.), *Interlanguage* (pp. 291–311). Edinburgh: Edinburgh University Press.

Hartshorn, J.K., Evans, N.W., Merrill, P.F., Sudweeks, R.R., Strong-Krause, D., & Anderson, N.J. (2010). The effects of dynamic corrective feedback on ESL writing accuracy. *TESOL Quarterly, 44,* 84–109.

Hartwell, P. (1985). Grammar, grammars, and the teaching of grammar. *College English, 47,* 105–127.

Haswell, R.H. (1983). Minimal marking. *College English, 45,* 600–604.

Havranek, G. (2002). When is corrective feedback most likely to succeed? *International Journal of Educational Research, 37*(3–4), 255–270. doi:10.1016/S0883–0355(03)00004–1

Heaton, J.B. & Turton, N.D. (1987). *Longman dictionary of common errors.* London: Pearson Longman.

Hedgcock, J. & Lefkowitz, N. (1994). Feedback on feedback: Assessing learner receptivity in second language writing. *Journal of Second Language Writing, 3,* 141–163.

Hedgcock, J. & Lefkowitz, N. (1996). Some input on input: Two analyses of student response to expert feedback on L2 writing. *Modern Language Journal, 80,* 287–308.

Hendrickson, J.M. (1977). Error analysis and selective correction in the adult ESL classroom: An experiment. ERIC: Centre for Applied Linguistics, Arlington, Virginia. EDRS: ED 135 260.

Hendrickson, J.M. (1978). Error correction in foreign language teaching: Recent theory, research, and practice. *Modern Language Journal, 62,* 387–398.

Hendrickson, J.M. (1980). The treatment of error in written work. *Modern Language Journal, 64,* 216–221.

Hendrickson, J.M. (1981). *Error analysis and error correction in language teaching.* SEAMEO Regional Language Centre.

Hillocks, G. Jr. (1986). *Research on written composition: New directions for teaching.* Urbana, IL: NCTE.

Hinkel, E. (2002). *Second language writers' text.* Mahwah, NJ: Lawrence Erlbaum Associates.

References **203**

Horner, B. (1992). Rethinking the "sociality" of error: Teaching editing as negotiation. *Rhetoric Review, 11*, 172–199.

Horner, B. (1994). Mapping errors and expectations for basic writing: From the "frontier field" to the "border country." *English Education* (Feb., 1994), 29–51.

Horowitz, D. (1986). Process not product: Less than meets the eye. *TESOL Quarterly, 20*, 141–144.

Hulstijn, J.H. (1995). Not all grammar rules are equal: Giving grammar instruction its proper place in foreign language teaching. In R. Schmidt (Ed.), *Attention and awareness in foreign language learning* (pp. 359–386). Honolulu: University of Hawaii.

Hussein, A.I. (1971). *Remedial English for speakers of Arabic: A psycholinguistic approach.* Unpublished Ph D dissertation. University of Texas at Austin.

Hyland, F. & Hyland, K. (2001). Sugaring the pill: Praise and criticism in written feedback. *Journal of Second Language Writing, 10*, 185–212.

Hyland, K. (2002). *Teaching and researching writing.* London: Longman.

Jacobs, G.M., Curtis, A., Braine, G., & Huang, S. (1998). Feedback on student writing: Taking the middle path. *Journal of Second Language Writing, 7*, 307–318.

Janopolous, M. (1992). University faculty tolerance of NS and NNS writing errors. *Journal of Second Language Writing, 1*, 109–122.

Johns, A.M. (1990). L1 composition theories: Implications for developing theories of L2 composition. In B. Kroll (Ed.), *Second language writing: Research insights for the classroom* (pp. 24–36). Cambridge: Cambridge University Press.

Johns, A.M. (1995). Genre and pedagogical purposes. *Journal of Second Language Writing, 4*, 181–190.

Johnson, D. & Roen, D. (Eds.). (1989). *Richness in writing: Empowering ESL students.* New York: Longman.

Johnson, K. (1996). *Language teaching and skill learning.* Oxford: Blackwell.

Johnston, M. (1985). *Syntactic and morphological progressions in learner English.* Canberra, Australia: Commonwealth Department of Immigration and Ethnic Affairs.

Kaplan, R.B. & Grabe, W. (2002). A modern history of written discourse analysis. *Journal of Second Language Writing, 11*, 191–223.

Kennedy, G. (1973). Conditions for language learning. In J.W. Oller, Jr. & J. Richards (Eds.), *Focus on the learner: Pragmatic perspectives for the language teacher* (pp. 66–82). New York: Newbury House.

Kepner, C.G. (1991). An experiment in the relationship of types of written feedback to the development of second-language writing skills. *Modern Language Journal, 5*, 305–313.

Klima, E. & Bellugi, V. (1966). Syntactic regularities in the speech of children. In J. Lyons & R. Wales (Eds.), *Psycholinguistic papers* (pp. 183–219). Edinburgh: Edinburgh University Press.

Knoblauch, C.H. & Brannon, L. (1981). Teacher commentary on student writing: The state of the art. *Freshman English News, 10* (Fall, 1981), 1–4.

Knoblauch, C.H. & Brannon, L. (2006a). Introduction: The emperor (still) has no clothes—revisiting the myth of improvement. In R. Straub (Ed.), *Key Works on Teacher Response* (pp. 1–16). Portsmouth, NH: Boynton/Cook Heinemann.

Knoblauch, C.H. & Brannon, L. (2006b). Teacher commentary on student writing: The state of the art. In R. Straub (Ed.), *Key works on teacher response: An anthology* (pp. 69–76). Portsmouth, NH: Boynton Cook/Heinemann.

Krashen, S.D. (1981). *Second language acquisition and second language learning.* Oxford: Pergamon.

204 References

Krashen, S.D. (1982). *Principles and practices in second language acquisition.* Oxford: Pergamon.

Krashen, S.D. (1984). *Writing: Research, theory, and application.* Oxford: Pergamon Press.

Krashen, S.D. (1985). *The input hypothesis: Issues and implications.* London: Longman.

Krashen, S.D. (2003). *Explorations in language acquisition and use: The Taipei lectures.* Portsmouth, NH: Heinemann.

Kroll, B. (Ed.). (1990). *Second language writing: Research insights for the classroom.* Cambridge: Cambridge University Press.

Kroll, B.M. & Schafer, J.C. (1978). Error-analysis and the teaching of composition. *College Composition and Communication, 29,* 242–248.

Kubota, R. (2001). Discursive construction of the images of U.S. classrooms. *TESOL Quarterly, 35,* 9–38.

Labov, W. (1972). *Language in the inner city: Studies in the Black English vernacular.* Philadelphia, PA: University of Philadelphia Press.

Lalande, J.F. II (1982). Reducing composition errors: An experiment. *Modern Language Journal, 66,* 140–149.

Lane, J. & Lange, E. (1993). *Writing clearly: An editing guide.* Boston, MA: Heinle & Heinle. (2nd ed. 1999).

Lantolf, J.P. (Ed.). (2000). *Sociocultural theory and second language learning.* Oxford: Oxford University Press.

Lantolf, J.P. & Appel, G. (1994). Theoretical frameworks: An introduction to Vygotskian perspectives on second language research. In J. Lantolf & G. Appel (Eds.), *Vygotskian approaches to second language research* (pp. 1–15). Norwood, NJ: Ablex.

Lantolf, J.P. & Thorne, S. (2007). Sociocultural theory. In B. VanPatten & J. Williams (Eds.), *Theories in second language acquisition: An introduction.* Mahwah, NJ: Lawrence Erlbaum Associates.

Lee, I. (2008). Understanding teachers' written feedback practices in Hong Kong secondary classrooms. *Journal of Second Language Writing, 17*(2), 69–85.

Lee, I. (2009). Ten mismatches between teachers' beliefs and written feedback practice. *ELT Journal, 63*(1), 13–22.

Leki, I. (1990a). Coaching from the margins: Issues in written response. In B. Kroll (Ed.), *Second language writing: Research insights for the classroom* (pp. 57–68). Cambridge: Cambridge University Press.

Leki, I. (1990b). Potential problems with peer responding in ESL writing classes. *CATESOL Journal, 3,* 5–19.

Leki, I. (1991). The preferences of ESL students for error correction in college-level writing classes. *Foreign Language Annals, 24,* 203–218.

Leki, I. (2004). Foreword. In S. Bruce & B. Rafoth (Eds.), *ESL writers: A guide for writing center tutors* (pp. xi–xii). Portsmouth, NH: Boynton/Cook Heinemann.

Leonard, S.A. & Moffett, H.Y. (1927). Current definitions of levels in English usage. *English Journal, 16,* 345–359.

Leontiev, A.A. (1981). *Psychology and the language learning process.* London: Pergamon.

Li, S. (2010). The effectiveness of corrective feedback in SLA: A meta-analysis. *Language Learning, 60,* 309–365.

Lightbown, P. & Spada, N. (2008). *How languages are learned.* Oxford: Oxford University Press.

Loewen, S. (2005). Incidental focus on form and second language learning. *Studies in Second Language Acquisition, 27,* 361–386.

Loewen, S. (2011). The role of feedback. In S. Gass & A. Mackey (Eds.), *The Routledge handbook of second language acquisition* (in press). New York: Routledge.

Loewen, S. & Nabei, T. (2007). Measuring the effects of oral corrective feedback on L2 knowledge. In A. Mackey (Ed.), *Conversational interaction in second language acquisition* (pp. 361–378). Oxford: Oxford University Press.

Long, M.H. (1991). Focus on form: A design feature in language teaching methodology. In K. de Bot, D. Coste, R. Ginsberg, & C. Kramsch (Eds.), *Foreign language research in cross-cultural perspectives* (pp. 39–52). Amsterdam/Philadelphia, PA: John Benjamins.

Long, M.H. (1996). The role of the linguistic environment in second language acquisition. In W. Ritchie & T. Bhatia (Eds.), *Handbook of second language acquisition.* San Diego, CA: Academic Press.

Long, M.H. & Robinson, P. (1998). Focus on form: Theory, research, and practice. In C. Doughty & J. Williams (Eds.), *Focus on form in second language acquisition* (pp. 15–41). Cambridge: Cambridge University Press.

Lunsford, A.A. & Lunsford, K.J. (2008). "Mistakes are a fact of life": A national comparative study. *College Composition and Communication, 59*, 781–806.

Lunsford, R.F. & Straub, R. (2006). *Twelve readers reading:* A survey of contemporary teachers' commenting strategies. In R. Straub (Ed.), *Key works on teacher response* (pp. 159–189). Portsmouth, NH: Boynton/Cook Heinemann.

MacDonald, S.P. (2007). The erasure of language. *College Composition and Communication, 58*, 585–625.

Mackey, A. & Goo, J. (2007). Interaction research in SLA: A meta-analysis and research synthesis. In A. Mackey (Ed.), *Conversational interaction in second language acquisition: A collection of empirical studies* (pp. 433–464). Oxford: Oxford University Press.

Mackey, A. & Oliver, R. (2002). Interactional feedback and children's L2 development. *System, 30*, 459–477.

Mackey, A. & Philp, J. (1998). Conversational interaction in second language development: Recasts, responses, and red herrings? *The Modern Language Journal, 82*, 338–356.

Mackey, A., Philp, J., Egi, T., Fujii, A., & Tatsumi, T. (2002). Individual differences in working memory, noticing of interactional feedback and L2 development. In P. Robinson (Ed.), *Individual differences and instructed language learning* (pp. 181–210). Philadelphia, PA: John Benjamins.

Matsuda, P.K. (2003a). Process and post-process: A discursive history. *Journal of Second Language Writing, 12*(1), 65–83.

Matsuda, P.K. (2003b). Second-language writing in the twentieth century: A situated historical perspective. In B. Kroll (Ed.), *Exploring the dynamics of second language writing* (pp. 15–34). Cambridge: Cambridge University Press.

McCrimmon, J.M. (1939). Commas and conformity. *College English, 1*(1), 68–70.

McDonough, K. (2006). Interaction and syntactic priming: English L2 speakers' production of dative constructions. *Studies in Second Language cquisition, 28*, 179–207.

McDonough, K. (2007). Interactional feedback and the emergence of simple past activity verbs in L2 English. In A. Mackey (Ed.), *Conversational interaction in second language acquisition* (pp. 323–338). Oxford: Oxford University Press.

McLaughlin, B. (1978). The Monitor Model: Some methodological considerations. *Language Learning, 28*, 309–332.

McLaughlin, B. (1980). Theory and research in second language learning: An emerging paradigm. *Language Learning, 30*, 331–350.

McLaughlin, B. (1987). *Theories of second language learning.* London: Edward Arnold.

McLaughlin, B. (1990). Restructuring. *Applied Linguistics, 11*, 113–128.

206 References

Mitchell, R. & Myles, F. (2004). *Second language learning theories*. London: Hodder Education.

Montgomery, J.L. & Baker, W. (2007). Teacher-written feedback: Student perceptions, teacher self-assessment, and actual teacher performance. *Journal of Second Language Writing, 16,* 82–99.

Nassaji, H. & Swain, M. (2000). A Vygotskian perspective on corrective feedback in L2: The effect of random versus negotiated help on the learning of English articles. *Language Awareness, 9*(1), 34–51. doi10.1080/09658410008667135.

National Council of Teachers of English (NCTE) (1974). Resolution on students' right to their own language. Retrieved from www.ncte.org/positions/statements/ righttoownlanguage (accessed February 20, 2010).

Ohta, A. (2000). Rethinking recasts: A learner-centred examination of corrective feedback in the Japanese classroom. In J.K. Hall & L. Verplaetse (Eds.), *Second and foreign language learning through classroom interaction* (pp. 47–71). Mahwah, NJ: Lawrence Erlbaum and Associates.

Ohta, A. (2001). *Second language acquisition processes in the classroom: Learning Japanese*. Mahwah, NJ: Lawrence Erlbaum and Associates.

Olsson, M. (1972). Intelligibility: A study of errors and their importance. *Research Bulletin No 12*, Department of Educational research, Gothenburg School of Education, Gothenburg, Sweden. EDRS: ED 072 681.

O'Malley, J. & Chamot, A. (1990). *Learning strategies in second language acquisition*. Cambridge: Cambridge University Press.

Patthey-Chavez, G.G. & Ferris, D.R. (1997). Writing conferences and the weaving of multi-voiced texts in college composition. *Research in the Teaching of English, 31,* 51–90.

Piaget, J. (1970). *Genetic epistemology*. Columbia, OH: Columbia University Press.

Piaget, J. & Inhelder, B. (1966). *The psychology of the child* (H. Weaver, Trans.). New York: Basic Books.

Pienemann, M. (1981). *Der Zweitsprachenerwerb auslandischer Arbeitskinder*. Bonn: Bouvier.

Pienemann, M. (1987). Determining the influence of instruction on L2 speech processing. *Australian Review of Applied Linguistics, 10,* 83–113.

Pienemann, M. (1989). Is language teachable? Psycholinguistic experiments and hypotheses. *Applied Linguistics, 10,* 52–79.

Pienemann, M. (1998). *Language processing and second language acquisition: Processability theory*. Amsterdam: John Benjamins.

Pienemann, M. & Mackey, A. (1993). An empirical study of children's ESL development and Rapid Profile. In P. McKay (Ed.), *ESL development: Language and literacy in schools* (Volume 2) (pp.115–259). Canberra: Commonwealth of Australia and National Languages and Literacy Institute of Australia.

Polio, C., Fleck, C., & Leder, N. (1998). "If only I had more time": ESL learners' changes in linguistic accuracy on essay revisions. *Journal of Second Language Writing, 7,* 43–68.

Politzer, R. & Ramirez, A. (1973). A error analysis of the spoken English of Mexican-American pupils in a bilingual school and a monolingual school. *Language Learning, 18,* 35–53.

Powell, P.B. (1973). *An investigation of selected syntactical and morphological structures in the conversation of secondary students after two years study of French*. Unpublished PhD dissertation. The Ohio State University.

Radecki, P. & Swales, J. (1988). ESL student reaction to written comments on their written work. *System, 16,* 355–365.

Raimes, A. (1985). What unskilled ESL students do as they write: A classroom study of composing. *TESOL Quarterly, 19,* 229–258.

Raimes, A. (1987). Language proficiency, writing ability, and composing strategies: A study of ESL college student writers. *TESOL Quarterly, 19,* 229–258.

Raimes, A. (1992). *Grammar troublespots.* New York: St. Martin's Press.

Ramanathan, V. & Atkinson, D. (1999). Individualism, academic writing, and ESL writers. *Journal of Second Language Writing, 8,* 45–75.

Reid, J. (1994). Responding to ESL students' texts: The myths of appropriation. *TESOL Quarterly, 28,* 273–292.

Reid, J. (1998). "Eye" learners and "ear" learners: Identifying the language needs of international students and U.S. resident writers. In P. Byrd & J.M. Reid (Eds.), *Grammar in the composition classroom: Essays on teaching ESL for college-bound students* (pp. 3–17). Boston: Heinle & Heinle.

Reid, J. (2005). "Ear" learners and error in US college writing. In P. Bruthiaux, D. Atkinson, W. Eggington, W. Crabbe, & V. Ramanathan. (Eds.), *Directions in Applied Linguistics* (pp.117–278). Toronto: Multilingual Matters.

Révész, A.J. & Han, Z. (2006). Task content familiarity, task type and efficacy of recasts. *Language Awareness, 15,* 160–178.

Richards, J.C. (1973a). Error analysis and second language strategies. In J.W. Oller, Jr. & J.C. Richards (Eds.), *Focus on the learner: Pragmatic perspectives for the language teacher* (pp. 114–135). New York: Newbury House.

Richards, J.C. (1973b). A non-contrastive approach to error analysis. In J.W. Oller, Jr. & J.C. Richards (Eds.), *Focus on the learner: Pragmatic perspectives for the language teacher* (pp. 96–113). New York: Newbury House.

Robb, T., Ross, S., & Shortreed, I. (1986). Salience of feedback on error and its effect on EFL writing quality. *TESOL Quarterly, 20,* 83–93.

Roberge, M. (2002). California's Generation 1.5 immigrants: What experiences, characteristics, and needs do they bring to our English classes? *CATESOL Journal, 14*(1), 107–129.

Roberge, M. (2009). A teacher's perspective on Generation 1.5. In M. Roberge, M. Siegal, & K. Losey (Eds.), *Generation 1.5 in college composition* (pp. 3–24). New York: Routledge.

Roberge, M., Siegal, M., & Harklau, L. (Eds.). (2009). *Generation 1.5 in college composition.* New York: Routledge.

Roberts, B. (1999). *Can error logs raise more than consciousness? The effects of error logs and grammar feedback on ESL students' final drafts.* Unpublished master's thesis, California State University, Sacramento.

Robinson, P. (1971). Oral expression tests: 2. *English Language Teaching Journal, 25,* 260–266.

Rouse, J. (1979). The politics of composition. *College Composition and Communication, 41,* 1–12.

Russell, J. & Spada, N. (2006). The effectiveness of corrective feedback for the acquisition of L2 grammar: A meta-analysis of the research. In J. Norris & L. Ortega (Eds.), *Synthesising research on language learning and teaching* (pp. 133–164). Amsterdam: John Benjamins.

Sachs, R. & Polio, C. (2007). Learners' uses of two types of written feedback on a L2 writing revision task. *Studies in Second Language Acquisition, 29*(1), 67–100.

Sachs, R. & Suh, B. (2007). Textually enhanced recasts, learner awareness, and L2 outcomes in synchronous computer-mediated interaction. In A. Mackey (Ed.),

208 References

Conversational interaction in second language acquisition (pp. 324–338). New York: Oxford University Press.

Saito, H. (1994). Teachers' practices and students' preferences for feedback on second language writing: A case study of adult ESL learners. *TESL Canada Journal, 11*(2), 46–70.

Santa, T. (2006). *Dead letters: Error in composition, 1873–2004.* Cresskill, NJ: Hampton Press.

Santos, T. (1988). Professors' reactions to the academic writing of nonnative-speaking students. *TESOL Quarterly, 22,* 69–90.

Sapir, E. (1921). *Language: An introduction to the study of speech.* New York: Harcourt.

Schmidt, R. (1990). The role of consciousness in second language learning. *Applied Linguistics, 11,* 129–158.

Schmidt, R. (1992). Psychological mechanisms underlying second language fluency. *Studies in Second Language Acquisition, 14,* 357–385.

Schmidt, R. (1994). Deconstructing consciousness in search of useful definitions for applied linguistics. *Aila Review, 11,* 11–26.

Schmidt, R. (1995). *Attention and awareness in foreign language learning.* Honolulu: University of Hawai'i Press.

Schmidt, R. & Frota, S. (1986). Developing basic conversational ability in a second language: A case of an adult learner of Portuguese. In R.R. Day (Ed.) *Talking to learn: Conversation in second language acquisition* (pp. 237–322). Rowley, MA: Newbury House.

Schuemann, C. (2008). Myth 2: Teaching citation is someone else's job. In J. Reid (Ed.), *Writing myths: Applying second language research to classroom teaching* (pp. 18–41). Ann Arbor, MI: University of Michigan Press.

Searle, D. & Dillon, D. (1980). The message of marking: Teacher written responses to student writing at intermediate grade levels. *Research in the Teaching of English, 14,* 233–242.

Searle, D. & Dillon, D. (2006). The message of marking: Teacher written responses to student writing at intermediate grade levels. In R. Straub (Ed.), *Key works on teacher response: An anthology* (pp. 57–68). Portsmouth, NH: Boynton Cook/Heinemann.

Selinker, L. (1969). Language transfer. *General Linguistics 9,* 67–92.

Semke, H. (1984). The effects of the red pen. *Foreign Language Annals, 17,* 195–202.

Sharwood Smith, M. (1981). Consciousness raising and the second language learner. *Applied Linguistics, 2,* 159–169.

Sharwood Smith, M. (1993). Input enhancement in instructed SLA: Theoretical bases. *Studies in Second Language Acquisition, 15*(2), 165–179.

Sharwood Smith, M. (1994). *Second language learning: Theoretical foundations.* Harlow: Longman.

Shaughnessy, M.P. (1977). *Errors and expectations.* New York: Oxford University Press.

Sheen, Y. (2007). The effect of focused written corrective feedback and language aptitude on ESL learners' acquisition of articles. *TESOL Quarterly, 41,* 255–283.

Sheen, Y. (2008). Recasts, language anxiety, modified output and L2 learning. *Language Learning, 58,* 835–874.

Sheen, Y. (2010). Differential effects of oral and written corrective feedback in the ESL classroom. *Studies in Second Language Acquisition, 32*(2), 201–234.

Sheen, Y., Wright, D., & Moldawa, A. (2009). Differential effects of focused and unfocused written correction on the accurate use of grammatical forms by adult ESL learners. *System, 37*(4), 556–569.

Sheppard, K. (1992). Two feedback types: Do they make a difference? *RELC Journal, 23,* 103–110.

Silva, T. (1988). Comments on Vivian Zamel's "Recent research on writing pedagogy". *TESOL Quarterly, 22*, 517–519.

Silva, T. (1990). Second language composition instruction: Developments, issues, and directions in ESL. In B. Kroll (Ed.), *Second language writing: Research insights for the classroom* (pp. 11–23). Cambridge: Cambridge University Press.

Silva, T. (1993). Toward an understanding of the distinct nature of L2 writing: The ESL research and its implications. *TESOL Quarterly, 27*, 657–677.

Silva, T. (1997). On the ethical treatment of ESL writers. *TESOL Quarterly, 31*, 359–363.

Silva, T. & Matsuda, P.K. (Eds.). (2005). *Second language writing research: Perspectives on the process of knowledge construction.* Mahwah, NJ: Erlbaum.

Silva, T. & Matsuda, P.K. (Eds.). (2010). *Practicing theory in second language writing.* West Lafayette, IN: Parlor Press.

Skehan, P. (1998). *A cognitive approach to language learning.* Oxford: Oxford University Press.

Skehan, P. & Forster, P. (2001). Cognition and tasks. In P. Robinson (Ed.), *Cognition and second language instruction* (pp. 183–205). Cambridge: Cambridge University Press.

Skinner, B.F. (1957). *Verbal behavior.* New York: Appleton-Century-Crofts.

Slobin, D. (1970). Universals of grammatical development in children. In G. Flores d'Arcais & W. Levelt (Eds.), *Advances in psycholinguistics.* Amsterdam: North-Holland Publishing.

Sommers, N. (1980). Revision strategies of student writers and experienced adult writers. *College Composition and Communication, 31*, 378–388.

Sommers, N. (1982). Responding to student writing. *College Composition and Communication, 33*, 148–156.

Storch, N. (2002). Patterns of interaction in ESL pair work. *Language Learning, 52*, 119–158.

Storch, N. & Wigglesworth, G. (2010a). Students engagement with feedback on writing: the role of learner agency. In R. Batstone (Ed.), *Sociocognitive perspectives on language use/learning* (pp. 166–185). Oxford: Oxford University Press.

Storch, N. & Wigglesworth, G. (2010b). Learners' processing, uptake, and retention of corrective feedback on writing: Case studies. *Studies in Second Language Acquisition, 32*(2), 303–334.

Straub, R. (1997). Students' reactions to teacher comments: An exploratory study. *Research in the Teaching of English, 31*, 91–119.

Straub, R. (2000). *The practice of response: Strategies for commenting on student writing.* Cresskill, NJ: Hampton Press.

Straub, R. (Ed.). (2006). *Key works on teacher response.* Portsmouth, NH: Boynton/Cook Heinemann.

Straub, R. & Lunsford, R.F. (1995). *Twelve readers reading: Responding to college student writing.* Creskill, NJ: Hampton Press.

Swain, M. (1985). Communicative competence: Some roles of comprehensible input and comprehensible output in its development. In S.M. Gass & C.G. Madden (Eds.), *Input in second language acquisition* (pp. 235–253). Rowley, MA: Newbury House.

Swain, M. & Lapkin, S. (1995). Problems in output and the cognitive processes they generate: A step towards second language learning. *Applied Linguistics, 16*, 371–391.

Swain, M. & Lapkin, S. (1998). Interaction and second language learning: Two adolescent French immersion students working together. *Modern Language Journal, 82*, 320–337.

Swain, M. & Lapkin, S. (2002). Talking it through: Two French immersion learners' response to reformulation. *International Journal of Educational Research, 37*(3–4), 285–304.

Swain, M., Brooks, L., & Tocalli-Beller, A. (2002). Peer-peer dialogue as a means of second language learning. *Annual Review of Applied Linguistics, 22*, 171–185.

210 References

Tate, G., Rupiper, A., & Schick, K. (Eds.). (2001). *A guide to composition pedagogies*. New York: Oxford University Press.

Taylor, B.P. (1981). Content and written form: A two-way street. *TESOL Quarterly, 15,* 5–13.

Towell, R. & Hawkins, R. (1994). *Approaches to second language acquisition*. Clevedon: Multilingual Matters.

Trofimiovitch, P., Ammar, A., & Gatbonton, E. (2007). How effective are recasts? The role of attention, memory, and analytical ability. In A. Mackey (Ed.), *Conversational interaction in second language acquisition: A series of empirical studies* (pp. 171–195). Oxford: Oxford University Press.

Truscott, J. (1996). The case against grammar correction in L2 writing classes. *Language Learning, 46,* 327–369.

Truscott, J. (1999). The case for "the case for grammar correction in L2 writing classes": A response to Ferris. *Journal of Second Language Writing, 8,* 111–122.

Truscott, J. (2004). Evidence and conjecture: A response to Chandler. *Journal of Second Language Writing, 13,* 337–343.

Truscott, J. (2007). The effect of error correction on learners' ability to write accurately. *Journal of Second Language Writing, 16,* 255–272.

Truscott, J. (2009). Arguments and appearances: A response to Chandler. *Journal of Second Language Writing, 18,* 59–60.

Truscott, J. & Hsu, A.Y-P. (2008). Error correction, revision, and learning. *Journal of Second Language Writing, 17,* 292–305.

Valdés, G. (1992). Bilingual minorities and language issues in writing: Toward professionwide responses to a new challenge. *Written Communication, 9* (1), 85–136.

van Beuningen, C., de Jong, N. H., & Kuiken, F. (2008). The effect of direct and indirect corrective feedback on L2 learners' written accuracy. *ITL International Journal of Applied Linguistics, 156,* 279–296.

van Beuningen, C., de Jong, N. H., & Kuiken, F. (2012). Evidence on the effectiveness of comprehensive error correction in Dutch multilingual classrooms. *Language Learning* (forthcoming).

Vann, R., Lorenz, F., & Meyer, D. (1991). Error gravity: Faculty response to errors in written discourse of nonnative speakers of English. In L. Hamp-Lyons (Ed.), *Assessing second language writing in academic contexts* (pp. 181–195). Norwood, NJ: Ablex.

Vann, R., Meyer, D., & Lorenz, F. (1984). Error gravity: A study of faculty opinion of ESL errors. *TESOL Quarterly, 18,* 427–440.

Wall, S. & Hull, G. (1989). The semantics of error: What do teachers know? In C.M. Anson (Ed.), *Writing and response: Theory, practice, and research* (pp. 261–292). Urbana, IL: NCTE.

Weaver, C. (1996). *Teaching grammar in context*. Portsmouth, NH: Boynton/Cook Heinemann.

Wilkins, D. (1968). A review of trends in language teaching. *International Review of Applied Linguistics, 6,* 99–107.

Williams, F. (Ed.). (1970). *Language and poverty*. Chicago: Markham Publishing Co.

Williams, J.M. (1981). The phenomenology of error. *College Composition and Communication, 32,* 152–168.

Wolfe, D.L. (1967). Some theoretical aspects of language learning and language teaching. *Language Learning, 17,* 173–188.

Wolfram, W. & Fasold, R.W. (1974). *The study of social dialects in American English*. Englewood Cliffs, NJ: Prentice-Hall.

Wykoff, G.S. (1939). An open letter to the educational experts on teaching composition. *College English, 1*(2), 140–146.

Xu, C. (2009). Overgeneralization from a narrow focus: A response to Ellis et al. (2008) and Bitchener (2008). *Journal of Second Language Writing, 18*(4), 270–275.

Yang, Y. & Lyster, R. (2010). Effects of form-focused practice and feedback on Chinese EFL learners' acquisition of regular and irregular past tense forms. *Studies in Second Language Acquisition, 32*, 235–263.

Zamel, V. (1976). Teaching composition in the ESL classroom: What we can learn from research in the teaching of English. *TESOL Quarterly, 10*, 67–76.

Zamel, V. (1982). Writing: The process of discovering meaning. *TESOL Quarterly, 16*, 195–209.

Zamel, V. (1983). The composing processes of advanced ESL students. Six case studies. *TESOL Quarterly, 17*, 165–187.

Zamel, V. (1985). Responding to student writing. *TESOL Quarterly, 19*, 79–102.

Zamel, V. (1987). Recent research on writing pedagogy. *TESOL Quarterly, 21*, 697–715.

Zhang, S. (1995). Reexamining the affective advantage of peer feedback in the ESL writing class. *Journal of Second Language Writing, 4*, 209–222.

Zhang, S. (1999). Thoughts on some recent evidence concerning the affective advantage of peer feedback. *Journal of Second Language Writing, 8*, 321–326.

INDEX

Page numbers in *italics* denotes a table/figure.

acquisition-learning hypothesis 9
activity theory 19, 106, 108
Adaptive Control of Thought (ACT)
  model 13–14
affective filter hypothesis 11
Aljaafreh, A. 72, 133
amount of written CF: and composition
  classes *109*, 113, 116–117, 144–145,
  163; and language classes 126,
  128–130; *see also*
  comprehensive/selective feedback
Anderson, J. 13–14
Anson, C.M. 28, 34, 35
approaches to written CF: studies of
  90–92, *91*
article system 58, *59*, 62, 63–64, 68, 74,
  104, 125, 129, 131
Ashwell, T. *83*
assessment: considering language issues in
  classroom 191–192; integrating a focus
  on accuracy into classroom 182–183,
  184
awareness 17, 18

Baker, W. 77, *78*
Baldwin, R.G. 30
Bartholomae, D.G. 32, 41
Beason, L. 33
behaviorist perspectives 4–6, 27
Bitchener, J. 4, 26, 52, 58, *59*, 60, 61, 63,
  66, 67–69, *67*, *68*, 69, 71, 100, 130, 136

Brannon, L. 36, 37, 38
Brooks, N. 4
Brown, Dan 6, 149, 152–153
Bruton, A. 52
Burt, M. 6, 7, 8

Canada: French immersion programs 17
Cathcart, R. 7
Chandler, J. 26, 86, 87, *88*, 111
character flaw: error as 29–30, 35
Chomsky, N. 5
City University of New York (CUNY)
  31
class error analysis 188, 194
cognitive perspectives 12–16; information
  processing models 12–14; Pienemann's
  processability theory 15–16
cognitive psycholinguistic perspective 21
College Composition and Communication
  (CCC) 30, 37
comments-on-content 55
'common errors' lesson 189
composition classes/studies 75–98,
  107–119, 125–126, 138–171;
  addressing the 'teacher variable'
  111–114; amount of teacher-provided
  written CF *109*, 113, 116–117,
  144–145, *163*; approaches and analysis
  76–77; arguments for continuing 96;
  comprehensive/selective written CF
  81, 92, 94, 116–117, 144–145,

214 Index

164–165; control groups in longitudinal designs 87, 110, 111; different approaches to written CF 90–92, *91*, 96, *97*, 116–117; direct/indirect correction 90, *91*, 92, 94, 116, *148*, 148–153, *150*, 168–170; effects of written CF on long-term improvement 87–90, *93*, 96, 110; effects of written CF on short-term revision 82–87, *83*, 95; error types marked by teachers 79–82, *80*, 95, 115–116; errors versus style feedback 146–147; explicit feedback 90, *91*, 116, 150–151, *163*; focus of teacher feedback 77–79, *78*, 95; focus of written CF 145–147, *163*; focused/unfocused written CF 92, 116; follow-up to written CF 161–162, *163*; forms of written CF 147–153, *163*; frequency of written CF 143–144, *163*; future directions 107–119; and grammar instruction 160–161; historical perspectives on error in L1 28–35; influence of L1 composition studies on L2 views of error treatment 40–44; instructor versus researcher feedback 111–113; integrating language instruction into syllabus 188–190; mechanical issues 151–153; preparing instructors for 183–192; purpose and goals of written CF 139–140, *163*; resolving methodological problems 110–111; sources of written CF 153–159, *163*; and strategy training 159–160; student differences 89, 118; student views of written CF 92–95, *93*, 96; support activities to build written accuracy 117–118; support beyond written CF 159–161, *163*; teacher response to error 35–40; timing of written CF 141–142, *163*; types of teacher-specific questions to consider 113–114
composition instructors: preparing of for written CF *see* preparing composition instructors for written CF
comprehensive/selective feedback: composition classes 81, 92, 94, 116–117, 144–145; language classes 22, 29, 53, 57, 62
Connors, R. 29, 30, 31, 39–40, *78*, 79, *80*, 81, 112
consciousness-raising 17–18
Constructive Analysis (CA) 4–5
content and form arguments *91*, 141–142

content-before-form arguments 141
control groups 26, 51, 56–57, 87, 110, 111
Corder, S.P. 7

de Villiers, P.A. 6
declarative knowledge 13, 14; conversion of into procedural knowledge 13, 14, 15, 20–21, 23, 50, 125
definite article 58, 64, 68, 115, 136
DeKeyser, R.M. 9, 14
delivery of written CF: options in 131–134; *see also* direct error feedback; indirect error feedback
developmental stage: error as 30–32
Dillon, D. 36, *78*
direct error feedback: and composition classes 90, *91*, 92, 94, 116, 148–153, *148*, *150*, 168–170; definition 65; definition of 131–132, 148; effectiveness of 67–70, 105, 132–133; factors determining use of 134; and language classes 54, 55, 64, 65–70, *67*, 74, 104–105, 131–134; students views of 94; theoretical arguments for 65
Donato, R. 72
Dulay, H. 6
dynamic corrective feedback 143

editing 22, 53, 86, 117–118, 143, 148; mini-lessons on 190–1; peer 155, *56*, 162, 189; *see also* self-editing
educational background (students): and receptiveness to written CF 70–72, 106
electronic text editors 158–159
Ellis, N.C. 57
Ellis, R. *59*, 60, 61–62
Error Analysis (EA) 5
error (composition studies) 28–45; as character flaw 29–30, 35; current views of 34–35; as developmental stage 30–32; influence of L1 composition on L2 views of 40–44; in L1 composition research 28–35, 44; L1 and L2 composition intersections in treatment of 42–43; as social construct 32–34; teacher response to 35–40; Top Twenty list 79–80; types of marked by teachers 79–82, 115–116
error conferences 136, 151, 154, 181–182; suggested procedures for 170–171
error gravity 32, 33–34
error (language learning) 3–27; behaviourist perspectives 4–6; cognitive perspectives 12–16, 27; early

perspectives on 4–11; and Krashen's Monitor Model 9–11; recent perspectives on 12–24
error-marking workshop activity sample 194–195
errors: versus style 146–147
explicit feedback: composition classes 90, *91*, 116, 150–151, *163*; language classes 52, 65, 72, 105, 128, 132

Fathman, A. *83*, 84
Ferris, D.R. 23, 42, 45, 54, 55, *78*, 79, 80, *80*, 81, *83*, 86, *88*, 89, 90, 92, 115, 117, 118, 142, 145, 149, 155
first-year composition (FYC) 29
focused written CF: composition classes 92, 116; language classes 57–62, 73–74, 103–104, 128–129, 130
Foin, A. *88*
follow-up to written CF 161–162, *163*
forms of written CF: and compositiom classes 147–153, *163*, and language classes 131–134; *see also* direct error feedback; indirect error feedback
Foster, P. 63
frequency of written CF: and composition classes 143–144, 163; and language classes 128
freshman composition 29
Frodesen, J. 142

George, H.V. 7, 8
global/local errors 115, 145–146
goals of written CF: composition classes 139–140; language classes 124–125
grading rubrics 35, 114, 161, 191
grammar: awareness of key issues in by composition instructors 186–187; language teachers' understanding of 177–178; mini-lessons 181, 182, 189, 190–191, 195–196; testing teachers' knowledge 177, 186; writing course instruction 160–161
grammar checkers 158
grammar point, researching 195–196
Grammar for Teachers courses 177
Grammar for Teachers Test 176
grammatical morphemes study 6
group work 135
Guénette, D. 55, 56, 66

Hairston, M. 34
Harap, H. 31
Hartshorn, J.K. 143, 188

Harvard University 29
Haswell, R.H. 38–39, *83*, 87, *88*, 90, 92, 162
Heaton, J.B. 8
Hedgecock, J. 70, 75
Hendrickson, J.M. 4, 6–7, 8, 19, 22, 148, 149
Hill, Adams Sherman 29
Holten, C. 142
Hsu, A.Y.-P. 52, 53, *83*, 84–85
Hull, G. 34
Hyland, F. *78*
Hyland, K. *78*

implicit feedback 72, 92, 116, 128, 132
improvement: effects of written CF on long-term 87–90
in-person error conferences 154
indefinite article 58, 64, 68, 115, 136
indirect error feedback: and composition classes 90, *91*, 116, 149–153, *150*; definition 65, 132, 149; explicitness of 150–151; factors determining use of 134; and language classes 64, 65–67, *67*, 74, 105, 130, 131–134; student views 94; theoretical arguments for 65; information processing models 12–14; Anderson's ACT model 13–14; McLaughlin's model 12–13
input enhancement 17–18
input hypothesis 10–11, 16
instructors *see* teachers
Interaction Hypothesis 16–17, 22
interactionist perspectives 16–20
interlanguage 6
international visa students 70, 71

Johnston, M. 15
Journal of Second Language Writing 41

Kennedy, G. 7
Kepner, C.G. 54, 75
Kiparsky, C. 8
Knoblauch, C.H. 36, 37
Knoch, U. 4, 26, 52, 58, *59*, 60, 66, *67*, *68*, 69, 71, 100, 105, 136
Krashen, S.D. 13, 16, 17, 22, 27, 43, 100; Monitor Model 9–11
Kroll, B.M. 32

L1 composition research: error in 28–35, 44; influence on L2 views of error treatment 40–44; interaction with L2 in treatment of error 42–43

216 Index

Labov, W. 40–41
Lalande, J.F. 66, *67*
Lange, E. *88*
Language Acquisition Device (LAD) 11
language classes/studies 49–74, 99–108,
107, 123–137, 123–171; amount of
written CF to provide 126, 128–130;
comprehensive/selective feedback 22,
24, 29, 53, 57, 62; delivery of written
CF options 131–134; design and
execution flaws in studies of 51–52;
development of current research
questions 100–108; development of a
theoretical basis for 100; direct/indirect
written CF 54, 55, 65–70, *67*, 74,
104–105, 131–134; early perspectives
on error and written CF 4–12;
effectiveness of written CF for different
domains and categories 62–64, 74, 102,
104; explicit feedback 52, 65, 72, 105,
128, 132; forms of written CF
131–134; future directions in research
89–108; and homework 137;
incorporating written CF into
179–180; influence of educational
background on receptiveness to written
CF 70–72, 74, 106; influence of
individual and contextual factors on
engagement of learner 108; oral CF
24–25; preparing teachers 173–183;
providers of written CF 134–135;
purpose and goals of providing written
CF 124–125; recent perspectives on
error and written CF 12–24; role of
written CF in acquisition of L2 forms
and structures 50–53, 73, 101–103;
short-term effectiveness of written CF
52–53, *53*, 73, 102; socio-cultural
theory and understanding of effective
written CF 72–73, 74, 106–107;
sources of CF 134–135; support of
written CF with other approaches to
accuracy 135–136; timing and
frequency of giving learners written
CF 125–128; types of linguistic
form and structure to focus on
130–131; unfocused/focused written
CF 57–62, 73–74, 103–104,
128–129, 130
language teachers: preparing for written
CF *see* preparing language teachers
Lantolf, J.P. 18, 72, 133
Lapkin, S. 72
Lefkowitz, N. 70, 75

linguistic error domains/categories:
effectiveness of written CF and 26,
53–54, 58, 60, 61, 62–64, 74, 102,
103–104, *107*, *109*, 129
linguistic form/structure: types to be
focused on 130–131
local/global errors 115, 145–146
Loewen, S. 25
Long, M.H. 16, 22
long-term improvement: effects of written
CF on 87–90, *93*, 96, 110
long-term memory (LTM) 13
Lunsford, A.A. 31, 35, 39–40, *78*, 79, *80*,
81, 112, 187
Lunsford, K.J. 35, 39, 40, 79, *80*, 81, 112
Lunsford, R.F. 38, *78*

McDonough, K. 63
Mackey, A. 15
McLaughlin, B. 9, 10, 12–13, 15
macros: use of for corrections 152
mechanical issues 82, 134, 151–153
migrant students 70–71
mini lessons: editing 190–1; grammar 181,
182, 189, 190–191, 195–196
minimal marking 38–39, 82, *88*, 90, 111,
150, 162, 170, 194
Mitchell, R. 14
Monitor Model 9–11, 27
Montgomery, J.L. 77, *78*
Myles, F. 14

Nassaji, H. 72, 73, 133
natural order hypothesis 10
needs analyses 130, 174, 175, 178–179,
187–188, 189
negative feedback 17, 18
noticing 17, 18
noun-verb agreements 130

Ohta, A. 72
Olsen, J. 7
one-to-one error conferences 136, 151,
181–182, 189
oral CF (corrective feedback) 18, 24–25,
50, 63, 64, 86, 100, 127, 129
oral meta-linguistic explanation 68, *68*,
69
out-of-class learning 137

pair work 135
passive voice 146–147
past simple tense 63, 68, 74, 104, 125,
127, 129, 130

Index 217

pedagogical advice: and early written CF
  8–9
peer editing workshops 155, *156*, 162,
  189
peer feedback/review 41, 108, 135, 154,
  155, 188
Piaget, J. 5
picture description task 136
Pienemann, M.C. 15–16, 73
plenary instruction 135–136
Polio, C. 85–86
practice: and theory 35, 45
preparing composition instructors for
  written CF 183–192; constraints
  183–184; designing mini-lessons on
  grammar and editing strategies
  190–191; grammar and language issue
  awareness 186–187; identifying gaps in
  knowledge 185; integrating language
  instruction into composition syllabus
  188–190; language issues in classroom
  assessment 191–192; needs analysis
  187–188; providing effective written
  CF on individual student papers 190;
  questionnaire *185*; reflecting upon and
  analyzing beliefs about written CF
  185–186, *186*; useful reference
  materials 193
preparing language teachers for written
  CF 173–183; assessment of error or
  accuracy 182–183; developing activities
  that support written CF 181–182;
  grammar/language issues 177–178;
  identifying gaps in knowledge
  175–176; integration of written CF
  into language-learning program
  179–180; needs analyses 178–179;
  providing effective written CF to
  individuals, groups and classes 180–181;
  questionnaire 175; understanding the
  role of written CF 176–177; useful
  reference materials 193
prepositions 26, 62, 63, 68, 104, 115, 149
procedural knowledge: conversion of
  declarative knowledge into 13, 14, 15,
  20–21, 23, 50, 125
process teaching 141
processability theory 15–16
processing capacity of learners 5, 16, 17,
  18, 128–129
proficiency level of learner: and written
  CF 7, 17, 24, 51, 58, 60, 105, 118,
  125, 126, 128–130, 131, 133, 179
providers of written CF 134–135

pseudo-learning 22
purpose of written CF: composition
  classes 139–140, *163*; language classes
  124–125

questionnaire for teachers 175, *185*

reference materials, useful 193
regulatory scale 72, 74, 108, 133
Reid, J. 142
researchers: perspectives on role of written
  CF 20–24
revision: effects of written CF on short-
  term 82–87, *83*
Robb, T. 26, *54*, 55–56, 66, *67*
Roberts, B.J. *83*, 188
Robinson, P. 7
Rouse, J. 32

Sachs, R. 85–86
sample student papers: and preparing
  composition instructors 186–187, 190,
  191–192
Santa, T. 29, 30, 31, 33, 34–35
scaffolding 18–19, 72–73, 74, 106, 133
Schafer, J.C. 32
Schmidt, R. 17, 53, 57
Searle, D. 36, *78*
selective/comprehensive feedback:
  composition classes 81, 92, 94,
  116–117, 144–145; language classes 22,
  29, 53, 57, 62
self-correction 8, 55, 57, 66, 71, 84,
  133–134, 135
self-editing 39, 44, 86, 95, 116, 140, 144,
  145, 150, 154, 159–160, *160*, 162;
  exercise 166
self-editing workshops 162, 189
self-study books 137
Selinker, L. 6
Semke, H. *54*, 55, 66, *67*
serious error 115, 146
Sharwood Smith, M. 17
Shaughnessy, Mina 30–33, 35, 40, 45
Sheen, Y. 24–25, *59*, 60, 62, *68*, 69, 105
Sheppard, K. 26, 54, 56
short-term memory (STM) 13
short-term revision: effect of written CF
  on 82–87, *83*, 95
Skehan, P. 63
Skinner, B.F. 5
SLA *see* language classes/studies
social construct: error as 32–34
socio-cognitive perspective 16–20

218 Index

socio-cultural perspective 12, 18–20, 27, 49, 50, 71, 72–73, 74, 100, 106, *107*, 108
Sommers, N. 37, 38
sources of written CF: composition classes 153–159, *163*; language classes 134–135
spell-checkers 158
stigmatizing error 7, 32, 92, 115–116, 146
Storch, N. 73
strategy training 157, 159–160
Straub, R. 38, *78*
students: educational background of and responsiveness to written CF 70–72, 74, 106; views of written CF 92–95, *93*, 96
style: versus feedback on errors 146–147
support activities 117–118; beyond written CF 159–161, *163*
Swain, M. 72, 73, 133
syntactic domains 6, 21, 63, 64, 65, 82, 101

teacher variable: addressing of in written CF 111–114
teacher-specific questions: consideration of in composition research 113–114
teachers 134, 154; focus of feedback in writing courses 77–79, *78*, 95; intersection of written CF practices with other response practices 114; philosophies towards written CF 114; preparation received for providing written CF 113–114; preparing for written CF in composition classes *see* preparing composition teachers for written CF; preparing for written CF in language classes *see* preparing language teachers for written CF;

response to error 35–40; types of errors marked by 79–82, *80*, 95, 115–116; versus researcher feedback 112–113
TESOL 41
theory: and practice 35, 45
timing of written CF: and composition classes 141–142, *163*; and language learning 125–128
'Top Twenty' list of frequent errors 39–40, 79–80
Truscott, J. 20–23, 25, 44, 50, 52, 53, 54, 55, 56, 57, 61, 63, 82, *83*, 84–85, 94, 95, 100, 113, 115
Turton, N.D. 8
tutors 135, 153, 156–157

unfocused written CF: and composition classes 92; and language classes 53–57, 61–62, 103, 128–129

van Beuningan, C. 28, 52, 57, 62, *67*, 100
Vygotsky 18

Wall, S. 34
Whalley, E. *83*, 84
Wigglesworth, G. 73
Williams, J.M. 33, 40, 95, 184
word processing tools 158–159
writing classes *see* composition classes/studies
writing theorists: perspectives on role of written CF 20–24
written meta-linguistic explanation *68*, 69

Xu, C. 61, 62

Zamel, V. 43
zone of proximal development (ZPD) 18, 72, 125

CPSIA information can be obtained
at www.ICGtesting.com
Printed in the USA
BVHW070331291118
534271BV00012B/121/P